CW00433460

The Edgeworth David Women

Cara Mallett

The Edgeworth David Women

Jennifer Horsfield

ROSENBERG

For Anne Edgeworth
1921–2011

First published in Australia in 2012
by Rosenberg Publishing Pty Ltd
PO Box 6125, Dural Delivery Centre NSW 2158
Phone: 61 2 9654 1502 Fax: 61 2 9654 1338
Email: rosenbergpub@smartchat.net.au
Web: www.rosenbergpub.com.au

Copyright © Jennifer Horsfield 2012

All rights reserved. No part of this publication may be reproduced, stored in a retrieval system, or transmitted, in any form or by any means, electronic, mechanical, photocopying, recording or otherwise, without the prior permission of the publisher in writing.

National Library of Australia Cataloguing-in-Publication entry

Author: Horsfield, Jennifer.
Title: The Edgeworth David women / Jennifer Horsfield.
ISBN: 9781921719516 (pbk.)
Notes: Includes bibliographical references and index.
Subjects: David, T. W. Edgeworth (Tannatt William Edgeworth), Sir,
      1858-1934--Family.
      David, T. Edgeworth, Mrs., b. 1856.
      Women--Australia--Biography.
      Wives--Australia--Biography.
      Daughters--Australia--Biography.

Dewey Number: 306.850994

Cover: Margaret, Cara, Billy, Molly and Mrs Attride the housekeeper, during
      David's absence in the Antarctic (NLA MS 8890)

Set in 12 on 16 point Arno Pro
Printed in China by Everbest Printing Co Limited

Contents

Acknowledgments

Some twenty-five years ago, Professor Noeline Kyle began gathering material for a biography of Cara David. Noeline was especially interested in Cara's work as a pioneering teacher within the NSW education system. A number of articles were written and published and a grant from the University of Wollongong allowed Noeline to travel to England and track down valuable information on Cara David's early years.

Noeline was unable to find a publisher who was interested in her work at that time. After I contacted her in 2009, she generously handed over all her research material to me, saying she wanted to see Cara David's life in print. I am greatly indebted to her for this.

Anne Edgeworth, though in failing health in the last years of her life, was actively supportive of my proposal to write the story of the David women and gave me access to both her own private papers and the extensive David Family Papers she had lodged in the National Library of Australia. This book is dedicated to Anne. In many ways, her life embodied the spirit and values of the three women whose stories are told in this book.

Members of the extended Edgeworth David and McIntyre family have been unfailingly helpful and supportive. I owe a special thanks to Anne Edgeworth's son, Tony Godfrey-Smith, always interested in the book's progress and encouraging of my efforts. Other family members who gave me their time and shared reminiscences with me were Dr David McIntyre and Philippa Sharman in Launceston, and Louise McIntyre of Melbourne.

David Branagan's wonderful biography of T.W. Edgeworth David first aroused my interest in this remarkable Australian family. I owe him many thanks for his ongoing encouragement, advice and interest. I hope my book will be a worthy partner on the shelves to his own.

In Canberra, Dr Peter Stanley gave me much expert advice and friendly support which I have greatly valued. Ian Morse shared stories of his grandfather, Major Victor Morse, friend and wartime colleague of Edgeworth David on the Western Front.

The Edgeworth David name is well-known in Sydney, and I found many people who were keen to assist my research. My thanks to Vicken Babkenian and Ann O'Connell of the Ashfield & District Historical Association, Jan Cowell, archivist at Abbotsleigh School, Pat Dale of Mosman Uniting Church, Tiffany Donnelly of the Women's College at the University of Sydney, University of Sydney Historian Julia Horn, Chesne Jones of the NSW Girl Guides Association, Mari Metzke of the Royal Australian Historical Association, Dick Morony of the Springwood Historical Association, Nyree Morrison, reference archivist at Sydney University, Gerri Nicholas, former archivist at Ascham School, Morwenna Pearce of Barker College and Dr Peter Rickwood of the Blue Mountains Historical Society. Mary Walters, whose family purchased the Edgeworth David home in Hornsby, shared memories of her friendship with Molly David. Emeritus Professor Jill Roe gave me helpful advice and encouragement; her biography of Miles Franklin opened a window into the world of some of the early Sydney feminists.

In Launceston, a keen group of local historians helped with my research: my thanks to Marita Bardenhargen, Dr Jillian Koshin and Dorothy Rosemann, and to Paul Edwards who introduced me to this circle.

My correspondence with Melbourne resident John Boddington gave me an insight into the history of Waratah and the Mount Bischoff mine. John's cousin, Cynthia Breheny, shared her memories of the C.V. Brooks School in Launceston.

In Canberra, Susan Hart read the draft manuscript and made many useful comments.

I wish to thank the following institutions for their helpful and efficient services: at the National Library of Australia – the staff of the Petherick Room, the Manuscripts and Pictorial Sections and the Newspapers collection; in Sydney – the State Records Office at Kingswood and the staff of the Mitchell Library. My thanks to the following institutions in the UK: the National Archives, Kew, the Suffolk County Council Records Office and the Whitelands College Archives in Chelsea.

Lastly, my loving thanks to my brother, Allan, who came with me on many journeys as we tracked down the Edgeworth David story; and to my husband, Rob, for his constant support.

Notes on the Text

Quotations in the text from the David family correspondence are all found in the David Family Papers at the National Library of Australia (MS 8890) unless otherwise acknowledged. Photographs are from Anne Edgeworth's collection unless otherwise attributed.

Tannatt William Edgeworth David is generally referred to in the text as David. His wife's affectionate name for him was Twed. He was widely and affectionately known as 'The Professor' to friends, colleagues and the public.

David's wife, Caroline, was universally known as Cara; her family's pet name for her was Mootie, from the German *Mutti*.

All measurements are given in Imperial form. The equivalents are set out below:

1 mile = 1.60 kilometres
1 acre = 0.40 hectares
1000 feet = 304.8 metres
£1 = $2 (in 1966)
For unskilled workers, a weekly wage in 1907 was about £3

The Edgeworth David children, about the time of their visit to Wales in 1895

Introduction

This book grew out of my conversations with a Canberra poet, Anne Edgeworth. Anne, until a recent illness which led to her death in 2011, had been actively engaged with Canberra cultural life since the 1950s as a theatre producer, a program presenter for community radio, and a respected poet. In 1994, she was named Canberra Citizen of the Year in recognition of these services.

In 2007 I was invited to help Anne put together a retrospective selection of her poetry, a selection that looks back over the issues that had engaged her passion and energies over many decades. Some of these poems celebrate Anne's remarkable forebears, especially her grandfather, the geologist and Antarctic explorer, Tannatt William Edgeworth David, and her own parents, Margaret and William Keverall (Bill) McIntyre. Anne always maintained a strong interest in the past generations of her family and became an active custodian of the Edgeworth David Papers in 1987, subsequently donating them to the National Library of Australia. A writer and teacher herself, Anne recognized the importance of the material contained within this family archive, which encapsulated over a hundred years of Australian history. She had a special interest in the lives of three women who played an important role in her own upbringing: her grandmother, Cara David; her own mother, Margaret McIntyre (née Edgeworth David); and her aunt, Mary (Molly) Edgeworth David. Through conversations with Anne over the course of six months, I learnt a great deal about these three women, who were united by close bonds of love and kinship. All three were highly intelligent and independent-minded women who did not always tread a conventional pathway. Over one hundred years ago, Anne's grandmother, Cara (whose story occupies the bulk of this book), broke off a promising educational career to marry but maintained a lifelong interest in the welfare and education of girls and young women, and was an influential figure in the early feminist movement. Cara's two daughters both became resourceful women in their own right, Margaret as an independent politician and community leader and Molly as a respected author and environmentalist. Cara's son, Billy David, has a minor but significant place in this family story.

Anne Edgeworth often reflected on the proud heritage these three women had left for her. Her grandmother, emigrating to Australia in the late Victorian era, proved to be a pioneer, establishing the first college in NSW to train women teachers. Her adventurous spirit found its match in a lifelong partnership with another émigré, T.W. Edgeworth David. They spent some of their early married life under canvas, when David worked as a surveyor for the NSW Department of Mines. Settling in Sydney when David became Professor of Geology at the University of Sydney in 1891, the couple raised three children there while actively engaged with many aspects of Sydney's cultural life. They were among an influential group of intellectuals – teachers, writers, lawyers and scientists – who were working to create a more enlightened and compassionate society, one in which a generous education would be the birthright of every child, and one where the old evils of exploitation and abuse would be reined in by just legislation. Cara David's own staunch feminism was to see her rise to leadership in one of the first significant political campaigns by women, that of the temperance movement. After the Great War, she played an influential role in the worldwide Girl Guides movement.

While her children were still young, Cara was to accompany her husband on a geological expedition to a Pacific island and later, on excursions to the Kosciuszko region in search of evidence for glaciation. Always of a strongly practical disposition, she was adept at all the domestic arts, mastered the skills required to run a small rural property, and managed the family finances and investments. She was also a passionate advocate for the rights and welfare of women and children and helped support legislation in this field.

Her two daughters grew up strongly influenced by this capable, warm-hearted and energetic woman. Both girls, educated largely at home, were able to matriculate quite young and in the 1900s were among the early women graduates of the University of Sydney, where their father's Department of Geology was a pioneer in its acceptance of women on the staff and as students. Both girls were encouraged by their parents to think of careers or active engagement with community life after they graduated; but in fact their young adult years were to be shadowed by events outside their control.

The first of these was the departure of their father with Ernest Shackleton to the Antarctic in 1908. During the long months of her husband's absence, with no communication possible with the outside world, Cara David, indomitable and outgoing in public, suffered a continuing private anguish that was expressed in insomnia and a range of physical ailments. Her elder daughter, Margaret, was especially aware of what her mother was suffering and did her best to support her during the sixteen months of David's absence. She was already engaged to marry, but put aside planning for her future life to stay by her mother's side. After the expedition's triumphant return to Australia in March 1909, Margaret married her fiancé, Bill McIntyre, and moved to the remote mining town of Mount Bischoff in Tasmania. There she nearly died of puerperal fever after the birth of her baby.

Horrified at this near fatality, her parents offered a loan to Bill so he could study medicine in Edinburgh. The McIntyres spent the war years there and after graduation, Bill served in Thessalonika with the British Army. After the war they returned to Tasmania where Bill became a respected family doctor and they raised four children. Margaret's considerable energies and creativity found expression in many ways: she directed the Launceston Repertory Company; she helped found a progressive school; and she became state commissioner for the Girl Guides. In 1948, she was asked to stand as an independent for the Tasmanian Legislative Council and was elected, the first woman elected in the state. She died a few months later in a plane crash.

Margaret's younger sister, Molly, was closely affected by the events of the Great War. Like many women of her generation, she was to lose the man she hoped to marry during those years; he was killed on Gallipoli. She spent the first years of the war helping her mother run a convalescent home for returned soldiers in the Blue Mountains; later she worked in a munitions factory in Canada and drove vehicles for the Women's Army Corps in Britain. Her talents as a writer emerged when she wrote her father's biography after his death in 1934. *Professor David* was published in England in 1938, to professional and personal acclaim. Molly went on to write two more books. *Passages of Time* – a memoir of her remarkable family – was published by University of Queensland Press in 1975 and was their 'best selling book ever' at that time. *Letters to Meg*, a series of imaginary and nostalgic letters to her sister 'in a far country', was written when she was in her nineties and published posthumously. Molly David was a well-known and much-loved identity in Hornsby where she lived an active, quietly self-sufficient life on a large semi-rural block until her death at 99.

Part 1: Cara

Prologue

In the northern spring of 1882, a distinguished colonial stepped ashore from a steamer at Liverpool and made his way to London. Illness and the stress of overwork had forced Sir Henry Parkes to take leave from his office as Premier of New South Wales and have an extended period of rest and a change of scene abroad.

In London, Parkes was feted as the Empire's most eminent colonial statesman. He dined with Mr Gladstone, discussed the purchase of art at the Royal Academy with the Prince of Wales and spent some days with the Poet Laureate, Lord Tennyson, at his home on the Isle of Wight.

In the midst of this social whirl – he confessed to his wife that he had had to open an engagement book – Sir Henry was mindful of the obligations of his office, and especially of the challenges provided by the new *Education Act* which had come into force in New South Wales in April 1880. The premier's own passionate interest in the importance of free, secular, public education for all young people had been the guiding force behind the passing of this Act which had brought widespread changes to education in the colony. State aid to church schools was abolished; public high schools for both boys and girls were established in the major towns; and a new college for training women teachers was to be opened in Sydney.

One task that Parkes hoped to perform in London was to engage a competent person to fill the office of principal of the new training college. Enquiries were made through the Right Honourable Anthony Mundella, president of the Committee of the Privy Council on Education. Having sat opposite Mr Mundella at a Royal Academy banquet, Parkes felt that here was a man whose judgment and experience he could trust. Mundella acted promptly and within a few days sent the premier a memo: 'Dear Sir Henry. I have found the right person for your Training College. When will you see her? I should like to tell you personally all I have learnt about her.'[1]

The young person in question was Miss Caroline Martha Mallett, a lecturer or 'governess' at the respected Whitelands Training College for women in Chelsea. Miss Mallett came with glowing references, having been a star pupil at the college before being appointed to the teaching staff. After her interview with Parkes, she accepted the position as the new principal of Hurlstone Training College in Sydney, at a salary of £300 per annum.

At the time of her appointment, Caroline Mallett was twenty-six years old. There was no sweetheart, nor any close family ties to keep her in England. Her records from Whitelands College state that she was an orphan. She told Parkes that personally, she was prepared to leave England at any time but could not honourably leave the college until she had concluded a course of lectures she was giving. A sense of duty kept her at Chelsea for another term, but after that, the new world beckoned, and with it, the challenge of an independent and prestigious career in a prosperous colony. She embarked on the steamship *Potosi* at Gravesend on 7 October 1882, bound for Sydney.

1 Early Years

Caroline Mallett was always known as Cara. She was not in fact an orphan, though she did lose her father very early in life. He drowned at sea, in the cold northern waters off the Suffolk coast.

Samuel Mallett was a fisherman. As a young man he worked in boats along the east coast off Southwold, where much of the bounty of the sea was harvested: sole, plaice and cod were hauled in every day and in autumn the drifters bought in heavy loads of mackerel and herring, to be gutted, sorted and salted into barrels by Scottish women who came down for the season, working on tables on the shingle just where the boats were drawn up. It must have been freezing work in the grey autumns of that district, the women up to their elbows in icy water and the winds blowing chill off the North Sea. The sea brought a livelihood to many of the labouring poor of the county, but it also brought death. The east coast was as dangerous as the stormy south-west and Southwold regularly lost its men and ships as they were blown by gales onto the treacherous sandbanks off shore.

Samuel married a local girl, Pamela Wright, at Kessingland, a village in Suffolk, in June 1853. Their first child, Thomas William Mallett, was born in May 1854, and Caroline Martha Mallett arrived two years later

The day's catch, Southwold (Noeline Kyle)

Packing herrings, Southwold (Noeline Kyle)

on 26 April 1856. By this stage the Malletts were living in Southwold. The third child, Sarah Elizabeth Mallet, was born on 5 September 1858. Six months later, on 9 March 1859, Samuel Mallett was drowned, swept off his ship near Flamborough Head. At the time of his death he was working as crew on the *Albion*, a steamer based at Southwold which took passengers to London from Yarmouth.

If Pamela Mallett mourned her husband's death, it was by seeking consolation in the arms of other men. Her fourth child, Martha Ann, was born in November 1860. The birth certificate refers to the baby as 'daughter of Samuel and Pamela Mallett' and states that her father, a fisherman, was deceased. No doubt this subterfuge was intended to give some respectability to the illegitimate birth but the deception would not have fooled her own family or the gossips of a close-knit community. Pamela lived with the three older children and the baby in one of a row of fishermen's cottages at Southwold, on the beach road facing the grey North Sea. Cara remembered her mother singing to her as a very young child.

A local mariner, Richard Skinner, took an interest in the young woman. He was a pilot, working on vessels off the Southwold coast. He was married at the time, but had no children.

In April 1866, Pamela gave birth to another child, named Elizabeth Skinner on the birth certificate, born at Wenhaston, a small village about five miles inland from Southwold. Then in September 1868, Richard Skinner was born, also at Wenhaston. By this stage Pamela was prepared to register children born out of wedlock and give them the father's name. In mid-Victorian days this would have been a most unusual decision. Was it an act of defiance or indifference? Her behaviour would have been a source both of shame and grief to her parents. Pamela's father, William Wright, was a schoolmaster, probably receiving a meagre income from running a school in his own premises in Southwold. He would have been literate but there is evidence to suggest that his wife, Caroline Wright, could not read. Both parents would have valued the modest respectability that William's position bestowed on the family. Their daughter's behaviour was not something they could accept or forgive and they cut themselves off from contact with her. However, they did stay closely in touch with one of her children. The young Cara Mallett was largely brought up by her grandmother, Caroline Wright, who recognized the girl's potential and hoped to help her rise in the world through education and thus avoid the unhappy destiny of her mother, Pamela. Cara grew up believing her mother was dead: in 1875, the eighteen-year-old Cara Mallett is listed in official records as an orphan yet her mother, Pamela Mallett, did not die until late 1877.[1]

Cara Mallett's early schooling took place at St Edmund's in Southwold. St Edmund's School was a 'National School', administered by the National Society for the Promotion of Education of the Poor in the Principles of the Established Church. The Church of England had established this society in 1811 to meet the need for elementary education of the working classes. By this means it was hoped to keep England free of the dangerous revolutionary fervour abroad in Europe.

Cara was a bright and determined young girl, who may have stood out from her peers in her eagerness to learn and to please. She acquired a cruel nickname, the Suffolk Punch, as the children mocked the thick ankles that showed under her pinafore. (The Suffolk Punch is a sturdy pony with thick hairy hocks.) Her competency and ambition led to an appointment in 1870 when she was still thirteen as a 'pupil-teacher' at St Edmund's. Cara was paid a salary of £10 per annum in return for her service in the classroom. There she helped the schoolmaster keep order, drilled the pupils in numbers and spelling, and instructed the young girls in sewing. At times it may have been uninspiring and repetitive work and yet it laid the basis of her lifelong interest in the education and nurture of children.

As a pupil-teacher, Cara boarded near the school in Victoria Street, with her uncle George Sturr, a fisherman, and his wife. Victoria

Street was home to the labouring poor. A rope-maker lived there with ten children to support; a thirty-nine-year-old widow worked as a charlady; there were men who worked as bricklayers, horse drivers, blacksmiths and fishermen, with young lads barely in their teens serving as apprentices. A number of girls became maidservants. The children of the street, improbably known as 'scholars' in the census records, attended St Edmund's, taking lessons under the watchful eye of the schoolmaster and his young assistant, pupil-teacher Cara Mallett.

At the time of the 1871 census, Pamela Mallett is also listed as living in Victoria Street. She was thirty-eight years old, a widow, with five children still under the same roof. Her son, Thomas, was sixteen and had become a shoemaker and the breadwinner for the family. Then there were the younger girls, Sarah and Martha, and the two children fathered by Richard Skinner.[2] Was Cara aware that her mother lived nearby, and that some of the youngsters in the schoolroom with her were her own kin? Anne Edgeworth says she certainly would have heard gossip about the family, cruelly magnified by childish tongues.

After four years of service as a pupil-teacher, Cara sat for a Queen's Scholarship late in 1874 and was one of sixty-four successful entrants to begin a two-year training course at Whitelands College in Chelsea. As well as gaining a scholarship, Cara won a prize of £3 given by the Society for the Propagation of Christian Knowledge for obtaining a first-class result in the Religious Knowledge exam.

Cara began her course at Whitelands in February 1875. All except four of the new students who started with her had been pupil-teachers before joining the college. Most of them came from respectable working-class families: the occupations of their parents included a railway official, a cabinetmaker, a schoolmaster, a watchmaker and a farmer. Nineteen of the students were listed as orphans, Cara Mallett among them. The provision of grants through the Queen's Scholarship, which allowed the best of the pupil-teachers to win an entry into training college, gave such parentless children every incentive to acquire an education and train as elementary schoolteachers. In Cara's case the scholarship provided for the young girl a step up into a different world. At a time when she would not have been able to study at university, a teacher training college offered Cara the only avenue to intellectual training of a formal kind. She was to respond to the opportunity with enthusiasm and passion.

Whitelands College had been founded in 1841 by the same national society which had administered St Edmund's at Southwold. Entrants to the college signed an undertaking to complete two years at Whitelands and also do two years teaching in a school for the poor or in any such school as the committee of the School Council should determine. The college aimed 'to produce a superior class of parochial School-mistresses … by affording them an appropriate education'.[3] If this sounds as though the college was limiting its students' prospects and confirming entrenched class divisions, this turned out not to be the case for many bright young women who entered its doors. A remarkable number of Whitelands graduates in the last quarter of the century eventually became headmistresses and many were also appointed as lecturers and principals at other training colleges in England and in the colonies. A few managed in later years to read for degrees at Oxford and Cambridge or from the University of St Andrews.

After 1870, elementary education became compulsory in England, so many more trained elementary schoolteachers were needed in both church schools and the new board schools.

The reputation which Whitelands College gained as a first-class teaching institute meant that its graduates were in high demand. Its good name owed much to the energy and initiative of its young principal, appointed just a year before Cara's arrival at the college. The Reverend John Faunthorpe was the first principal to be appointed at Whitelands; before that the college had been under the direction of a Church of England curate with a lady superintendent to manage the daily life of the students. Faunthorpe was a graduate of London

Miss Mallett, the young teacher

University and a trained teacher. He was determined that Whitelands should become the best training college in England. In addition to the basic government syllabus, Faunthorpe added French to the timetable, Latin (for selected students), several science subjects, especially botany, additional English literature, additional art, algebra and geometry and kindergarten theory. That Cara Mallett absorbed and valued this wealth and breadth of knowledge is evident from the hundreds of books she brought out with her to New South Wales in 1882, books which ranged over the full spectrum of courses she had studied and then taught,under John Faunthorpe.

The teaching at the college was carried out by 'governesses'. This was the term used to describe women who would now be known as lecturers, and who had the full responsibility for the academic progress of the students. The teaching methods were thorough and to modern eyes rather regimented. There was reading and repetition from memory, grammar and composition, geography, history, arithmetic, sewing and cutting out and domestic economy. Each Saturday morning there was an examination and students who gained less than half marks had to repeat the examination on Saturday afternoon. There was much emphasis on rote learning and drill, but it brought results, with many students winning prizes at government examinations. Military drill was the only form of vigorous outdoor exercise provided and was conducted by a regimental sergeant major, Mr Elliot. The daily timetable also included much of the cleaning and cooking at the college, so that the trainees would be able to teach their students the basics of household care. This served to reinforce their lower middle-class character as such menial tasks would never have been asked of women higher up the social scale. But a love of the arts and a wider cultural vision were also seen as important elements in their education and were encouraged by Faunthorpe. In 1881, a fine chapel was erected in the grounds, in later years to be beautified by windows and interior designed by William Morris. Faunthorpe also started a well-equipped Sunday Library for the students.

One distinguished Victorian who took a keen interest in the progress of Whitelands was John Ruskin, who gave hundreds of books and pictures to the college, including a cabinet specially made to display forty-eight engravings and copies of paintings by Turner. An embossed version of the Koran was one of Ruskin's gifts on display, as well as a mediaeval Bible and a superb collection of bird paintings by John Gould. A letter survives from Ruskin expressing pleasure in the gift of a beautiful embroidered vest made by the students and presented to him by Miss Stanley, the assistant governess. The college had a reputation for high standards in needlework and also choral music. If these were conventional feminine accomplishments in the Victorian era, they would also have represented a gracious and civilizing influence in the lives of many of these young women.

The report of Her Majesty's Inspector for 1882 noted that at the college 'extreme kindness is combined with eager industry'. Such characteristics were possible because Whitelands was run along the lines of a large Victorian family home. The principal did not live there but worked a twelve-hour day and the resident governesses and lady superintendent exercised a strong influence over almost every aspect of student life, with compulsory daily prayers and scripture readings, one and a half hours a day of lesson preparation under the supervision of a governess, 'Drilling' on Tuesday and Thursday nights and on other evenings, Singing Practice.

Cara Mallett flourished in this benign and orderly environment if we are to judge by her academic successes. In her first year she won a prize for French, receiving a copy of Racine's plays, a drawing prize and one for School Management. In her second year she won prizes for Domestic Economy, Sanitary Science, Needlework, Cutting-Out, Knitting and Drawing. The college often selected her work to show to distinguished guests as an example of high academic standards at the college. For her prize for educational theory she received a copy of Palgrave's *Golden Treasury*, one of the many books that accompanied her on her journey to New South Wales.

Upon graduating from Whitelands in 1876, Cara Mallett was chosen to stay on as governess. Miss Matilda Gillott, the head governess, had been killed in a road accident that year and in October Miss Kate

Stanley, an assistant governess, was appointed head governess with a salary of £100 a year, to start from Christmas 1876. Miss Stanley's own position was to be filled by Miss Cara Mallett, appointed as fifth governess with a salary of £40 a year including board and lodging, to rise by £5 a year at the recommendation of the principal. Cara had not yet sat for her end of year exams but Faunthorpe recommended her appointment on the basis of her previous results.

Cara Mallett taught at Whitelands College for six years. During that time she was also furthering her own education. She gained a first-class certificate in Advanced Animal Physiology at the Normal School of Science at South Kensington (where the British Department of Science and Art conducted exams), won prizes for her studies in Sanitary Science and gained an award from the St John Ambulance Association. She received a promotion every year and by 1881 her salary had been increased to £95, which included a bonus voted by the council for the teaching of science. This was a considerable amount for a young woman to be earning at this time.

On being offered the position as principal at Hurlstone College in Sydney at the excellent salary of £300 per annum, Cara accepted immediately. There was nothing holding her except the obligation to finish the course of lectures she was giving. There were many reasons why she felt ready to leave England. As a young woman she already had a clear understanding of the class system in which she'd grown up. In 1887, she wrote from New South Wales to her younger sister, Sarah, after Sarah's marriage to Elgin Carter, a master bricklayer and bellringer at St Edmund's Church in Southwold. She urged Sarah and her husband 'to raise yourselves by every honest means, so that there are fewer in the family afflicted with want, which is such a dreadful crime in England'.

Cara must have known that she could never go back to Suffolk. She could not marry into that community of manual workers and fishermen and would not have cared to work there again. She had

Whitelands exterior (Whitelands College archives)

Whitelands garden (Whitelands College archives)

Whitelands staffroom (Whitelands College archives)

Whitelands street (Whitelands College archives)

left her respectable working-class origins behind when she came to London as a student, but she remembered the poverty and limited horizons that had defined the world of her childhood. Her education at Whitelands and her years as a governess there had equipped her to be at ease among educated middle-class individuals and to move confidently in a variety of social and professional circles. Anne Edgeworth recalls that Cara as an older woman had no trace of a Suffolk dialect but spoke pleasant, unaffected English. Perhaps her grandmother taught her to speak standard English: as a child this would have set her apart from the fishermen's children of the town with their heavy Suffolk burrs.

Given the class system in England at the time, Cara would not have been able to marry 'above her station', in a society where lowly social origins were a handicap for a woman, however assured and accomplished.

Cara knew of the difficulties facing middle-class female teachers in England and of the low status most of them were accorded. Maud, a fellow-student and friend of hers, was the daughter of a poor country vicar. With her training at Whitelands finished, Maud obtained a position with one of the newly established local board schools, a well-paid position with a relatively high salary and good working conditions. But her mother was ostracized by the local gentry when it was discovered that her daughter was working at a board school. There was no alternative for Maud but to give up her position and seek more socially acceptable, though less well-paid, work as a private governess. Cara visited her friend some time after this to find her in very reduced circumstances.[4] Experiences of this kind instilled in Cara a lifelong loathing of social pretension and snobbery, and she passed this attitude on to her two daughters.

As a well-paid professional woman, Cara was able to help support her grandmother, who had married again after the death of Cara's grandfather, William. The one written reference to this matter, in a letter to her sister, Sarah, suggests that Cara felt a certain bitterness at the demands this new relative has put on her. In 1887 she wrote, 'My grandmother and her husband were a great expense to me before I was married. I find it very hard that after giving so much to a man who was no relation at all, I should not be able to help the one whom I love.' (Cara had hoped to visit Sarah in England but did not have the funds to do so.)

There were other factors prompting Cara's decision to leave England. The threat of inherited lung disease lay like a dark cloud over her family. She called it 'the curse of our family ... it has taken off a great many of our relatives'. Her beloved sister, Sarah, was to be among those who succumbed to tuberculosis, and her own mother's death in 1877 was allegedly caused by it. Cara's daughter, Molly, recalled her mother's reasons for applying for the Hurlstone position. She said her mother had fallen ill during the London winter from overwork, staying up late at nights correcting examination papers. Her doctor, when she recovered, informed her that if she didn't leave England for a healthier climate – he suggested Canada or Australia – she would have about six months to live. Even for more robust constitutions, the foggy London winters would have been hard to endure in the Victorian era.

After Cara left England in 1882, she did not see her immediate Mallett relatives again. Any communication with her grandmother was through Sarah. At some stage in her adolescence or later, Cara must have re-established contact with her siblings. She loved Sarah above all and called her 'my favourite and dear, good-hearted sister'. Her brother, Thomas, had a history that troubled her, as he was said to be an alcoholic.

Thirty years later, in 1912, Cara's younger daughter, Molly, visited England to see her sister, Margaret, and to stay with relatives of her father. While there, Molly got in touch with a cousin, one of her mother's nieces, who worked in a Midlands town as a shop assistant. They met for lunch. It was a painful, embarrassing occasion. Evidently the niece interpreted Molly's educated accent and reserved demeanour as signs of patronizing snobbery, and Molly, painfully shy as a young woman, would have found friendly contact even harder to achieve in the face of this response. There was no further contact with any Mallett relatives in England.[5]

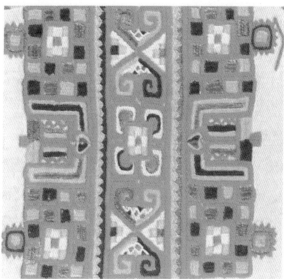

Samples of needlework from Whitelands College (Whitelands College Archives)

2   Lady Principal

In 1880, Sir Saul Samuel was appointed as Agent General for New South Wales in London. In the colony he had made his name as an astute and successful businessman and politician: in the 1870s he served in Henry Parkes' government as postmaster-general. He was Agent-General in London till 1897 and during that time vigorously advanced the claims of the colony. He negotiated hefty government loans to assist the state's development, fostered assisted immigration and negotiated with the P&O shipping company for weekly mail services to New South Wales.

Samuel took a personal interest in the story of Miss Caroline Mallett. He gave Cara a letter of introduction to people of influence in Sydney which she later found most useful in getting to know people. He arranged her passage on the steamship *Potosi*, the New South Wales government paying for the ticket, and accompanied her to the ship on departure day.

Whitelands College staff said goodbye to Cara with reluctance. John Faunthorpe wrote a warm reference for her which he sent to Henry Parkes to help him make his choice. He detailed a long list of prizes and first-class results that Cara had gained as a student and as a governess. He then admitted, 'I am the more regretful after seeing this list of certificates than I was before that she is leaving me.'[1] Kate Stanley, the head governess, testified to Cara's high personal character as well as her unusual ability as a teacher, and wrote of the love and respect she inspired in her students.

The young woman who embarked with her luggage at Gravesend on 7 October 1882 was one of many such educated, single women teachers who emigrated in that period to the far reaches of the Empire or to North America to work as 'governesses'. Some were sponsored by the Middle Class Emigration Society, which was set up in 1862 to help educated young women find work in the colonies; others left England with only their own resources. Some were going to prestigious positions, as Cara Mallett was. Miss Carr, head governess of the Derby Training College, left England at the same time as Cara to take up a position in India as principal of the Government Female Normal School in Madras.[2]

At twenty-six, Cara Mallett was no longer a young woman; indeed by nineteenth-century standards she was nearing the age when she might be termed an 'old maid'. But she was a personable and good-looking woman. Her daughter, Molly, quoted friends who spoke of her beauty. In her photos she appeared assured, even regal, with fine skin and bone structure, a luxuriant head of hair and dark, questioning eyes. She wore stylish clothes without frills or flounces. Undoubtedly, she had presence. John Faunthorpe said that she would be 'an ornament to any College'. In his letter to Henry Parkes, Sir Saul Samuel wrote of her in flattering but patronizing terms: 'You made an excellent choice and I admire your taste … she is a most charming young woman, and I do not think that you will have her very long in the Government Service. I shall be very much surprised if she does not very soon after her arrival change her name.'[3]

Besides her personal luggage, Cara took with her on the journey trunks full of books. They tell a story in themselves. Many of them had been gifts from her principal, Mr Faunthorpe, among them *Cromwell's Letters*, *Animal Physiology* and *Notes on Nursing* (by Miss Nightingale).

Cara Mallett, about the time of her appointment to Hurlstone College

Then there were many prizes: Shakespeare's *Collected Plays*, *The Jewish Nation*, *Mrs Beeton's Cookery Book*. The books ranged across natural history, religious studies, the classics (in French and English), German and Italian grammars, elementary chemistry, anatomy and botany. John Ruskin was represented by *The Stones of Venice* and *Modern Painters*. *Plain Needlework* and *Young Housewives' Assistant* were there to remind her of the important role 'domestic economy' would still play in the curriculum for female teachers; but other books must surely have been Cara's own favourites and included for just that reason: Mark Twain's *The Innocents Abroad*, Jane Austen's *Mansfield Park*, all of George Eliot's novels and a complete set of Dickens.

There were thirteen books by Charles Darwin in her luggage, including *On the Origin of Species*, *Geological Observations*, *Fertilisation of Orchids* and *The Descent of Man*. One of the unresolved tensions of Cara's life was in trying to reconcile a fervent desire for religious certainty with contemporary scientific theories.

The 'domestic sanitation' courses at Whitelands had a strong temperance emphasis and two of the books Cara brought with her were *The Temperance Lesson Book* and *Dialogues on Drink*. Whitelands was a Church of England establishment and its church-going leaders shared the concerns of many educated middle-class people that alcohol was destroying the social and moral fabric of working-class life. In May 1878, the principal, teachers and pupils at Whitelands prepared a petition to go to the House of Commons seeking the closing of public houses on Sundays.[4]

On Cara's arrival in Sydney she stayed in an apartment arranged for her by Henry Parkes. But her home for the next two and a half years was to be at Hurlstone College in Ashfield. In the 1860s, Ashfield was an agricultural district given over to orchards and market gardening. In the next decade and with the colony's increasing prosperity, much of the open space was subdivided to provide suburban retreats for wealthy Sydney businessmen and officials. They built grand homes on the pleasantly undulating land with its fine vistas towards the city and the Parramatta River. The Hurlstone estate sat on the high ground between what are now the suburbs of Ashfield and Canterbury. In 1874 John Kinlock, an itinerant mathematics and physical education teacher, purchased part of an area known as the Canterbury Estate and drew up ambitious plans to build and run his own school there. It was to be called the Hurlstone School and College. However, before long Kinloch ran into financial difficulties. He decided to subdivide the estate and keep only nine acres for the college. It was at this point that the New South Wales government stepped in, offering to purchase the whole estate in 1880 for the purposes of establishing the state's first training college for female teachers.

There was much to be done at the new college, and Cara had to be the guiding force pushing for change or improvements. She found that the existing buildings, while pleasantly situated on a rise with a northerly aspect, were not entirely suitable for the efficient running of a residential college. There was no sick room for an emergency; there were too few bathrooms and the college was completely dependent on erratic Sydney rainfall for its water supply; there were no storerooms for linen or household provisions; the kitchen was small and the scullery merely a rough shed. The twenty-eight students shared large dormitories, each with their own small cubicle but with very little privacy. They had no sitting room so had nowhere to spend their leisure time except in the lecture room or dining room, which were bare of any creature comforts apart from a piano in the dining room. At times Cara must have thought back wistfully to the quiet, well-equipped library at Whitelands, the art studio with its tall windows, the gymnasium, the well-furnished and book-lined staff sitting room. The department promised extensive alterations but they were slow in coming. Cara sent an exasperated memo to the under-secretary, Peter Board, in April 1883: 'The building additions to Hurlstone College, which were approved by the Minister some three months ago, are really

Hurlstone College, 1883 (*Sydney Mail*)

Hurlstone College (Ashfield & District Historical Society)

too necessary to admit of infinite delay. Will you be good enough to order that they be done immediately?'[5] The leaking walls were finally waterproofed by the start of 1884. The building additions completed during that year included bedrooms and sitting rooms for teachers, extra dormitories and storerooms. A windmill had been installed but the grounds were still 'sadly in need of attention'.

As in any Victorian establishment, there were servants aplenty: six altogether, including a caretaker, and a lady superintendent to manage them and the domestic arrangements for the college. And because this was New South Wales in an era of cheap and abundant food, the meals would have been the envy of many English people: porridge and meat at breakfast, 'hot joint and two vegetables and pudding' every dinnertime, honey, stewed fruit and cakes, tea and cocoa, bread and butter for tea. There was a fowl-yard standing empty on the property when Cara arrived. She promptly put in a request to the department to purchase fowls: 'the scraps of food would feed a good number of [them]'. She also asked for a cow, so by the end of the year most of the milk and eggs required were produced on the property. Meat and vegetables had to be delivered as there was no vegetable garden, though Cara reported dryly that six sets of garden tools had been provided 'as a means of amusement' for the students.[6]

During her first year at Hurlstone, Cara not only managed student and business affairs but taught the students for the bulk of their curriculum. She taught English Literature, Geography, Reading and Elocution, and Domestic Economy, which included cookery and needlework. In her annual report Cara noted that the crowded timetable did not allow space for much practical work in these areas, but the students did sweep out their own cubicles, dust the dormitories and lecture room, and take it in turns to cook Monday's dinner for the establishment. A resident governess superintended the students for private study for two hours every evening except Saturdays and every alternate Wednesday, and also taught them Arithmetic, Grammar and

History. Four visiting teachers came in to instruct in French, Drawing, Music and Drill. The accepted form of Physical Education was, as at Whitelands, a form of military drill, which was considered in that era to inculcate the self-discipline a schoolteacher would require and also improve the students' 'deportment and physique'. During her second year Cara arranged for a croquet lawn and a lawn tennis court to be built for the students to use.

It was a disappointment to her that there was no science in the one-year curriculum, but the timetable was already overcrowded and it was not considered a priority for trainee teachers. In accordance with the secular aims of the *Education Act* of 1880, no religious instruction of any description was given in the college, though prayers were read twice a day, at 8.30 am and 9 pm; students could please themselves about attending them.

Who were these young women who came under Cara Mallett's guidance? The great majority of them were pupil-teachers from humble backgrounds. From very early in their teens they had been apprenticed for three or four years to a schoolmaster and worked in a large mixed classroom under his guidance. They were supposed to be given at least one hour a day of after-school instruction to help them in their school duties and to prepare them for the entrance exam to the training college. But real intellectual training was non-existent. Once they arrived at the training school much of the material in a crowded curriculum was leant by rote and probably had very little significance for them because they had neither the maturity nor the leisure to make sense of it. These aspects of the curriculum troubled Cara but she did not have the authority to change this entrenched system of pedagogy.

An early source of frustration to her at Hurlstone was the need to approach the department in writing for every piece of petty expenditure, until George Reid, the Minister for Education, gave instructions to allow some discretionary spending. From the start, Reid was a strong supporter of Cara and her initiatives at the new college. He personally authorized her to set up a 'demonstration school' in a building erected in the college grounds, where the students would gain practical experience of working with children in a classroom.

It wasn't long into the teaching year before Cara's spirited convictions brought her into conflict with the public servants who ran the Department of Public Instruction in Bridge Street. She was especially concerned at the narrow focus of the course she was required to teach in English literature. In her first year, nineteen of her twenty-eight pupils came to her after six months' study at Fort Street Training School, which up till then trained public school teachers, both men and women. For reasons of continuity Cara decided to let the students proceed with the courses they had been studying. She was not impressed by what she saw and in June 1883 wrote a sharply worded letter to the departmental head:

> The 'literature' consists in learning up the lives of all the literary men from the earliest Saxon times to the present day. I beg leave to submit that such a cramming of literary biography is not a study of literature; that so many hundreds of biographies are rather crushing when added to the other work of the term … they are no value to mental training, and are not likely long to enrich the memories of the hapless students. I have therefore to suggest that the study of literature at Hurlstone should mean, in the future, the study of one or two books prescribed by the Department.[7]

The head of studies at Fort Street, John Wright, hastened to send a reply defending his program and enclosing a copy of his 1882 English literature exam paper. In the end, however, Cara's voice was heard in the department. After being asked to submit detailed suggestions for a change of syllabus, she was gratified to learn in July 1883 that the Hurlstone students would be allowed to study a period of English literature in depth and read closely two works from the period. The chief examiner suggested the period 1560–1680: the works to be portions of Milton's *A Masque of Comus* and Shakespeare's *Julius Caesar.* But this change of policy was to cost her dearly and earn her enemies among the senior men in the department, some of whom had been in positions of authority for years.

In June 1883, Cara was advised that mid-year exams for the Hurlstone students would take place in the Fort Street School in the city. She had a request to make: could the students be allowed to sit the exams at Hurlstone? The expense of a return train fare to the city, and the added expense of buying lunch, was beyond the means of many of her students. As well, a twenty-minute walk from the station left them with wet and muddy shoes all day if it rained. This request brought a heated and defensive retort from the chief examiner, John Gardiner:

> For seventeen years it has been my duty to deal with all matters pertaining to the Training and Classification of students. Never until Miss Mallett's appearance at Hurlstone has any attempt been made to invade it. But now, after having had so much conceded to her, she seeks to ignore the Department … I sincerely trust that the Minister will not yield to such an ill-advised and unreasonable application.[8]

The minister decreed that the exams were to continue at Fort Street as arranged but that students were to be given expenses for travel and lunch. He also regretted the unnecessary 'warmth' expressed in the minutes coming from the Examiner's Branch.

A less strong-minded woman than Cara Mallett might have found the job at Hurlstone both daunting and demoralizing. Bridge Street's hostility took a public form, with an article in the *Sydney Mail* in May 1883 describing the new college. It was clear where the paper's sympathies lay. The article expressed reservations about the lady principal whose views of the nature of her office seemed to be so at odds with that of her superiors and warned that 'the experience of an old official, who has either grown up under a system, or the system has grown up under him, is a valuable check upon hasty reforms'.[9]

We have no record of Cara's private, inner life during her years at Hurlstone. At times she must have wanted to escape the confines of the boarding school atmosphere and the emotional solitude which was the lot of the single teacher. Certainly she had letters of introduction to people of influence in Sydney, but later evidence shows that she disliked formal social gatherings. Shortly after arriving at Hurlstone Cara acquired a white horse called Bunyip and residents recalled seeing her cantering out of the college gates and off into the Canterbury bushland. Perhaps these were her only real moments of uncomplicated pleasure.

Her second year at Hurlstone, 1884, must have been something of a nightmare for Cara. The criticisms and innuendos coming from Bridge Street intensified, as John Wright, the Fort Street principal, and John Gardiner, the chief examiner, both felt their credibility and position to have been compromised by a young and outspoken woman. They took their revenge in June 1884, when the results came out of the yearly exams of the intake of students from June 1883. These young women had been studying under Cara's newly designed English program. With a barely disguised note of triumph, Gardiner reported on the poor results: 'the results indicate that the students were unable to deal with the questions set' and accused Cara of 'supplying a program of studies that was not adhered to'. [10] John Wright went further: 'There should be a searching enquiry in to the workings of the College'.[11] Gardiner, gaining courage from what he saw as evidence of Cara's failings, wrote a fourteen page letter to the Under Secretary in September 1884, damning the lady principal in highly personal terms: she always chose 'to do as she thought fit, to have her own way in everything, and to be responsible to none but the Minister'.[12]

How did Cara respond to these accusations? We know from her

earlier comments that she was faced with a difficult task, of cramming into one year a course of study that to modern eyes seems onerous in the extreme. This was to be presented to young women in their teens who had little intellectual preparation for it, having come from a three or four year apprenticeship in the crowded classrooms of rural or suburban New South Wales. Having experienced a more liberal education at Whitelands, Cara wanted something better than the old system. She had hoped to read *Comus* and *Julius Caesar* with her students – had ordered thirty copies of each text to be available for the college library – only to find that there was little time for such luxuries in the crowded timetable. In a minute to the chief inspector in September 1884, and smarting under the attacks of John Gardiner, Cara let down her guard. She confessed to finding the results of all the exams 'painfully depressing … what ought I to do, what *can* I do, under the circumstances'.[13] As she had done before, she requested that the training program be extended to two years or else the standard of entry into the college be raised. Neither request was considered feasible by the department. With reference to the students' poor results in the June 1884 exams, the chief inspector recommended they be given a chance to re-set the exam in December that year. Cara, in a tone expressing both defeat and despair, wrote in November, 'I can add nothing to my minute of 15 September. Let the students attend the December exam if they desire to do so.'[14]

The chief inspector, perhaps finding the personal nature of the attack on Cara distasteful, terminated the correspondence and closed this file in November 1884.

Cara Mallett's work was vindicated in the inspectors' reports of May 1884 and April 1885, which warmly commended the positive atmosphere of the school, its efficient management and excellent teaching program. One of her successful innovations was the introduction of a kindergarten class as part of the demonstration school, under the direction of a teacher trained in this system. The *Kindergarten* was a German invention, and therefore viewed with much suspicion in the English-speaking world. Friedrich Froebel had developed the philosophy behind it, in the belief that very young children develop and flourish in an environment of playful and unfettered discovery. This was a very big contrast to the regimented world of the Victorian schoolroom, and many educators in England looked askance at the whole concept, regarding it as expensive to run and unproductive. One of Her Majesty's Inspectors of Schools in England had this to say about the system as he'd seen it implemented in limited form in some schools. He claimed that young children 'are not being well prepared for the serious work of school or of after life, if all that they are required to do looks like amusement and play. The kindergarten gives them nothing which seems like work – it does not train them to overcome difficulties.'[15]

Cara David was to develop a close circle of women friends in Sydney, many of whom were passionate about the welfare of women and children. They were fully supportive of the kindergarten philosophy and in fact Cara's friend, Maybanke Wolstenholme, established the colony's first free kindergarten in Sydney in 1896. Cara had studied the principles of the kindergarten movement at Whitelands and brought out with her to the colony a number of books about its theory and practice. She was glad to be able to implement some of these principles at Hurlstone.

By the end of 1884, Hurlstone College had expanded to fifty students in two classes. A second teaching assistant had been appointed. Miss Jane Webster was also a Whitelands graduate. Cara herself had recommended Miss Webster's appointment, having taught her at Whitelands when Jane had been training there in 1881. She must have found that the younger woman brought companionship and shared experiences to what was a lonely position as principal. In her book-lined study Cara now had the chance to mull over the events of the day with a congenial female friend. There were dramas enough to consume their energies: a student diagnosed with typhoid fever whose parents accused Cara of inadequate 'duty of care'; a complaint from a parent that his child had been unfairly expelled by Miss Bluett for writing 'dirty notes'; the college cook 'going on strike' for higher wages.

By the beginning of 1885, the building program at the college had been completed. There was a new lecture hall and a properly furnished dining room. As well, two large airy and well-lit dormitories were built where each student had her own cubicle and some degree of privacy. Cara reported that the students were working diligently and conscientiously and their conduct was excellent. Many of the pupil-teachers still came to the college with great gaps in their knowledge, especially in history; but she was confident that that would be resolved now that the subject of history was to be included in the training and examination for pupil-teachers. By the end of 1884, the departmental report submitted to the minister had nothing but praise for the young principal. That year, Cara was accepted into the prestigious British association of teachers, the Royal College of Preceptors, and could henceforth use the initials MRCP after her name. Colonial administrators would have been impressed: they still looked for the British stamp of approval on all their endeavours. The young Miss Mallett was earning a name for herself in educational circles. She was, in fact, one of the colony's first independent, highly qualified professional women.

3 Courtship and Marriage

A young Welshman, Tannatt William Edgeworth David, had travelled to New South Wales in October 1882 on the same ship as Cara Mallett. David was twenty-four years of age, a tall, slightly built figure, with the fresh complexion of northern climes and keen, deep-set blue eyes. People found him to be a courteous, easygoing but rather shy young man, bookish in inclination, but with surprising reserves of physical energy and stamina. He had been a scholar at Oxford, trained in the Classics, and his father, a Church of England minister, had expected David to enter holy orders after his undergraduate studies. Instead, David was embarking for the new world and a very different life to that to be found in a comfortable country rectory in Wales. He was to work as a surveyor with the New South Wales Geological Survey, in a colony experiencing a burst of growth and prosperity and, with it, the need to exploit its untapped mineral resources.

Sir Saul Samuel, who arranged David's passage and paid for his saloon-class ticket, also gave him a letter of introduction to Miss Cara Mallett. 'Miss Mallett who is going to Sydney under engagement with the New South Wales Government will be a fellow passenger of yours … I shall feel obliged by your rendering her any assistance or attention within your power'.[1] A match-making scheme was in the air. Samuel assured Sir Henry Parkes that David was 'an exceedingly *good* young man. She will be quite safe under his care if she chooses to accept it.'[2]

David had already spent some time abroad. A breakdown in his health before he graduated at Oxford required him to seek a more congenial climate than England. In 1878, he spent some time in Canada with his maternal relatives and later, two months in the colony of Victoria. When he resumed his studies in 1880 it was to sit the exams and graduate as a Bachelor of Arts. But in terms of a vocation his interests now lay elsewhere. As a student at Oxford in the 1870s, David had been developing a growing interest in geology, inspired partly by the lectures of Joseph Prestwich, newly appointed Professor of Geology, and by the inspiring blend of science and art that marked the lectures of John Ruskin, Slade Professor of Fine Arts. Ruskin was a keen student of mineralogy and geology and introduced the romance of geology into his university lectures in a way that appealed to the impressionable undergraduate. During his university vacations, and in the remainder of his period of leave from his studies after returning from abroad, David pursued his own geological discoveries by foot and horseback in the region of St Fagans near Cardiff, where his father was a minister. He joined the Cardiff Naturalists' Society and soon made his mark as a promising amateur geologist, reading a paper to the society and leading a 'field day' to the Brecon Beacons to investigate evidence of ice dispersal in the region – the beginning of his lifelong interest in the study of glaciation.

David was beginning to think seriously about a career in geology. On the advice of Professor Prestwich, he undertook class work for about six months at the Royal School of Mines in London, under Professor J.W. Judd. While not completing a degree there, David was enthused by the prospect of professional work in that field.

The opportunity to work in New South Wales came about after the New South Wales Geological Survey lost one of their few trained geologists, Henry Lamont Young, in a drowning misadventure. Charles Wilkinson, the Government Geologist, looked abroad for a replacement and the young Edgeworth David was offered the job, having been recommended for it by a number of distinguished men including Professors Prestwich and Judd. Through the agency of Sir Saul Samuel, David was appointed as an Assistant Geological Surveyor at an annual salary of £300, the same as Cara Mallett was to receive. As well, as a working geologist David would receive an allowance of £250 for equipment such as horses and tents.

After accepting the appointment to the Geological Survey of New South Wales, David gained further practical experience of the kind of work he'd be doing in the colony by visiting some working tin mines in the Cornwell region in August 1882 and by making a study of mining methods and production. He left his family home at St Fagans on 4 October 1882 and embarked a few days later on the SS *Potosi* at Gravesend, carrying with him the letter of introduction to Miss Mallett.

The first encounter of the young couple on board ship was an accidental one. Taking in the sea air on deck one blustery autumn day shortly after leaving Gravesend, David saw a pale, dark-eyed young woman struggling to open her umbrella as she faced the stiff sea breeze on deck. He went immediately to her aid. It was only a few days later that he realized that this young woman was the Miss Mallett whose welfare Samuel had commended to him. They became good friends on the long sea voyage. David wrote home to his Aunt Sarah, 'By the time we reached Naples I had got to know some of the people on board. Secondly, I became acquainted with a young lady, named Miss Mallett. She is one of the nicest ladies on board.' Once the ship steamed into the Mediterranean the weather settled and deck sports began in earnest. David threw himself into these with great energy, competing with his cabin mate, Cecil Sharp, in high jumps, 'potato races' and rope-climbing.[3] Cara Mallett was not a good sea traveller and motion sickness was an ordeal on every voyage she took. But once she found her sea-legs she did become involved in some of the shipboard entertainment on the *Potosi*, which included concerts, 'mock court-martials and Theatricals'. A reading of *The Merchant of Venice* was staged, with Cara playing Portia, David, Shylock and Cecil Sharp, Antonio.[4]

Cara left no diaries or letters from the voyage, but the tone of David's letters home are coloured by a sense of romance and adventure. He was already in love, but wasn't to declare his feelings for several years. He joined Cara on a shore party to visit Naples, and wrote home to his Uncle Charles, 'I shall never forget the effect of the sun rising behind Mount Vesuvius and lighting up the huge cloud of steam and smoke coming from the crater'. Sailing through the Straits of Messina, he was up at sunrise to observe the passage: 'the most beautiful view I have seen ... the Sicilian coast crowded with white, red-roofed houses and snow-capped Etna brooding over all, dark smoke coming from its summit'.

As the ship approached Sydney, Cara and David prepared to go their separate ways. David made a note in his diary to return to Miss Mallett her copy of W.C. Wentworth's *New South Wales*. When the Potosi docked at Sydney Harbour on 27 November 1882, he was met by his new chief, Charles Wilkinson, head of the New South Wales Geological Survey, and within a few days had found digs of his own with the Misses Tindell in Macquarie Street. He settled straight into departmental work in their offices, also in Macquarie Street, and within a few weeks had set off for the Yass district on a map-making assignment. In early March 1883, he set off for the New England district, where he was to spend seventeen months on his first major project for the department, a systematic study of the tin-mining deposits of the region. It is probable that on his brief returns to Sydney he made a number of visits to Miss Mallett at Hurlstone College. He may have been in love but his natural shyness and almost exaggerated sense of courtesy kept him from pushing his case.

Cara's daughter, Molly, states that Cara had many admirers who visited her at the college and went riding with her. One young man, out riding with Cara, noticed that her long locks of hair that had worked loose and he offered to pin them up for her. Cara turned around to see him surreptitiously kissing the lustrous manes of dark hair.

David, aware that he faced competition, must eventually have decided it was time to act before he lost Cara to another admirer. His daughter tells the story of his visit in early 1885:

> [David] called at Hurlstone College one evening with the intention of asking [Miss Mallett] to become his wife. When he arrived, there were several other visitors present. He made up his mind that the vital question of his engagement must be settled that evening, as his duties compelled him to leave Sydney the next morning for a long sojourn in the field. The strength of his determination may be gauged by the fact that he overcame his natural reserve and shyness … [and] having waited for some time in vain for the other guests to leave, he asked them politely but firmly to leave, explaining to them the object of his visit.[5]

His courage was rewarded and Cara agreed to become his wife.

Only one letter survives from Cara during her engagement. It was found by her daughter in David's 'locked book of treasures' after his death. It gives us an insight into an issue with which many thoughtful people were grappling in late Victorian times: the fading credibility of orthodox Christianity. Many of Cara's friends were to be drawn to Theosophy or Spiritualism, and Cara herself in later year was restless in her quest for authentic religious experience. Her daughter writes with affectionate irony of her mother's 'involvement in various religious sects. All were tried and found wanting – Christadelphians, Methodists, Seventh Day Adventists, Unitarians, Quakers, Baptists …'[6] Having been immersed in orthodox Anglicanism at Whitelands College, Cara brought these beliefs and practices with her to the colony, though religious observance was certainly not a requirement in the new public education system. It must have become clear to her that her future husband was not a conventional Christian. Cara's granddaughter, Anne Edgeworth, speculates that David's early breakdown in health as a university student was in reality a crisis of faith, as his geological studies increasingly shaped his world view and made it impossible for him to think of following his father into the church. David, throughout his life, paid reverent homage to the traditions and ethics of Christianity but his faith was probably that of a deist – a believer in some 'Higher Power' – rather than that of the established church. This was a source of worry to Cara: 'Since you have told me that you don't altogether believe in Christ as perfect God – I have a little feeling of terror for you. I am sure *my* faith in Christianity has increased since I loved you'. This may have been an issue on which the couple agreed to differ, though many years later it was to become a problem when Cara attempted to write a biography of her late husband.

Cara Mallett married T.W. Edgeworth David on 30 July 1885 at St Paul's Church of England in Canterbury – then an outer Sydney suburb. It was a quiet wedding, with two of David's friends as groomsmen: Owen Blacket, son of the former colonial architect, Edmund Blacket, and Charles Wilkinson, David's departmental chief. David had kept his family in Wales informed about his engagement and forthcoming marriage. He was necessarily reticent in talking about Cara's family. He wrote to his Aunt Sarah about Cara:

> most people say she is pretty, I certainly think she is, but you shall judge for yourself when I send you her photograph. She is not of what is generally called good family, but has been brought up as a lady and lived in nice society at Whitelands College in London where she seems to have been a general favourite. Since she has been in Australia she has made many nice friends in the best society in Sydney, chiefly through the introductions which Sir Saul Samuel gave her.

David's father, William, seems to have approved of the marriage, though his mother, from a prominent Anglo-Irish family, had reservations which were to make themselves felt when Cara took her family over to Wales some years later.

Cara had been required to resign from Hurlstone College on her marriage but the couple chose to stay in the district. Their first home was a cottage at 1 Elizabeth Street in Ashfield, which was developing into a pleasantly leafy suburb with many fine homes and easy access to the city by rail. David returned from fieldwork in time for Christmas 1885 and in a letter to his Aunt Sarah he paints an appealing and quite unstuffy picture of married life. Cara told him of her visit the previous night to see *The Mikado* at the Regent Theatre with a group of friends – Miss Webster from the college, Miss Nicolls (a new teaching assistant at Hurstone), Owen Blacket and his wife, and Edward Touche, a bachelor friend of David and later their neighbour in Ashfield. In the summer evenings after his return, David and his wife sat out on the balcony with views to the purple hills on the far side of the Parramatta River and he read aloud till the noise of the cicadas drove them indoors. He confessed to his aunt that he was very happy. Early in 1886, the Davids purchased their own home which they called the Gunyah on the corner of Church and Alt Streets in Ashfield.

David's chief, Charles Wilkinson, a bachelor till 1887, had advised him that 'surveyors oughtn't to get married as they had to camp out so much'. David's solution was to take his wife with him. In April 1886, he began a new and important project with the Geological Survey: exploring and mapping the Hunter River coal measures, a survey driven by the need for new coal reserves to feed the colony's expanding railway system and growing industry. When it was clear that this was to be a long project, the couple agreed that they would stay together in the field camps and rent out their Ashfield home. By this stage Cara was pregnant. It is an early reflection of her pioneering and adaptable spirit that she entered into this arrangement with zest. Years later Cara told her grandchildren, 'I loved camping with him those first few years before the three children arrived'. With the help of David's campkeeper, they set up camp near Farley railway station, not far from West Maitland. Here Cara took up her botanical interests and together the couple began (in David's few after-work hours) to translate from the French the relevant parts of an important publication by Belgian palaeontologist L.G. de Koninck. While there, David spent a number of weeks examining the coal measures on the cliffs extending from Newcastle south to Redhead, a wonderful geological feature that had previously been examined by Ludwig Leichhardt.

Shortly before the baby was due, Cara moved from the field camp at Farley into Wallis House, a guest house at Victoria Bridge near Maitland. Here her daughter, Margaret Edgeworth, was born on 28 November 1886. She was christened at the parish church of St Mary's and a celebration followed at Wallis House with christening cake, afternoon tea and wine. Cara stayed on at the guest house during the hot months of January and February before rejoining David at Farley.

Family trio: 'the holy family' as Cara dubbed them as they tried strenuously to get baby Margaret's attention for the camera

Camp life seemed to agree with 'little Madge', as the baby girl was always called. She slept in a candle box in the survey camp while her mother 'botanized' and 'kept house' for some months before returning to Ashfield. Early in March 1887, despite the hot weather, Cara and Madge rejoined David at Farley, but several days later the new family moved south to Mount Vincent (near present-day Cessnock) placing their tents at the foot of a range of wooded sandstone hills. For a new and inexperienced mother there was plenty to fret about: the mosquitoes were bad on the humid plain, and there were great numbers of poisonous snakes. Cara disturbed one that had crawled under some washing blown off the line.

During the months they spent there, David gave an address to the Maitland Scientific Society which proved a great success and prompted him to think about a future career in lecturing and academic life.

He broke camp on 12 November 1887 and the family returned to what promised to be a more settled life in their new home in Ashfield. Cara was exhausted by the struggle of caring for a lively toddler in an unpredictable environment and was demoralized to discover she was pregnant again. On receiving a letter from her newly-married sister, Sarah, she wrote back:

> I am very glad indeed to hear from you, and to know that so far, you are not in danger of infants. Unfortunately I expect again at the end of April. I vow number two shall be the last. Madge is eleven months old today, a regular little pickle, I have been obliged to get a nurse for her as I am not well enough to look after her entirely myself.

With his wife's welfare in mind, David looked around for two 'strong country girls' who could accompany them to Sydney. The eldest girl, at eighteen, was to help with the cooking and housework. Bridget Devereux, a sixteen-year-old Irish girl, was engaged as nurse. She became very fond of the baby and stayed on with the Davids to nurse and look after all three of their children.

Life at the Gunyah was anything but serene for the first few months. They discovered major whiteant damage to the house and the whole of the kitchen, dining room and bathroom floors, plus some of the door and window frame, had to be burnt. Their neighbour, Edward Touche, was a good handyman and proved an invaluable source of help and advice at this time. He became a lifelong friend of the Davids.

Before the house repairs began, there were patriotic celebrations to enjoy in Sydney, with the centenary of the founding of the colony on 26 January 1888. The Governor's wife, Lady Carrington, had unveiled a bronze statue of the queen in Macquarie Street the day before and now a new public park, to be called Centennial Park, was proclaimed. Cara and David watched the processions from the balcony of Miss Tindell's house, where David had lodged as a bachelor. Sydney loved the pomp and display of these imperial events. Cheering crowds lined the streets as they were to do eleven years later when the New South Wales contingent left for South Africa. David reported to his aunt that 'all the British dignitaries were there, plus most of the Bishops of the Church of England and Rome in NSW'. The Imperial squadron, together with the New Zealand governor on the Admiral's ship, unfortunately arrived late for the proceedings, having encountered heavy weather.

Then came the house renovations and the replacing of the timber floors. Cara may have been feeling tired and nauseated in the midsummer heat of Sydney but a restful pregnancy was out of the question. She still had to do a great deal of the housework herself in that age before labour-saving devices came on the market. In addition, her husband was soon out in the field again and she took over the organization of the household. February 1888 saw David based at the Great Northern Colliery near Lake Macquarie, where he discovered many fellow Welshmen working as miners: the landlord of his hotel came from the Rhondda Valley. In June he was camping near Tumut with views to the snow-capped Alps; in August, superintending the boring of a coal seam at Woodford in the Blue Mountains.

The second baby, Mary (Molly) Edgeworth David, was born on 4 May in Sydney, while David was up country over a hundred miles from Sydney. By chance he came to Maitland and on hearing the news caught the night train back to Sydney for what must have been a fairly brief stay at home with his young family. The strain showed through in a letter to his aunt, written in June that year: 'I have never had so much incessant work necessitating constant travelling as I have since the time that little Mary was born'. He was conscious of the toll his frequent and prolonged absences had on the family and must also have been aware of his wife's physical and emotional vulnerability during those years of childbearing. Cara confessed in a letter to Touche that she 'had been out of health for some time'. In December 1889, she had taken the two little girls up to Lawson in the Blue Mountains for an extended break from the coastal humidity. Her indifferent health may well have been due to the exhaustion and loneliness of coping with young children as a single mother – which she was virtually for much of that period after Mary's birth.

In January 1890, David was advised of a move back to Maitland where the mapping of the Hunter Valley coal measures was proceeding. Cara was resigned to more domestic upheavals, but the underlying worry and frustration she was experiencing is evident in her letters to Touche. By this stage he had left Sydney for New Zealand, where he was trying to start a business. Cara missed his friendship and good practical business sense as well as his handyman's skills:

> going over and packing our tools – everything we handled spoke of you. We leave here on Thursday for Maitland for from one to three years, as the fates decree. We hope to let the Gunyah of course. Twed [her name for David] is looking very thin and worn – he works too hard as usual, and I have come to the conclusion that I must let him go his own way over that, and try to wear myself out in the same length of time.

There was another hot summer to endure in Maitland. And Cara was pregnant again, despite her earlier vows. They were living at Como, a rented house in East Maitland. The little girls, restless in the sticky evenings, were lulled off to sleep by their father singing them nursery rhymes and hymns. Cara's son, William David (Billy), was born at

Como on 1 April 1890. Anne Edgeworth was told by Molly David that Cara, in addition to breast-feeding her own children, took on for a couple of months the baby son of a miner whose wife was too ill to feed the infant. If this was the case, it illustrates a generous spirit as well as a happy lack of middle-class consciousness in the young Mrs David.

Bridget Devereux accompanied them to Maitland and must have been a lifesaver to Cara in what proved to be a daunting year. Molly David remembered Bridget as 'an excellent cook [who] loved and understood children.'[7] A month after Billy was born, David was recalled to Sydney to act as Geological Surveyor-in-Charge when Charles Wilkinson took off overseas to care for the colony's displays at the International Mining and Metallurgy Exhibition in London. He was to be in Sydney, working at a frantic pace both on office matters and in the field, till late October.

Some time during that difficult year, David must have decided that the welfare of his family required him to seek a more settled form of employment. An opening arose in Sydney in November 1890, with the death of Professor William Stephens, Professor of Natural History at the university. Stephens had lectured in Palaeontology and General Geology, subjects in which he was not academically trained but in which he'd taken a great amateur interest. The University Senate decided the new incumbent to the post would be known as Professor of Geology and Physical Geography. They set up a 'Home' appointment committee through Sir Saul Samuel, and David decided to apply for the post. Neither he nor Cara were hopeful of his chances as the Home Committee consisted of men based in England but David had powerful supporters in the colony, including Mr Justice William Windeyer of the University Senate. It was Windeyer's vote that proved crucial in the Senate's decision to appoint David because of 'his great practical acquaintance with the geology of Australia.'[8]

The family had moved back to Sydney in December 1890. The Gunyah was still rented out, so they moved into an old stone cottage called Merivale, in nearby Church Street. There were five and a half acres of land attached and an untidy garden. Molly's earliest memories were of this home, where Cara's old white horse, Bunyip, had learnt to trot safely between the shafts of a buggy and would take the four-year-old Margaret and her young sister out for rides (whether with an adult along is not made clear). David, still employed at this stage by the Department of Mines, was travelling incessantly on more fieldwork. He was run down and suffering from rheumatism.

From Merivale, Cara confided in Touche, a sense of loneliness and anguish not far beneath the surface of her letters:

> Sometimes I feel as if I shall go out of my senses with grief when I look forward to his probable breakdown. His brother, Arthur, has broken down from overwork, had haemorrhage of the lungs and been ordered to Australia. I wish you could run and see us as you used to do, we miss you so much.

There were financial worries for the couple on top of the incessant travelling. In 1888, Touche had persuaded David to join him in an investment in land: they purchased two adjacent blocks at St Marys near Penrith at the foot of the Blue Mountains, and some at Mortlake on the Parramatta River. David hoped that they might be able to use the Penrith block to set up a wattle bark farm. However, the land brought more troubles than it was worth. Neighbours helped themselves to all the timber on the Penrith block and though the land declined in value with the 1890s depression, rates still had to be paid every year. In 1903, after a visit to the two deforested, drought-ridden and mosquito-infested blocks at St Marys, Cara wrote in exasperation to Touche: 'It was a gorgeous bargain. I congratulate both you and Twed on your tremendous foresight in purchasing land. It may be of value in 3003 and some of our remote descendents will benefit from it.'

Another problem was David's well-known absent-mindedness

Arthur David

concerning money. According to his granddaughter, Anne, David 'wasn't remotely interested in managing money, though very conscious that one must keep within one's means'. When Ned Touche left for overseas, David offered to pay Touche's yearly rates on the blocks, but often forgot to pay these on time. It was a sore point to Touche though he expressed his feelings graciously to Cara: 'In many respects Twed is the best fellow I know, but when a man is so absorbed by science that he can't or won't properly attend to matters of business, one cannot give him carte blanche to act on one's behalf'. Cara often paid the rates from her own bank account.

Another worrying financial venture involved a search for payable coal in Queensland. In late 1888, David had embarked on a project to be called the Queensland Coal Venture, in conjunction with Touche and other friends including his chief, Charles Wilkinson. David undertook to do the prospecting and in his annual leave from the Department of Mines he set off for Central Queensland in December 1888 with an engineer friend, Alfred Cadell. Other members of the syndicate joined them in Brisbane. Forty-six square miles of land were taken up north of Rockhampton, in an area David was sure contained payable coal though he had not actually seen any outcrops. It was an arduous trip. The party covered 'over 120 miles of chaining, a great deal of it through thick mangrove scrub, and deep tenacious mud, in which we sometimes bogged up to our thighs. As the salt-water creeks and estuaries abounded in sharks and alligators, it lent a little excitement to the prosaic routine.'

David confessed to Touche after this venture that he 'had missed the wife and little ones fearfully … I think it will be a long time before I am again lured away on a similar expedition.' Cara, coping on her own with a baby and toddler, no doubt entertained a similar wish.

The Queensland coal venture continued until 1891 under the name of the Broad Sound Coal Co. David travelled up to Central Queensland to check it out shortly after taking up his new position at the University of Sydney. He reported that the coal was of good quality but the water at the mine was a problem. The company was floated but it did not prosper and the scheme collapsed a year later. A viable coal industry in that remote area was not feasible in competition with the well-established Newcastle and Hunter Valley fields.

The crash affected David deeply, especially on behalf of his friends who had lost their investments. With his own highly developed sense of obligation to people, he was determined to pay them back for losses incurred, and drew on the family's own resources to do so. By then, in late 1892, he was receiving a professorial salary, adequate but hardly a large sum with three children to bring up and no savings to fall back upon. If Cara accepted the losses philosophically, she also felt the burden it imposed on her own family. In 1892 she received news that her sister, Sarah, was ill: it was later confirmed that Sarah was suffering from tuberculosis. Cara wrote to her, 'I never felt how far away Australia was until I heard that you were ill, and I wanted to come to see you so much. I would have come in spite of the distance if I could have afforded it, but we have had losses lately and that is out of the question.' Sarah's life from her marriage to Elgin Carter in 1887 had been a litany of incessant childbearing, infant deaths and struggles with her own inherited illness. She died of tuberculosis in late 1892, shortly after giving birth to her fifth child, who died a few months later. Three of her other children also died of tuberculosis. Cara was desolated. She must have reflected at some stage in her grief that she might have shared Sarah's sad destiny if she had not been given such opportunities for education and travel.

Sarah's remaining child, Elsie Lillian Carter, was two years old when her mother died. Elgin Carter's stepmother, Susan Carter, took on the job of caring for her granddaughter, and it was to Susan Carter that Cara made an offer to bring up Elsie as one of her own children, if Elgin ever wished to marry again.[9]

Some time in early 1892, the family moved back into the Gunyah. Cara, relieved at being in her own home again, began a flurry of house renovations. These included a new parental bedroom and a maid's room. From this stage in their marriage it was Cara who generally took on the management of the family budget. The Davids had separate bank accounts, which would have been quite rare in those days. In later life Cara told her granddaughter, Anne, that she felt sorry for wives who had never signed a cheque in their lives and had to go cap in hand to their husband for money. Cara managed the household very capably on David's salary and they were never in debt, though David may have borrowed a sum of money from his father, William David, to help with repayments to his syndicate of investors. Anne believed that her grandparents always discussed any planned outlay of money, but in the end the decision was left to Cara. In later life she managed to keep their bank balance in a healthy state by investing in a number of properties. Anne was convinced that, had her grandmother 'been of the post-WW2 generation … she would have been running a business of some kind very efficiently'.

The Gunyah entrance: the tiling, nameplate, windows and brickwork are original (Author's photo)

4 The Professor's Wife

On a Monday evening in May 1894, a group of men and women gathered in the drawing room at the Davids' home for one of the monthly meetings of the Ashfield Literary Circle. It was to be a 'Tennyson Evening', with readings of some of the Poet Laureate's best-known works and some musical recitations as well. The seats were scattered informally around the room – some of the gentlemen may even have relaxed on the floor – and for an hour or so the group enjoyed the program, which included Professor David's moving recitation of 'Ulysses', Miss Taplin's musical interpretation of 'Sweet and Low' and Mrs David's reading of 'The Revenge'. An animated discussion followed, with much laughter and interchange of ideas. The evening finished

Cara sewing, 1910

with the appearance of coffee and cakes, the signal for a general movement and further buzz of conversation.

Cara David was the organizer and lively centre of this gathering. She was an entertaining and witty public speaker and no doubt a popular hostess in such an environment. (Formal social gatherings had very little appeal for her, however, and she always remained indifferent to the soirees and dinners held by wealthy Sydneysiders.) Her Ashfield literary circle was one of the most popular in Sydney, regularly drawing thirty or so people. It was held at a different house each month, with the hostess providing a modest supper after the group had listened to a paper (on topics that ranged from Shakespeare's tragedies to the poetry of Robert Browning), followed by a lively discussion. Such an intellectual and social milieu would have been rare enough in the colony in the closing years of the century, but it was decidedly middle-class in character.

The Literary Circle was part of an ambitious enterprise called the Australasian Home Reading Union (AHRU) a loose confederation of like-minded groups throughout the colonies and New Zealand. Initiated by influential and educated professional people in the 1890s as the colonies moved towards federation, the union was unashamedly idealistic. It aimed to become 'a great educating power and spread knowledge throughout the Colonies not only in the great cities but through the remote back settlements wherever there are men and women who wish to learn'.[1] For a small subscription of half a crown a year, people could enrol in a course of their choice, receive a list of recommended books to read, and in the monthly journal find articles of interest related to their home study. The courses of reading and study in science, history and general literature were to be sufficiently popular to be intelligible to those who hadn't had any higher education 'but sufficiently thorough to instruct and interest the more learned'. An important part of the course was the 'assemblies' where people in one area could meet for monthly discussions, readings and social exchange.

This required an enthusiastic and hard-working organizer who would be responsible for the group in their area or suburb.

Cara and David were both to contribute considerable time and energy to this project over the course of the next six years. Cara organized the 'modern English Literature' course and David prepared a five-part course of study of geology, the chapters of which appeared regularly in the *Reader*, the AHRU journal. The professor was president of the New South Wales section of the union for a number of years and his wife served on the executive committee.

One of the founding members and most influential voices in the AHRU was Maybanke Wolstenholme. She was already in her forties when Cara met her in the 1890s, and her life thus far had taken an extraordinary and tragic course. Like Cara, she had been a pupil-teacher – at Fort Street Model School – but unlike Cara, Maybanke had grown up in a loving and educated middle-class family, the Selfes, who had emigrated from London to Sydney in 1858. She married in 1867, when she was twenty-two. The husband, Edmund Wolstenholme, was a handsome but shiftless timber merchant. Maybanke's maternal history echoes that of Sarah Mallett but was to have a very different outcome. She bore seven children in the space of eleven years, of whom only three lived longer than three years. Four of her infants died of tuberculosis. Besides dealing with her own losses, Maybanke found that her husband was drinking heavily and he eventually deserted her. She made the decision to bring up the surviving children on her own and take in boarders at her Marrickville home. Her mother, Bessie Selfe, came to live with her and together they provided the three surviving boys with a secure and stable home life and education. Maybanke had to wait till the end of 1892 to petition for divorce under the newly passed legislation, the *Divorce Amendment and Extension Act*. This legislation allowed women trapped in a loveless and often abusive marriage to obtain their freedom on the grounds of three years' desertion.

Once her eldest boy started at Newington College, she converted her large home into a fee-paying school for girls. Maybanke College survived for sixteen years and became well known for its high standards. During that time, Maybanke became a vocal campaigner for planned parenthood and sex education as well as reform of the many laws affecting women and children. Her own blighted marriage and her tragic experiences as a mother gave her life a drive and passion it was never to lose. During the 1890s, she emerged as a leader in Sydney's intellectual and educational circles, combining the roles of headmistress and female suffragist. She wrote a touching poem for the December 1892 edition of the AHRU journal, 'So Many Years Ago', about the drowning of a young child; another poem, 'In the Twilight', was published in the *Illustrated Sydney News* in 1884. These were some of her only personal expressions of grief in a long public life. In 1899, now a divorced and free woman, she married Francis Anderson, the Professor of Philosophy at the University of Sydney – whom she had met through their common involvement in the AHRU – and found a new happiness in this partnership.

Maybanke was probably the guiding force behind the formation of the New South Wales branch of the AHRU. She served for some years as its general secretary and also as treasurer. She wrote the introductory article to the *Reader* expressing her belief in the civilizing power of education for all people, no matter what their social class. The tenor of the journal was optimistic and high-minded. In August 1892, she wrote of future plans: there was talk of a January 'summer assembly – possibly a literary entertainment on the wooded shores of Port Jackson ... and an excursion by rail to the Illawarra district for geological and botanical studies'.[2] The June edition contained an article on 'A visit to Greece' by Louisa Macdonald, founding principal of Sydney University Women's College. (Louisa had taught and researched classical antiquities with A.S. Murray at the British Museum.) Professor Mungo MacCallum, Professor of Modern Literature at the university, wrote on 'French Literature: Romanticism in France'. Rolf Boldrewood wrote an article for 1894 extolling the joys of reading and giving his 'warmest approval and sympathy' to the AHRU's aims.[3]

The first annual assembly of the AHRU was held at Sydney University in April 1893. The gathering included many of Sydney's liberal intellectuals, and certainly some of the women who were to become a force in the suffrage movement and in education for women: Lady Manning (whose husband opened the University of Sydney to women students in 1888), Lady Mary Windeyer, Miss Macdonald, Mrs Wolstenholme and Mrs David.

Maybanke Wolstenholme was conscious of the narrow reach of the union. In 1892, she'd sent out invitations to all the trade unions of New South Wales (about eighty in number) to attend a meeting of the AHRU, but though all present 'pledged to endeavour to form circles in their own neighbourhood', nothing resulted from this effort. Undaunted, Maybanke still held out hopes for wider membership and she made a suggestion in an editorial in 1893:

> In a Circle where some members have a little time to spare, one evening during the month might be devoted to a small Circle of men and women in the lower walks of life. Among those who serve us in shops and warehouses, who come to our doors with goods or wait at out tables, there are many well able to appreciate high thinking ... Certainly the results could not fail to be good. If a strike were threatening and employer and employee could remember with pleasure a friendly conversation – whether on Shakespeare's Tempest or the 'Fabian essays', would matter little – the memory of happy intercourse would gild the blackness of the strife, and much sorrow might be averted.[4]

Given the bitterness of the labour struggles of the 1890s, one can appreciate that the AHRU held little attraction for working people, who would have seen it as a club for the rich and privileged. Even the regional centres in places like Mudgee and Armidale were run by academics, teachers or clergymen. In 1893 and 1894, the union was also involved in arranging University Extension lectures in Sydney suburbs and country towns, but there is no evidence that these lectures attracted a different clientele to that of the 'circles'.

Maybanke Wolstenholme recognized that the union was unable to attract the poor and uneducated but she remained a loyal and hardworking member until 1898. Cara and her husband also continued their staunch support for the AHRU. In 1894, Cara prepared a study course on 'education' and David was still running his popular geology courses.

The AHRU continued, in a very modified and diminished form until 1912, to be followed in 1913 by the Workers Educational Association (WEA). But by the end of the 1890s it was clear that the union was becoming less viable. By 1897, New South Wales, Queensland and South Australia were the only colonies left to carry on the scheme which its founders had hoped would become a 'literary federation', linking people across the land and in New Zealand in a unique educational experiment. In 1898, the monthly *Reader* was discontinued and in its place a 'Year Book' was to be issued. In fact no year books were issued after 1898, when David was chair of the Executive Committee.

The fact that David took on major executive and teaching roles in the AHRU soon after assuming his professorial appointment suggests the kind of punishing work schedule he set himself. In September 1891, he had written cheerfully to his Aunt Sarah that he was looking forward to having leisure for original scientific work in the new job. But already in August that year he admitted to Ned Touche to being severely overworked: 'I have constantly to go into the lecture room with my lecture only half prepared in spite of my working hard early and late'. This was partly because he had work to complete for the Department of Mines, mapping the coal measures of the Hunter Valley. But David was also a man who could not resist a commitment to many and varied projects including the writing of numerous scholarly papers, service on scientific boards and the preparation of popular public lectures. By 1892, he was already a key speaker for the proceedings of the Australasian Association for the Advancement of Science and was writing articles for geological societies in London and Sydney.

Cara had hoped that David's move to the university would give him 'a better chance in life' as she confided in Ned Touche. And indeed it did. The Edgeworth Davids became involved in many different aspects of Sydney's intellectual and cultural life and were able to contribute to scientific and social programs that they cared strongly about. But Cara had the measure of her husband and knew that whatever he took on he would pursue without regard to self-interest: she surmised, correctly, that if he got the job 'he would manage to do too much even then'.

One issue in which both David and Cara took a close interest was the women's suffrage movement. In August 1894, their friend Maybanke Wolstenholme started her own feminist newspaper, *A Woman's Voice*. Conscious that the AHRU had failed in its mission to reach 'the back blocks' and the narrow streets of working-class life, she hoped to reach a wider audience through this new publication, sold at railway bookstalls and by sympathetic retailers throughout Sydney and beyond. Subscription was a modest two shillings a year and there were a few reliable advertisers who loyally supported the venture. Though Maybanke claimed that it was the first such journal of its kind, in fact Louisa Lawson's publication *The Dawn*, which ran from 1888 to 1905, was aimed at a similar readership. Thoughtful women (and some men) were increasingly troubled by the lack of freedom and the social and legal inequities that women faced in the workplace, in the home and in public life. As the colonies moved towards federation, a groundswell of support gathered for including female suffrage in any planned federal constitution. (The colony of South Australia was held up as an enlightened forerunner of change: its citizens had voted for female suffrage in 1894, one of the first states in the world to grant these rights to women.) *The Dawn* and after it, *A Woman's Voice*, provided a forum to explore what voting rights for women would mean, and how they might lead to radical and far-reaching changes in women's lives. The *Voice* strongly promoted the work of the Womanhood Suffrage League, established in 1891.

A Woman's Voice had its first issue in August 1894 and ran till December 1895. Cara David took out a subscription and read it closely till her departure overseas in January 1895. She followed the debate in its pages on 'sweatshop' conditions for women seamstresses and wrote a forceful letter to the editor for the September 1894 issue in which she voiced support for a minimum rate of wages for needlewomen. She urged her wealthier sisters to think twice before buying 'bargain' clothes that had been produced at 'semi-starvation wages' by women who had no say in their conditions of work.

Many of the issues which the paper explored were ones that were dear to her own heart, especially those promoting education for girls. Cara would not have seen the article published in the May 1895 issue, but it would have had her approval: it concerned the new Domestic Economy classes at Sydney Technical College, where schoolgirls and older women could gain new domestic skills, at a very small fee and with half-price travel on tram and train to attend the classes. Cara did not see such skills as restricting a woman's life choices – she was equally passionate about their education in the arts and sciences – but she supported practical training, being of an innate practical bent herself and knowing how much her own family had benefited by the skills she could bring to family management.

A Woman's Voice explored, bravely for its time, the sexual hypocrisy and double standards of the age. Respectable men took mistresses, visited prostitutes, spread sexually transmitted diseases and held socially and legally sanctioned powers over the home and their wives, while at the same time young girls who were unfortunate enough to become pregnant out of wedlock were vilified and left to fend for themselves with no social or institutional support. Even within the framework of marriage, a woman had absolutely no legal identity in New South Wales until 1879. She could not enter a binding contract, possess any property except land or make a will unless her husband agreed to it. A series of acts passed after this date gave married women the same legal rights as unmarried women, but it was not until the *Divorce Extension Act* of 1892 that women could initiate divorce and escape from an abusive marriage on grounds other than adultery. Maybanke's own bitter experiences left her well aware of the hidden misery women might be enduring in 'respectable' marriages; and she knew also of the vulnerability of a woman abandoned by a drunken or shiftless husband and left to fend for herself and her children with no means of support. For this reason her newspaper strongly promoted support for women in the workplace, the Free Kindergarten movement and the establishment of a Women's Hospital. Maybanke wrote many songs and stories for young children and also published a series of *Voicelets*, or sex education leaflets for parents. Two of them, 'Shall we confide in the Girls?' and 'Shall we talk to the Boys?' were reproduced in part in the October and November issues of the *Voice* in 1895. To a modern reader they seem impossibly coy, but in fact were a brave attempt to push aside the veil of secrecy and hypocrisy that meant all talk of sexual subjects was taboo in polite society and in respectable homes.[5]

In August 1895, Maybanke's second son, Arthur, was drowned when the SS *Catterthun* was wrecked off Newcastle. It was the fifth death of a child she had had to face. Knowing this, we wonder at Maybanke's continuing endurance, keeping the *Voice* alive and in publication for the rest of that terrible year. Her final editorial had this to say:

> The Voice may have to cease. The subscription list is not large enough to pay for its publication. I cannot get advertisements which would help support it, and I can no longer largely supplement its income.

If the Voice must cease I shall not regret it but shall conclude that it was born ten years in advance of the times … I shall know I have done a little of the rough work of the pioneer and have made the path a trifle clearer for the women who in a few years will follow. [6]

The *Voice* was silenced after 1895 but the late 1890s were to see the growth of new and influential women's groups, to which both Cara David and Maybanke Wolstenholme were to contribute.

One of the many community projects which the Davids supported during their years at the Gunyah was the Ashfield Infants' Home. The home had been founded in 1874 as a refuge for unmarried mothers and their infants, and in response to the appalling incidence of infanticide and infant mortality in the colony. Victorian morality had no sympathy for unmarried mothers, who were generally vulnerable young working-class women, often made pregnant while working as domestics in respectable middle-class homes. When the home was first established there was very little public support for it as it was felt that institutions which cared for mothers and their illegitimate babies only 'condoned immorality'. The government refused to supply funds but it did attract influential private supporters. Mrs Mary Windeyer was the committee treasurer from 1879. Dorette MacCallum, the wife of Professor Mungo MacCallum of the University of Sydney, was also on the committee of the Infants' Home and served on it for twenty-five years.

The home began life in Darlinghurst but soon needed larger premises and in 1876, the committee purchased Gorton, a large residence in extensive grounds fronting Parramatta Road and not far from the Davids' home. Louise Taplin, a trained nurse, was recruited in England in 1888 to manage the home, which she did with single-minded dedication for the next twelve years until her death in 1901, apart from a brief trip to England in 1886. From 1897, the committee decided to run a kindergarten for all children of a suitable age at the home for two hours daily, and a trained kindergarten teacher was employed. The Davids, close friends of Louise Taplin, gave their financial support to the Infants' Home for many years and their daughter, Molly, was still sending yearly donations in the 1970s.

In January 1895, the Ashfield Circle of the AHRU held a farewell gathering before Cara David left for the United Kingdom. She took the three children, now aged nine, seven and five, and planned to spend

Margaret David (née Thompson), Cara's mother-in-law

most of the year with David's family in Wales. David was to join them at the end of the year. 'The house seems so lonely and desolate without them,' wrote David wistfully to his Aunt Sarah. He would not have had much time to dwell on their absence since he was working at his usual frantic pace once the university term began. He was unable to get extended leave that year so had to make a quick dash over to join the family and his ageing parents in the December holidays. His ailing father died two years later.

Willie David, Cara's favourite in-law

David's parents lived near Cardiff at Llandaff, in the church rectory, a picturesque two-storey homestead next to the old church of St Fagans where William David had been rector. His unmarried daughter, Ethel, lived at home. Arthur, the eldest son, was a clergyman based at that time in Queensland where he had gone for his health. Edmund, the second son, was a businessman with a family and Cara warmed to Edmund's wife 'once I've had time to understand her'. The other son, Willie, had been in trade in Madras and was home on leave. He was Cara's favourite: 'very nice – not quite as nice as Twed of course – but very likeable,' she confessed to Ned Touche. Relations with Margaret David, her mother-in-law, were less straightforward. Coming from a prominent Anglo-Irish family, the Thompsons, Margaret David must have felt that her son had married beneath him. Cara Mallett had no 'connections' and may have been regarded by Margaret David as a bit of an adventuress ... wasn't she an orphan who had set off alone to the colonies? Cara sensed her disapproval: 'The ice is thin between my feet and the deep pool of my mother-in-law's displeasure,' she wrote to Touche. The three children, however, had a glorious time. 'They never had such a Christmas (toys!)'. Cara and the children and Bridget travelled home with David on the *Himalaya* in February 1896. The ship called at Colombo, where David was tempted to purchase a live cheetah but thought better of it, considering that it might 'become a dangerous playmate for the children when he grew up'.

Cara was relieved to be back in New South Wales in time for a balmy Sydney autumn. She told Touche, 'I feel terribly run down after the year's flight to England – it is so nice to see the sun and the nice high sky. I was so glad to get home again and to thaw in mind as well as in body.'

St Fagans rectory
(NLA MS 8890)

5   Funafuti

In 1897, David volunteered to lead a scientific expedition to Funafuti in the Gilbert and Ellice Islands and asked his wife to go with him. Funafuti (now Tuvalu) is the largest island in a ring of about thirty-five coral atolls of that name, 700 miles due north of Fiji. The purpose of the expedition was to test Darwin's theory on the formation of coral atolls. Darwin surmised that they had originally been fringing reefs around volcanic peaks rising from the ocean; as the peaks gradually subsided and sank below the sea, the reefs – so the theory went – were transformed into ring-like atolls of great depth.

In 1896, a British expedition to Funafuti led by Professor William Sollas had attempted to test Darwin's theory of subsidence by boring into the reef rock to confirm its great thickness and discover the volcanic substratum. His expedition ran into unforeseen problems and the drilling operation was abandoned after reaching a depth of no more than 105 feet. David had been one of the Sydney-based executive committee for Sollas's project, having extensive experience in drilling operations from his days working with the Department of Mines. For the 1897 expedition, David acquired machinery that he hoped was better adapted to the task of drilling the hard coral rock. The scientific team under his leadership consisted of George Sweet, a geologist from

Melbourne, and two undergraduates from Sydney University, William Poole and Walter Woolnough. Foremen John Hall and George Burns of the Diamond Drill Branch of the NSW Department of Mines, plus four workmen, formed the drilling team. The expedition was financed partly by the Royal Society of London and partly by the New South Wales government and a group of wealthy private citizens. The scientific team all paid their own expenses.

Cara had heard first-hand about the remote coral atoll and the scientific world's interest in it when she and David hosted a two-week visit from Professor Sollas in April 1896. He stayed with them at Ashfield en route to Funafuti. So when David asked Cara to come along as expedition cook, nurse and keeper of stores, she had a fairly clear idea of what was involved. Writing to Touche shortly before their departure, she was matter-of fact, even brutally candid, about the likely hazards and discomforts she could expect. Her language is coloured by a sturdy British contempt for the islanders who would host them, an attitude that was to be considerably modified during her time on the island:

> The island is in the Ellice Group – is about half a mile wide and 2 miles long[1] … grows pigs and cocoanut, fish and taro – and 200 niggers with itch and ringworm – and nothing else but coral. No meat, milk, fresh fruit, vegetable or bread to be had. We take everything except servants – live in a native hut and knock as much fun out of it as we can.

It was a 'mad thing' they were doing, she added, with a mixture of high spirits and apprehension. She was anxious about David's welfare: she knew from past experience that he was notoriously neglectful of his health once he became involved in fieldwork. Her own presence on the expedition would at least ensure that there were regular mealtimes.

They left Sydney on 2 June 1897 on the SS *Taviuni* for Fiji, from where they would travel to Funafuti. They were to return in late

Funafuti group: the official photo of the 1897 expedition

September, David having been given a term's leave of absence by the university. Bridget was to stay with the children in Sydney and a 'dour' Scottish lady, Mrs Sharp, was also engaged to live in.

Cara kept a detailed diary of her stay on Funafuti. It is refreshingly frank and down to earth in its tone and reveals a great deal about the diarist and also the man she married. She promised David before the trip that she 'wouldn't grumble', but the journey and the expedition were to call upon all her reserves of patience and good humour – qualities that often wore thin. It is likely that if she had been a more pampered and fussy woman she might have found the whole experience an intolerable challenge. As it was she took an intense and lively interest in the human aspects of the expedition, and her diary reflects this. Cara had a strong pioneering spirit, evident in her readiness to travel out alone to the colony as a young woman and to rough it with David in survey camps. To be sure, the Ellice Islands were no longer an unknown and exotic culture, having been the subject of British colonizing and missionary activity since the 1860s. But there was no denying that the months of travel and work on Funafuti would be very different from the orderly routines of life in Church Street, Ashfield.

Funafuti was a British protectorate. The British Commissioner based in Fiji was responsible for ensuring its peaceful governance through the local native leaders. The island was governed by an elderly king whose role was largely ceremonial; the real leader of the community of about 250 was the sub-chief, a resourceful and intelligent man named Opataia, who was responsible to the Commissioner for enforcing all laws. There was only one white man on the island, an Irish-Australian trader named O'Brien who had married a local woman many years before. He acted as guide and interpreter to the party.

The first few days tested everyone's humour. A rough and stormy voyage from Fiji on the SS *Maori* meant the party couldn't wash or change into fresh clothes for six days – a particular ordeal for a Victorian woman with her long hair and cumbersome outfits, and Cara inevitably suffered from seasickness. Then wet and squally weather left them soaked to the skin while disembarking. They rowed ashore after the steamship was steered inside the ring of islands and anchored in the eleven-mile wide lagoon. The village itself, dominated by the large whitewashed mission church, consisted of a straggly line of huts and palm trees and faced inward over the lagoon. Cara discovered to her relief that the expedition base camp was to be set up on the other side of the island half a mile away facing the ocean: there the sea breezes provided some protection from the flies, mosquitoes, smells and sticky heat of the village. A native hut with thatched roof became the Davids' home for the next few months with a nearby shelter serving as a cooking hut. A corrugated-iron shed was built for the stores, tents were erected for the men and work soon began on constructing the drilling apparatus, whose successes and malfunctions were to dominate their lives for the next three months. Once drilling began it often continued well into the night and the sight from the beach of the derrick with its noise and lights and activity reminded Cara of the Black Country of the industrial Midlands.

The organizing of stores, washing and drying their mildewed garments and cooking meals dominated her routine for the early days. Extensive stores of tinned and dried food had been brought with them and Cara was a resourceful cook, using native ingredients to provide variety and freshness to their diet: 'curried yams and bacon' were on the menu some days, as well as a vegetable dish made from boiled breadfruit and coconut. For the first week Cara cooked for the scientific team as well and found it heavy work in that enervating climate. David, conscious of their limited time on the island, was driving the team – and himself – relentlessly, and did not give them time at first to cook. Cara noted in her diary after the first week, 'Twed … overworking more than ever – would have nothing to eat but tinned stuff and ship biscuit if I were not here, and would eat that standing over his drill'.

The villagers, fascinated by the goings-on above the beach and drawn to the company of this tall and energetic white woman, crowded into the doorway or around the open windows of the hut at all hours until Cara prevailed upon Opataia to explain and enforce their need for privacy. But she herself sought out the women of the village on her afternoon walks and enjoyed chatting with them with a lingua

Cara and David's hut, Funafuti

franca of pidgin English. She was especially interested in their cooking methods and domestic skills, and her diary is full of traditional recipes for preparing fish, coconuts, yams and breadfruit and as well lists all manner of phrases and terms commonly used by the people in their domestic affairs. She described in detail the mission-inspired costume of the women, a skirt of leaves and an apron-like garment on top that sat loosely over their neck and shoulders and as she noted, '[did] not conceal the charms of the dark-skinned beauties as much as they might do'. She was very amused to watch the flirtatious behaviour of thirteen-year-old Naina, who took a shine to young Poole the undergraduate. Going into the lagoon to fish one day, she laughingly flung her garment at him as she raced into the water.

A century ago these Pacific islands provided a variety and abundance of natural resources which is almost unimaginable in our present world – though Cara points out that it was only after the British required all landowners to keep their land planted with food-producing trees that a reliable source of taro and breadfruit was always available. The villagers were not interested in 'the plodding industry of Europeans'. She noted with amusement that the little mission school where children were taught to read and write only functioned for little over an hour each day, before the children were released to race off gleefully for the lagoon. There Cara David, elegant schoolmistress and professor's wife – discarding her long garments? She must have surely have stripped to a chemise and bloomers – raced with them into the water and played 'spouting games' in a circle. The children laughed at her clumsy swimming … she swam like a monkey, they said. She tried once to prepare a fish she'd caught, only to have it grabbed by a young girl who with one swift movement of her dainty teeth bit off the head of the fish and gutted it with expert fingers. The children came to watch her bake bread in the cooking shed and they helped her fan the coals to keep them hot. She sang them nursery songs: 'Old MacDonald Had a Farm' complete with all the clucking and mooing, foreign sounds that the children found hilarious. She showed young Naina how to patch and mend her chemise, but at having to take up needle and thread 'a look of unutterable boredom' came over the young girl's face and Cara relented. 'After all, why should one consider rag-mending such a sterling virtue? When I maliciously suggested another patch … she looked at me pathetically and said "Bine-by" so "Bine-by" I let it remain. Happy little Naina!'

The women taught her to weave the pandanus mats that provided floor coverings for the huts and they presented her with a woven 'birth mat' on which a newborn baby was placed. They loved looking at the illustrated journals Cara had brought with her and marvelled at the wasp-like waists of women in the fashion plates. When Cara described the function of whalebone corsets they were horrified that women would allow this torture to their bodies. With the tolerant old trader, O'Brien, as their chronicler she heard stories of love, jealousy and sexual betrayal. It was clear to her that life on Funafuti was every bit as complicated as in more sophisticated cultures.

Cara came to know and enjoy the company of the islanders in a way that was not possible for her husband, whose energies were totally consumed by the fortunes of the diamond drill. There were innumerable breakdowns and jamming of equipment as the drill tried to penetrate deeper into the coral rock below the atoll. On 10 July Cara confided to her diary: 'Twed gets thinner every day, but his marvellous hopefulness flags none. I am down in the depths of dark despair about the bores but try not to show it. Walk by moonlight with the hopeful one.'

They celebrated their twelfth wedding anniversary that month. They still enjoyed each other's company, occasionally snatching time alone together for an evening swim in the lagoon. Cara marvelled at David's capacities of endurance and fortitude. Sometimes he was up most of the night writing his notes and repairing equipment and then would set off wearily to the drill camp after a couple of hours' sleep. All physical work was exhausting in that steamy climate. She recognized with wonder and dismay that the man she loved would always be driven to sacrifice his own personal comfort in pursuit of some higher goal. Was this his father's legacy to him, with science taking the place of a religious vocation? Cara was to see in the years ahead how much of David's life and work was devoted to disinterested scientific enquiry: a journey over that 'illimitable ocean of the unknown'.

The project continued into August, gradually making headway against the coral rock. By the end of August the drillers had reached 500 feet. At intervals Cara sailed with the team to some of the outlying islets around the lagoon, where David mapped the reefs and Cara botanized. She had a strong interest in plants from Whitelands days and had brought many botanical books out to the colony. She learnt all the Samoan names for common plants and collected them assiduously, planning to take them back to Sydney in a waterproof tin box. One memorable night she sailed with Opataia and his men to Fuafatu, one of the islets in the north, to join the survey team which was camped there. The tiny islet had an entrance from the lagoon just wide enough to let in a small boat. If it missed that tiny passage it would be swept out of the lagoon onto the reef or drift north over the open Pacific. Cara recorded in her diary the vivid impressions of the journey, all her senses sharpened by knowledge of the dangers they faced. It was an eleven-mile journey over the lagoon in the small sailing boat, tearing along in the darkness with a few stars showing through broken cloud and the white horses of the waves racing past them. 'A queer feeling of elation took me … It seemed as if one had gone on like that – in the roar of the wind, the swish of the sea, and the darkness – for ages, and that one would continue to go on and on like that for ever.'

Opataia, seasoned navigator and sailor that he was, brought them safely to the tiny harbour and late at night they joined the survey team at their beach camp. Cara crawled into David's bivouac shelter in her wet skirts and regaled her sleepy husband with tales of the crossing. In the middle of her tale, a squally tropical storm swept through and collapsed all the tents and the party spent the rest of the night huddling under the wet canvas.

She often pined for the comforts of home and missed the children intensely. Seeing the dreadful skin diseases that affected many of the islanders – caused mainly by poor hygiene and washing practices – Cara worried that she might carry a serious infection back to her family. She regularly spent time ministering to the tropical sores and ulcers of the islanders and tried to impress on them the importance of better washing practices. She made a terse comment in her diary that the missionaries would have been better teaching the natives cleanliness 'instead of the fourth commandment'. Her feelings about the missionary influence on the islanders were ambivalent. The Christian mission was under the control of a native pastor, Simona, appointed by the London Missionary Society. Cara took a strong dislike to this man, finding him obsequious and self-centred. 'A greedy brute,' she confided to her diary; and the many hours he spent in her hut improving his English skills became an exercise in forbearance for Cara. But on the other hand it was clear to her that Opataia's leadership was due in part to his committed Christian faith and his wisdom and generosity of spirit. She noted that on work parties where he led the early morning prayers, a note of 'thanksgiving' was always prominent in his prayers.

The traditional island culture was based on communal sharing of many resources like cooking facilities and harvests of fish. Theft was unknown. Even the elderly king shared all the gifts presented to him with the rest of his people and took no special privileges for himself. Inevitably this simple communal life was changing under the impact of increased trade with westerners and the introduction of commercial life: many of the men could now earn money by working for the survey team or could trade with visiting foreign ships. The islanders saw a strong connection between Christianity and prosperity. Cara noted caustically that they had been taught 'to read the Bible, sing hymns and be greedy'.

As leaders of the survey team David and his wife attended the mission church every Sunday and found there a very different environment to the sober Anglican churches they were used to. Women suckled babies on the floor and the music that rang out in the airy building was wild and strange to their ears, with a vibrant reedy quality. The visitors were also guests of honour at a village party at the school and were entertained by the 'rich and barbarous' singing and dancing of the boys and girls.

Their months on the island came to an early end when the mission ship, the SS *John Williams*, arrived a week early on 5 September and they had to rush to embark. The Davids, with Woolnough and Poole, were to return to Sydney and the rest were to stay on under Sweet's charge and complete the drilling, which David believed would soon reach the underlying basalt rock.[2] Cara confessed to 'heart-longings' for her children. A little native baby aroused her maternal feelings as it held out its arms to be cuddled. 'I think of dear little Molly and her wish to have a black baby, but dare not risk it lest the little exotic should die'.

The journey back to Sydney was tedious and frustrating, marked for Cara by the inevitable seasickness and an attack of pleurisy. She was acutely anxious about the delays. A slow passage meant that they would not arrive in Sydney till weeks into the new term. David took it all in his stride: he read *Martin Chuzzlewit* to the passengers and took a church service on deck, having already established a reputation as a wonderful orator.

The children were overjoyed to have their mother back at the Gunyah, even if she arrived without a little black baby for Molly. 'How we missed and longed for her!' wrote Molly. 'Victorian fathers, however kindly, were august beings, never really in touch with their children as mothers were. Home without our mother was indeed a desolate place.'[3]

Cara was soon in demand as a guest speaker for she was a born storyteller and could hold an audience with her vivid, forthright language. She gave a talk to Sydney University Women's Association shortly after her return: the audience was reported to be spellbound. She also contributed a paper to the *Australian Christian World* journal that year. Given that she was writing for a committed Christian readership, the article makes interesting reading. It took a coolly impartial and unsentimental view of the missionary activity on Funafuti. Cara was quite blunt in her criticisms of Simona the native pastor and pointed out some of the irregularities under his leadership: for example, he was given supplies of medicines by the London Missionary Society but did not use them, begging supplies from the survey team instead. She also quoted examples of his 'idleness and greed'. She mentioned, however, that the two previous pastors had been considered trustworthy and faithful servants of their people. She noted that the islanders were reverent churchgoers and she wrote – with a degree of sophistry – that there was no sexual immorality in the place, a state of affairs brought about by missionary influence. Overall, her approach to the topic is that of an anthropologist rather than a Christian apologist. It would be interesting to know how the journal's readership responded to Mrs David's views, but there were no follow-up letters in the 1898 editions of the journal.

Cara's botanical collections were to contribute to a paper subsequently written by Joseph Henry Maiden and published in 1904 by the Linnaean Society of New South Wales. Maiden was the Director of the Botanic Gardens in Sydney and was a lifetime friend and professional associate of David. Both men were passionate about their scientific calling and both maintained a lifelong curiosity and interest in the natural world as expressed in the unique Australian landscape and its flora. It is clear that Cara David had an equally strong interest in these pursuits.

Maiden and his wife, Jeanie, had five children who were much the same age as the David children and the families became quite close, the Davids often visiting their friends at the official gardens residence, a gracious home in the Domain. Maiden had a particular interest in the *Acacia* and *Eucalyptus* species and wrote a number of important textbooks and popular works about native flora, so he was the obvious person for Cara to consult about her collection of Funafuti plants. She was to collaborate with Maiden again in the coming years with the founding of the Wattle Day movement.

After her return from Funafuti Cara must have decided, perhaps in view of the obvious public interest in the trip, that her diary notes were worth working up into a book. This became *Funafuti, or Three Months on a Coral Island: An Unscientific Account of a Scientific Expedition.* She turned for editorial help to her colleague in the AHRU, Professor Walter Scott of Sydney University. Scott toned down the manuscript by cutting out some of Cara's observations about the islanders' sexuality and also some of her less favourable remarks about the missions. The publishers Smith, Elder and Co. declined to publish the work, to Cara's disappointment, but it was then accepted by John Murray and the text was revised by an English friend, Mrs G.R. Scott, of Merton College, Cambridge. Cara was delighted to have such a prestigious publisher though she regretted the further liberties taken with the text. She confessed in a letter to Touche that 'in considering the delicacy of the spiritual and moral constitution of the British Public, one is apt to lose the vividly truthful picture of the island as it really is … if I could afford it, I would risk publishing all the indelicate facts – because they are full of teaching what is needed.'

The book's reception amazed her. Within a year of its publication in 1899, it had garnered respectful reviews in scores of English, colonial and French publications and gave her an entry into writing a weekly column for the Melbourne *Age*. 'Notes from Sydney' ran for only a few months in 1900: perhaps the time that went into researching her material proved too demanding for a woman still running a busy household with three young children.

The columns covered material that a modern journalist might be employed full-time to research. They addressed the politics of the day in Sydney: the delivery of the state budget; lack of adequate planning for the city's roads; the debate over free trade. The wider interests of the new nation were also covered, as in the creation and naming of the new federal electorates. Cara wrote about the proposal for giving electorates Aboriginal names, and she described the scorn with which this proposal was generally met. Her own view was that 'there are those who see beauty and propriety in the native nomenclature.'[4]

Cara David was known among family and friends to be always ready to speak her mind, and there were some tartly worded commentaries in her columns on Sydney's social scene and its pretensions. She also wrote a scathing column about a group of British officers dining at the Hotel Australia and their 'taunts' directed at a private soldier (recently returned from South Africa and dining with his sister and a wounded officer) in the hotel. Their snobbery was an example of the class divisions which she and her family found so distasteful in British life.[5]

'Notes from Sydney' were published anonymously, so very few of Cara's friends would have known of her work in this field. But the favourable publicity given to the Funafuti book certainly raised her profile as an interesting woman in her own right among the academics and community leaders who formed the Davids' friendship group in Sydney. In idle moments during those years of the South African War,

Cara even dreamed of becoming a war correspondent and writing home exciting accounts from the Transvaal.

6 The Blue Mountains

In the 1890s, the inner-city suburbs of Balmain, Paddington, Woolloomooloo and Glebe were severely overcrowded, their tenements, cesspits and back alleys breeding places for typhoid and even bubonic plague. No wonder the open spaces, quiet streets and leafy gardens of Ashfield made it seem such a desirable and health-giving place to live. Even so, it did not escape the muggy and often stifling heat of a Sydney summer.

From 1894, the David family spent time every summer in the Blue Mountains. The health of the young children was one factor that drew them there. That year, their four-year-old son, Billy, had had a serious attack of pleurisy and on his recovery David sent Cara with Bridget and the three children to the mountains for a summer holiday, where he joined them in the university vacation. They rented a place called Shiloh in Blackheath, a small cottage about a mile from the railway station commanding a lovely view of the deep valleys below.

By late 1896 they had purchased their own cottage at Woodford to serve as a holiday home. They celebrated Christmas there, exploring the sandstone cliffs and ferny gullies below their bushland block.

Sydney residents had long known of the attractions of the Blue Mountains. The crisp air was considered health-giving, especially for those inclined to chest conditions or who were 'delicate'. The grandeur of the landscape inspired many artists. One of the earliest and most distinguished was Eugène von Guérard; his 1862 sunset vista of the Jamieson Valley, *Weather Board Creek Falls*, anticipated later 'views' that were to draw tourists to the region in increasing numbers. David himself, taking his brother Arthur for a walk down a steep path from Leura in 1897, called the Jamieson Valley 'one of the most beautiful places I have ever seen'.

From the 1880s, Sydney real estate agents began offering free train trips to Springwood and Woodford where residential lots had just been released for sale. Until then the area had been unavailable for development, being reserved for Sydney's possible water supply till about 1876 when the decision was made to base Sydney's supply on the Nepean/Wollondilly Rivers to the south. Messrs Richardson and Wrench invited potential buyers to have a pleasant day out, inspect the land and then attend an auction in Sydney, though in some cases auctions were held on the ground. For many years the people who bought blocks of land in this part of the mountains were professional people or prominent businessmen, and the cottages were generally kept as weekenders.

The Davids had already purchased their land when a large number of allotments were advertised for sale in Woodford in about 1899. David's block had belonged originally to a wealthy Sydney businessman, Alfred Fairfax. For an outlay of £135, the Davids purchased twenty-four acres on Woodbury Street. Three of the acres were flat, typical of the poor heath-covered soils on the sandstone plateau; the rest, in Cara's words, was 'picturesque but unmarketable gully'. The land they purchased still retains much of the character it would have had one hundred years ago. Woodbury Street is a quiet cul-de-sac, heading north not far from the Great Western Highway which crosses the mountains to Bathurst. The street ends at a wall of bush. This is now part of the Woodford Special Reserve, as the gullies form the water catchment for Lake Woodford, the region's drinking water. Beyond the reserve, the land drops steeply over the sandstone escarpment into the Grose River, that winds its way through some of the most dramatic and beautiful scenery in Australia.[1] It is part of the great arc of wilderness that forms the Blue Mountains National Park. Molly David spoke of the place with great affection in her memoirs:

> I think our holidays at Woodford, as very young children, were an important stage in our lives, because we lived close to the earth there. When I say 'earth' I don't mean ploughed fields and hedges, but the primitive, untouched earth. It was poor country but we came to know it intimately, whatever flowers, trees and shrubs grew there, and the small life that inhabited it.[2]

Bush near Mabel's Pool: Molly's 'primitive, untouched earth' (Author's photo)

For Molly, those years laid the foundation of a passionate love for her native bushland and shaped her strong environmental concerns in later life.

Mabel's Pool: Margaret, Miss Stockfelt, Arthur David, Cara, Molly, Bridget Devereux and Billy

Mabel's Pool (Author's photo)

The children learnt to swim at Mabel's Pool, a deep swimming hole about a mile down the gully, where Woodford Creek spills over a sandstone ledge and drops about 30 feet in a waterfall. The track down to the pool and the sandstone steps to it were built by Alfred Fairfax in the 1870s and it is a feature marked on all the local maps of the time. The pool has a sandy bottom and is fringed by the lush vegetation of a Blue Mountains gully. Flood debris and regrowth over a hundred years have shrunk its size but it is still a beautiful waterhole. Fairfax's sandstone blocks are still in place, though worn and mossy now. Woodford soldiers serving with the First AIF in France wrote home with nostalgia about this spot and the golden wattle that bloomed in September along the rough bush track leading down to it.

The cottage on the Davids' property was a simple weatherboard dwelling of four rooms. They named it Tyn-y-Coed, a Welsh name meaning 'hut in the trees'. They relined the rooms and put in a new stove and Cara soon had plans for enlarging it into a comfortable home. Molly tells us that once she found a reliable bush carpenter, her mother saved up the money to have progressive additions made to the cottage: a wide verandah and six new rooms were added plus outhouses, stables and two large water tanks. Ever the pioneer, she set about creating a tiny farm, establishing an orchard with a wide variety of fruit trees, a large vegetable patch and a fowlyard with fifty hens.

Some time around 1899, the family decided to make Tyn-y-Coed their permanent home, though regular trips to Sydney were still possible with the reliable train service that ran between the mountains and the city. David had a small flat at Forest Lodge near the university for his base during the week. He came home by train on weekends and for holidays. Young Billy began boarding at Sydney Grammar School from the age of eight (about 1898) so Cara and the two girls had the place to themselves for most of the time. Because she was on the spot Cara was the one who largely directed the renovations.

The two girls were taught by their mother at home from an early age. After a brief stint in Ashfield at a small private school the girls were withdrawn. (Molly David recalls that she had been victimized by the teacher for innocently questioning the teacher's judgment on some matter; her mother, when she discovered this, immediately withdrew the girls from the school.) A young Scottish woman, Miss Wilson, was engaged as governess at Ashfield and came up to Woodford with them in 1896, when Molly was eight and Margaret ten. From 1904 the family planned to have a suite of rooms in town where the girls could stay when Margaret started university.

Most of our knowledge of the Davids' years at Woodford comes from Molly's memoirs, *Passages of Time*, where in lucid and nostalgic prose she writes of that country childhood seen from the perspective of a ninety-year-old woman. There are many anecdotes about Margaret because the two sisters were very close. Billy, being younger and away at boarding school, does not figure much in the book.

The girls spent their later childhood and early adolescence at Tyn-y-Coed and in that formative environment they acquired a set of practical skills and a certain resourcefulness that stayed with them in later life.

Molly, David, Jeanie Alexander and Margaret, 1900 (NLA MS 8890)

As well as learning to swim they learnt the bushman's skills of handling tools including axes and, later, firearms. When their parents acquired a couple of ponies they learnt to ride bareback and spent much of their free time riding unchaperoned in the bush around Woodford and along the Bathurst Road. Harnessing one or other of the ponies to their two-wheeled box cart, the girls would be sent to do the shopping further up the main road at Lawson. When the ponies had to be re-shod, it was Molly's task, riding one horse and leading the other by a halter, to take them the eight miles down the winding road to Springwood to the nearest blacksmith. The girls rode astride, which was still not considered quite decent. Cara David had firm opinions about suitable dress and behaviour for females and she scorned the conventions that saw young women confined since adolescence in fashionable garments that hobbled their movements. While she rode sidesaddle when an unmarried woman at Hurlstone, after her marriage she had divided skirts made to wear when she accompanied David on field excursions to the Snowy Mountains. Cara also believed that young women should not be encased in whalebone, and her two daughters were lucky to grow up uncorseted. Again, this was considered scandalous by some of Molly's peers who thought it was little better than going naked. Cara David shared Maybanke Wolstenholme's opinion that wearing corsets was the Victorian equivalent of the Chinese practice of binding women's feet.[3]

Woodford in the 1900s was a sleepy hamlet. Permanent residents were few and far between: the voting population of the area was still only 41 in 1906. The train station was a rough wooden platform with a small shelter shed perched in its middle. A 'stalwart young girl acted as stationmistress'.[4] The western railway was a single line, with trains having to use sidings to pass. Duplication of the line took place while the Davids were at Woodford and fettlers' camps, complete with wives and children, sprang up along the road. There was only one large house on the main road. Woodford House, first built as an inn serving travellers, had been acquired as a 'country residence' for Alfred Fairfax, but in the 1890s it had become a boarding house. The only other large house in Woodford was that owned by Gustavus Waterhouse, a wealthy local dignitary and pillar of the Methodist Church. He was to play a part in the Davids' story during the coming war.

Through the eyes of the young Molly we see her mother as the very centre of family life at Woodford: seething with vitality and enthusiasm but with a definite practical bent to her nature. While designing and supervising the extensions to Tyn-y-Coed, Cara was also running the household with Bridget living in and with the occasional help of a young village girl. In a letter to Ned Touche in 1899, Cara described her role as 'gardener, hen wife, dressmaker, cook, housemaid and general odd man about the place – no single male or female will come to such a lonely place'. She was adept at all the kitchen arts of jam making, preserving fruit and eggs, bread making and preparing meals. She also worked long hours in the garden and orchard, often rising at dawn in the hot summer months to do some useful labour in the cool of the morning. The kitchen garden was soon producing enough to meet half of the family's needs for the year. Cara was also an excellent needlewoman (a skill gained at Whitelands) and her family still has fine examples of her work, such as linen embroidered for tablecloths and pillow cases. She made all her children's and her husband's underwear and shirts, having regular sessions once or twice a year when fifteen pairs of underpants would be turned out on her treadle sewing machine; and she also knitted their socks and pullovers – including a balaclava which David was to take to Antarctica in 1908. The professor's hair was also cut at home by his wife, who no doubt was a brisk and skilled worker with scissors. Once a year Cara placed an order for English tailor-made suits for David, through the services of the obliging Touche who was then based in London. Cara's attempts to have her husband presentably attired didn't succeed. David really did fit the image of an 'absent-minded professor': not only was he prone to mislaying papers, umbrellas and bags but his pockets always bulged with geological specimens and he much preferred the comfort of well worn and shapeless coats and hats to any smart new attire. Cara confessed to Touche in 1900 that she'd been trying hard for fifteen years 'to make him take even a mild interest in his appearance – but he is more and more interested in his work and less interested in everything else. But there – this is about his only fault so I have a good deal more to be thankful for than to grumble over.'[5]

At Woodford, Cara was someone the local women came to with a range of problems, having a great respect for her abilities in domestic arts and in practical management of a household. Everyone knew Professor David and they were all proud to have him living in their midst – the local maps of the time all have 'Professor David's residence' clearly marked. But for much of the year he was absent in Sydney and it was Cara David whom the locals had most to do with. Molly recalled one incident on a hot summer's day when a funeral was to take place: the coffin was taken to the railway station to await the train to Rookwood cemetery, when the elderly parson found he'd forgotten his spectacles and couldn't read the prayers. Cara David took the prayer book from 'the trembling and agitated old man and read the service for him. She was always a tower of strength in a crisis.'[6]

Some of Cara's habits would have appeared eccentric to the locals: she was a vegetarian for many years (she found it helped cure her migraines) and also an enthusiast for 'physical culture' and fresh air. At one stage she had all the glass window panes removed from the bedrooms at Tyn-y-Coed, much to the dismay of a visiting university professor. The David family regularly attended local church services when in the district and, as was customary within the Church of England, arranged for their two daughters to be confirmed and accepted as members of faith into the church. Cara obtained permission to instruct her daughters herself in church doctrine, as 'she held very strong anti-hell opinions, and was afraid [they] might be introduced to the devil and church doctrine relating to him.'[7] For this reason the girls were never allowed to attend Sunday school either, though Margaret certainly helped with the teaching of Sunday school at Woodford after she finished university.

Early in 1899, the family was asked by friends in Fiji to take into their home a young member of the Fijian royalty, whose parents wanted her to have a European education. Elenoa came to live with the Davids around 1900 and in that time became a well-loved member of the family. The children were in awe of her wonderful swimming prowess: she would dive into the pool and retrieve live crayfish with her teeth. Some time into her stay, Elenoa returned to Fiji to visit her family and while there contracted pneumonia and died. The news came as a great shock to the David girls, who had come to regard her as their sister. Cara would also have mourned her death, though true to the spirit of the times she did not see Elenoa as quite the equal of her white offspring. 'Our princess is a jolly little girl, obedient and lovable, and as nice as any *white* gentleman's child could be,' she had informed Touche during Elenoa's stay.

In May 1906, David left for an international geological conference in Mexico, where he was to deliver a paper on his findings on glaciation. He travelled via India, England and North America to visit family and colleagues. In a letter that was to set the tone and pattern for many in the ensuing years, the absent husband sent his love to his wife and the children and expressed serene confidence in Cara's ability to manage three teenage children, the bush dwelling and its garden, family finances, local tradesmen and house renovations during his absence. Cara was always very proud of David's academic and scientific success and seemed to accept that she would always be the one 'left behind to look after the farm'. As she put it in a letter written many years later to a grandchild, 'special brains are needed for special work'. She had been willing to give up her own promising teaching career to marry David, but there was no sense of having 'missed out' in life. Why would there be? She was the wife of a distinguished professional who trusted her and treated her as his equal, instilling in her a belief in her own power as an educated woman. And she had access to those most precious commodities: servants, her own home and a degree of financial independence, none of which could be taken for granted by working-class women.[8] She also had the determination to make the most of what life offered and engage in full measure with issues she cared about. The Edwardian woman's life of tennis, tea parties and complaints about the servants held no appeal for Cara David.

With all the responsibilities of domestic life at Tyn-y-Coed, the adventurous Cara was more than willing to escape its demands from time to time, leave the house and teenage children in Bridget's care and accompany David on his geological excursions. She came to share his fascination with geology and wrote an article about some local geological features for a Blue Mountains newspaper in 1903.[9] She went along as chaperone on the university field trips which became a popular feature of the academic year for geology undergraduates, both men and women. There was a week's camping trip to Kiama on the South Coast in August 1902, an excursion to Jenolan Caves in September 1903 and another week's camp at Pokolbin near Cessnock in 1907. On a day's geologizing in the lower Blue Mountains in May 1896, David collected in his pockets 'weight enough of rocks to kill two ordinary men'.

Cara also relished the challenge and adventure of trips to the Southern Alps, which David visited regularly as part of his lifelong interest in glaciation. His first trip to the Kosciuszko region was in February 1901. At that stage there were still conflicting reports about whether the Australian Alps had been subject to glacial action in the past and David wished to make his own observations of the region. He was accompanied by Richard Helms from the Australian Museum and E.F. Pittman of the Department of Mines. He continued his survey of the Kosciuszko plateau in the long vacation of 1905/6. He was particularly interested in proving the glacial origins of the deep lake, known as Blue Lake, that lies to the south-west of Mount Twynam, the third highest feature in that sweep of mountain country. In January 1906, under the snowy bluffs of Twynam, David launched his coracle made out of interwoven twigs, wire netting and waterproof cloth, and risking life and limb ventured out onto the deep waters of the lake to take soundings. The coracle made it back to shore and the trial was pronounced a success: David's measurements showed the lake's steep descent to a maximum depth of 75 feet. He came back at the end of the month with Cara along this time, as well as two scientists, W. Hedley of the Australian Museum and G.A. Waterhouse.

The party collected horses at Jindabyne and rode up along the old bullock track on the Crackenback Range with their mountain guide, James Spencer. Camp was made in a glade of snow gums next to the old Bett's camp, near the head of the Perisher Valley. A photograph taken by David shows his wife standing by the tent in early morning sunshine, brushing out her hair. The image hints at feelings of freedom and joy in the outdoors that one doesn't associate with Edwardian women. These feelings are also evident in Cara's Funafuti diaries. Her love of an active outdoor life was to be passed on in full measure to her two daughters.

Bett's Camp; Cara and David on horseback (Kosciuszko Huts Association, PIC 8329/1-92 National Library of Australia)

Cara holding horses while David 'geologized' (SU P11)

Cara brushing her hair, camp in snow gums (SU P11)

From Bett's camp, the party rode up to the trig point on Kosciuszko's summit, where the old weather station established by Clement Wragge in the 1880s still stood, abandoned since 1902.[10] Cara held the horses while David 'geologized'. Many photographs in David's collection show his careful observation of the striated grooves on rock surfaces, evidence of glacial movement over them in the past. Cara pursued her own botanical interests, with the alpine region at the height of its brief summer flowering.

In January 1907, they both returned to the mountains for a ten-day excursion with David's geology students. A full account of this trip exists, recorded in a bound volume and presented to Professor and Mrs David by the students. Twenty men and eight women formed the student group: a testimony to the remarkable popularity of this course with both sexes. They travelled by steam train to Cooma, and a horse-drawn coach took them beyond Jindabyne to the Thredbo River. From there the party was to walk up in stages to the Kosciuszko plateau, with the tents and provisions being hauled up by a bullock team, two horse teams and carriages also accompanying them. The bullock team found it heavy going and was badly bogged a number of times, delaying their trip by a day while all the party helped unload the wagon to lighten it.

Bett's Camp was again the base for their mountain adventures. They spent a day at Blue Lake remaking David's coracle, which had been left there from the previous expedition and crushed flat by snow. This time it was christened *The Cara*. Once again David ventured out onto the lake to take soundings, with some of his students taking bearings and recording the results. The highlight of the excursion was a twenty-four-mile walk to the summit of Kosciuszko. Clad in hobnailed boots and wide-brimmed hats, the party trudged up slopes of snow grass and around rocky outcrops, a stout staff providing support where needed. The women draped their wide hats in veils of red muslin which protected them from both the March flies and the fierce mountain sun. At tea breaks the men drew on the comfort of their pipes and they cradled pannikins of hot tea brewed up by Will Connors, their cook and handyman. From Charlotte's Pass, they trekked over Mount Clarke and had lunch at Lake Albina that lies beneath Townsend's northern flanks. There the group bathed (perhaps just the men … the water would have been icy) and they inspected evidence of glaciation in the rock pavements. Afternoon tea was enjoyed on the breezy summit of Kosciuszko and the obligatory group photo was taken next to the summit trig. As it was Accession Day (the anniversary of Edward VII's coronation) they all sang 'God Save the King'. Returning to camp at 9 pm, they saw glimpses in the late evening light of the Thredbo Valley, still heavily timbered, remote and untouched by development apart from grazing on the valley floor.

On the return journey to Jindabyne and while awaiting the arrival of the bullock wagon, the group met the New South Wales Premier, Joseph Carruthers, and his daughter and accompanying party who were returning from Kosciuszko. Carruthers has ridden from Jindabyne to inspect the progress of the new road which was being built up the Perisher Valley to Charlotte's Pass and then on to Kosciuszko's summit. He was hopeful that a great new era of tourist development was about to begin in this remote region and on his return to Jindabyne he regaled eager journalists with tales of his ride and the magnificent prospects to be viewed from the mountain summit. He was keen to show the world, and in particular, British investors, that New South Wales was not just a drought-plagued sheep walk; surely its winter attractions would rival those of Europe once the planned Kosciuszko Hotel was completed.

On their return to Sydney David's students presented Cara with a medal to commemorate the 'first ascent' of Kosciuszko by a woman. They may not have been aware that the mountain had been climbed by Charlotte Adams in 1881; there was also of course no recognition by the students that Aboriginal people had roamed these mountains in summer for generations.

Further annual trips to the mountains followed for David, with Cara accompanying him in January 1915. This was a motoring trip along the new road to a camp below Charlotte's Pass. The weather, unlike that of the 1907 trip, was wet and cold and they cooked and camped one night in a heavy snowstorm. The students were predominantly female on that trip, many of the young male undergraduates having already enlisted in the AIF. A photograph of the group at the camp shows them in a cheerful mood but Cara's diary is full of black remarks about David's new, young laboratory assistant, Eric Jones, who accompanied them on the trip and hoped to achieve his scout's badge for campcraft. He proved to be hopelessly incompetent, incapable of cutting firewood, lighting a fire, making bread or cooking. He refused to leave his tent in the morning chill and David was left to start most of the morning activities. Nevertheless the excursion was a success with the usual highlight being a round trip to Kosciuszko. In a spirit of charity Cara and David signed Eric's scout papers, no doubt aware that the young man would never venture into this challenging terrain again.

Snowstorm, geology camp, January 1915 (SU P11)

7   New Directions

The 1890s were a period of great activity for women in the colonies and a number of groups were formed to agitate for political reform and social change in many areas of women's lives. Cara David was to be involved with a wide range of these groups from the 1890s onwards. This independent intellectual life and commitment to voluntary public service were to be important features of her marriage and were to help her weather some of the difficult times that lay ahead for her.

She retained an intense interest in the colony's education system. Cara had made her mark professionally in establishing Hurlstone College, actively pursuing higher standards and better training for young women teachers even though it was clear that she was faced with structural barriers and resistance to change within the department. She and the women who followed her at Hurlstone as principals to 1903 were among the first tertiary trained women professionals in Australia and therefore had a degree of influence in the educational world.

In 1894, Cara joined the new professional association of teachers, initially called the Teachers' Guild of NSW, and soon after known as the NSW Teachers Association. Though no longer a teacher herself, she was able to share her professional knowledge with her peers. Cara's friends, Maybanke Wolstenholme and Louisa Macdonald, were also members of the guild and David was one of its founding members. Membership was held mainly by professors and staff from the University of Sydney, principals of state and independent schools and staff from most non-government schools. State schoolteachers were encouraged to join, but not many did: perhaps they sensed class barriers. They were to reserve their loyalties for the NSW Public School Teachers Association which began in 1895 and which became the NSW Teachers Federation in 1918.

In 1894, Cara wrote a paper for the Guild's newsletter, *Australian Teacher*, putting forward some practical suggestions for the training of teachers outside the established state system. She was thinking especially of the hundreds of small private schools in the colony that were in the hands of totally untrained people, and of the many tutors and governesses employed in private homes that 'have not the least notion how to train children's minds'.[1] The discredited pupil-teacher system, under which Cara herself had worked as a young girl, was still for many private

Louisa Macdonald (Sydney University Women's College)

schools in the colony the only method they used for training new teachers, a state which Cara considered 'a disgrace'. She suggested a joint endeavour by the Education Department, the university and the Teachers' Association: the establishment of a Board of Management that would arrange for the design of curricula, hold training courses, appoint examiners, arrange practical teaching sessions in schools and award diplomas for students who wished to teach outside the state schools. Her suggestions must have been favourably received by the department as by 1895 the board had been appointed. The ten members of the board included David's university colleagues, Professors Scott and MacCallum, Miss Louisa Macdonald of the University Women's College, a school inspector and Cara herself. In April 1895, *The Teacher* was advertising a Course of Training for the year for candidates for the Kindergarten Diploma. This was to include lectures in the Psychology and History of Education and a course of training, both practical and theoretical, under a Kindergarten teacher approved by the board. The theories of Friedrich Froebel, with their far-reaching implications for the nurture of young children, were finally achieving acceptance in educational circles in the colony – a move for which Cara David must take much of the credit.

The following year, courses for Primary and Lower Secondary Diplomas were also offered; for these, candidates needed to spend twelve months observing and teaching under supervision in a school approved by the board as well as undertake theoretical studies and examinations in education and school management. By 1899, the scheme was well under way, offering training and certification of teachers from kindergarten to secondary level. Cara, together with Professor Francis Anderson and noted kindergarten expert, Elizabeth Banks, examined candidates for the Diplomas in Kindergarten and Primary grades. Cara held this honorary position for two years. By this stage there were forty-five students on the roll, forty of them kindergarten students, three working for the Primary and two for the Secondary Diploma.[2] The Kindergarten graduates were all female, as this area of education was still considered an extension of a woman's innate nurturing gifts. At the end of the courses came presentation nights when the students received their diplomas and awards. In 1899, Mrs David offered an unusual prize: a guinea 'for the best collection of purely *Australian* songs and stories, suitable for Kindergarten classes, written by young Australian students. Many of the songs now in use are absurd and unsuitable, and there are none on Australian subjects.'[3] Like many of her friends with artistic or literary interests, Cara was feeling the influence of a strengthening wave of national sentiment as the colonies moved towards federation. (Maybanke Anderson also wrote and published a collection of Australian children's songs.) Cara was a keen member of the new Wattle Day League, which encouraged schoolchildren (and their parents) to protect native bushland and to take an interest in their local native flora. The league also aimed to instil patriotic ideals in children.

Cara David always had a strong practical orientation and was suspicious of abstract theories that did not meet the needs of real people. She saw the practical training of a student teacher in a classroom under the guidance of an experienced senior teacher as all-important, and the board was at pains to seek out suitable schools which could be the venue for practice teaching. The training programs were also to have a solid foundation in good theory. What surprises a modern reader are the close links set up by the association between prestigious university academics and the more humble world of the kindergarten and primary schoolteacher. The programs of lectures were run by the University Extension Board, with Professors Scott, MacCallum and Anderson (heads of Classics, Modern Languages and Philosophy, respectively) lecturing to the students. These three men were all good friends of the Davids and like them were involved in the Australasian Home Reading Union. All shared the belief, common to many educated people before the Great War, that the key to social reform and a more ethical future for humanity lay in education and in the provision of a healthy, nurturing environment for all citizens from babyhood on.

One issue that was to preoccupy Cara from her Hurlstone days onward was the need for better training for women running a household. In our labour-saving homes it is easy to forget just how much of domestic life, a hundred years ago, revolved around the continuing labour of women. It's worth spending a moment looking at what was involved in the time-consuming chores that constituted housework: the weekly wash, starching, ironing and mending clothes, cleaning and blacking stoves and hearths, cooking for large families, beating rugs and dusting and sweeping cluttered home interiors. Then there was the poultry yard to care for, vegetables to be picked, fruit bottled and jam made. Family ailments needed the simple medical remedies which mothers were expected to provide, and invalids or elderly dependent relatives needed special cookery and care. Women who could not afford to hire any help spent their days in an endless round of exhausting physical chores as well as looking after their children.

In 1888, Sydney Technical College established cookery classes for working-class women and Cara David was asked to be an examiner. There was a disappointingly small attendance at the daytime classes. On being asked to suggest a solution to this, Cara pointed out that women who were working were unlikely to be able to attend classes held in the afternoon, and she suggested the times be changed to an evening. These were successfully introduced in 1889.

Cara had many other practical suggestions to make to the department. The classes should be as cheap as possible, with one good textbook suitable for colonial conditions. The cooking classes could become self-supporting by selling their produce to the public as sixpenny lunches. Cara also advised the teachers to be encouraging to their students, and not to show contempt for 'colonial ways'.[4]

It is no surprise that domestic life in Australia at the turn of the century was inevitably bound up with 'the servant question'. Any sensible middle-class woman would have done her best to employ reliable servants, and Cara was one of these. She came to rely heavily on Bridget Devereux in running her Ashfield home, in cooking meals and in looking after the children when they were young, though she stayed very active herself in running the household. As well, a woman came in once a week to do the heavy washing.

It seemed clear to everyone that there would be a need for reliable household help for many years to come in Australia. (No one at that stage anticipated the upheavals of the Great War and the changes it would bring in the role of women, nor the introduction of new labour-saving devices that would revolutionize domestic life.) Cara wrote a paper she called 'Housewifery Schools', published in the *Australasian Nurses Journal* in 1906 and first presented as an address given to the National Council of Women that year. In the paper Cara advocated the establishment of a school to train women in all the skills needed for running a household efficiently, whether as the head of the household or as a woman in paid employment in someone else's home. She listed fifteen areas of expertise, which included skills we would now expect from a range of professionals, including health services, horticulture, accountancy and budgeting, dietary skills, and clothes making: all of these were skills Cara herself practised very competently. She wanted to see women learn how to feed a family in healthy and economical ways: 'the daily waste of food through ignorance in the average Australian household would shock either the French or Belgian housewife,' she claimed during the war.[5] It was important to raise the confidence and competence of women in what was still their major sphere of life and work; she suggested that 'girls of all social grades' would benefit by attendance at such a school and improve their chance of economic independence. Her experience led her to believe that Australian women were more adaptable and enterprising than many of their sex in the Old World and that young housewives or young girls seeking domestic positions would respond with intelligence and enthusiasm if given the chance to be trained in these skills. The school remained an idea only. After the Great War, as women turned away from domestic service to jobs in factories and department stores, the notion of such training for girls in service began to seem out of date.[6]

By the early 1900s, Cara had a strong circle of like-minded women friends in Sydney. At this stage the family was living at Woodford but Cara seems to have spent many busy weekdays based in Sydney. It was easy enough to catch an early train down to the city and return late in the evening; or perhaps she spent the night at David's lodgings.

Cara was one of the founding members of the Women's Club in 1901. Initiated by Dr Mary Booth who had consulting rooms in the city, it was to provide a place where women interested in public, professional, scientific, literary or artistic work might spend their leisure moments and associate on equal terms. Like the Women's Literary Society, founded in Sydney in 1889, the Women's Club provided an independent space for women and their interests, one that did not depend on male patronage. It was definitely a product of the new age, the work of women empowered by education and the prospect of the coming suffrage. One of the club's many attractions for Cara was that it provided a peaceful place to relax after a hectic day of meetings in the city; and it was also a stimulating social venue. The club, which met in rooms in Rowe Street in the city, contained a library, a debating circle, a circle for social and political discussion and a lecturer circle for visiting speakers. Some of these circles met at night so working women could attend. Cara was a lively member of the debating circle and also involved in arranging guest speakers. She was president of the club in 1907 and vice-president in 1910.

Another founding member of the Women's Club was Miss Rose Scott, one of the key figures in the early feminist movement in New South Wales. In 1891, she had helped found the Womanhood Suffrage League, which aimed to advance the cause of female suffrage as the colonies prepared for federation and the drafting of a new constitution. A charismatic and cultured woman, Scott drew a whole network of people to her side. She had never married and had inherited the large family home, Lynton, in Jersey Road, Edgecliff, in Sydney's Eastern Suburbs. There she held informal Friday evenings 'at home', which were considered to have all the attractions of a European salon and where political and social issues of the day were debated. While radical in many of her views – she was a pronounced pacifist in the years leading up the Great War – she was a welcoming host to all age groups and social types. Mrs Molyneaux Parkes who founded the conservative

Women's Liberal League in 1902 was her friend, as was the suffragist Vida Goldstein, independent candidate for the Federal Senate in 1903. Anglican, Roman Catholic, Presbyterian and Methodist clergy were all welcome at Lynton. Scott invited factory girls to come along to discuss their working conditions with members of parliament, a move that had helped bring about the *Early Closing Act* of 1899 which required shops to close at 6 pm.

Louisa Macdonald, the influential head of the Sydney University Women's College, was one of Rose Scott's lifelong friends. The men in the early Labor movement – Billy Hughes, William Holman, George Reid – all knew her well; the legal fraternity, including Sir William Windeyer, Alfred Deakin and Sir Robert Garran, were her friends. Her appreciation of Australian art and literature drew many creative people to Lynton, including Henry Lawson, A.B. Paterson, Alex Chisholm, Jeanie Gunn and Miles (Stella) Franklin. Rose Scott, enchanted by *My Brilliant Career* and by the 'dear young girl' who was its author, became a protégé of this talented but headstrong young woman and invited Stella to stay with her in Sydney when she visited the city. At that time Stella Franklin was still living with her parents on their impoverished dairy farm near Goulburn.

The Edgeworth Davids were also counted as friends of Rose Scott. Both the Davids supported the suffrage movement and the professor lent his name and prestige to the cause by giving an address at a Suffrage League gathering at Ashfield Town Hall in 1893 and another at the Ashfield School of Arts in 1894. The David women certainly visited Lynton from time to time and there they met the young Stella Franklin, probably in August 1902. Rose Scott was anxious that Stella meet some of her older feminist friends, particularly Cara David and Dr Mary Booth: 'Friends of mine, such dear women, want to know you.'[7] Cara and her two daughters had read *My Brilliant Career* and loved it.

The book itself was causing quite a stir in Sydney. Professor MacCallum confessed to Cara David that *My Brilliant Career* had genius in it. The new Governor-General, Baron Hallam Tennyson (the poet's son) read this 'story of bush life' with much pleasure, and shared his enthusiasm about it with the Davids. In August 1903, he wrote directly to Miles Franklin, letting her know of his interest in her work and offering to help secure publication of her next book in England.[8] Cara also wrote a letter to Miss Franklin conveying Tennyson's admiration for the new writer, but that letter seems to have been undelivered: by this stage the Franklins had left their farm near Goulburn and moved to Penrith, driven off the land by the great drought of the federation years.

Both Rose Scott and Cara David were anxious to offer editorial advice to the young writer when she told them of her new project. This is assumed to be one of two manuscripts, since lost: either 'On the Outside Track' or 'The End of My Career'. By August 1903, Rose was eagerly awaiting the arrival of the manuscript from Penrith. She promised to read it aloud to her cousin, David Scott Mitchell, and then forward it promptly to Mrs David at Woodford.

Cara read the manuscript intently but was dismayed at what she found: crude caricatures, a commonplace ending, banality, too narrow a focus … a work, in summary, that needed a complete redrafting. Cara advised her young friend not to risk her reputation by publishing it. 'If you could come to me, and go over it with me … there are a number of very important things I could point out to you – to avoid in any new book.' She was taken aback by the sense of bitter pessimism in the book and its 'concentration on man's vileness' (a theme she attributed, in a gentle gibe, 'to Miss Scott's influence'). 'O child!! I *do* wish you would come to me … I do think I could help you a wee bit – not by trying to tie the wings of your genius but helping to teach your genius how to guide its own flight.'[9]

Cara David was not alone in her judgment that this latest offering from Miles Franklin was unpublishable. Edward Garnett, reader for the new English publishing house of Duckworth, considered 'On the Outside Track' an 'inflated' book which needed 'more sense and more modesty'.[10] Nothing was heard of either manuscript for some years and both evolved into very different books before reaching publication. Meanwhile, the young writer, undaunted, was gathering material for another book, based on her year's experiences in 1903 working in Sydney and Melbourne as a housemaid. Her 'Mary-Anne' diary was intended to give an honest picture of the grim conditions under which young women worked in domestic service. This was a theme close to the heart of many feminists at the time. They saw that women in service were particularly vulnerable to economic and sexual exploitation by men. They were 'voiceless' at a time when male workers were gathering power and solidarity through the union movement. Cara David certainly warmed to Miles Franklin's new project. Raising the status and credentials of women domestic workers was a mission she had been involved with ever since her days at Hurlstone.

In April 1904, Cara invited Miles Franklin to Woodford for an extended stay, explaining that the family was generally down in Sydney during the week. Their 'Blue Mtn shanty' would be an ideal place for Miles to finish the 'Mary-Anne' project in uninterrupted peace and quiet. She expressed her delight at the new project: 'If Mary Anne is a success, nothing will go against your future ... we all hope for a brilliant hit for it.'[11]

Miles Franklin did not take up the invitation and in early 1906 she left Australia to try her fortunes in America. Her departure left Rose Scott desolate. This wealthy, cultivated and clever woman had a wide range of social and political causes that she cared about, yet it is clear from her letters to Miles that she was troubled at this time by an acute sense of personal loneliness.

Scott's missionary work for women continued unabated. Much of her energy in those years after federation was directed to running the Women's Political Educational League (WPEL), which she had founded in October 1902, to educate women about how to use their newly won voting powers and to inform them what issues were worth fighting for. There were many problems concerning the welfare of women and children that needed attention but that had received little support from an all-male legislature.

Thoughtful women saw evidence all around them of the glaring inequalities between the sexes. They were dismayed at the special vulnerability of women and children in a society with double standards of sexual morality. It was widely believed that men's sexual appetites were too powerful to restrain and that it was natural for them to seek satisfaction among prostitutes and servant girls. At the turn of the century the 'age of consent' in New South Wales was fourteen years, which was legally the age at which a girl could choose to become a prostitute and men could pay for her services without committing an offence. As a result there were extremely high rates of abortions, infanticide and maternal and infant mortality, as young girls were abandoned to unwanted pregnancies with no man interested in supporting them. Another legal anomaly was that while a woman had to register a baby in her own name, the father's name did not have to appear on the birth certificate if it was illegitimate: this made it very hard to require fathers to provide maintenance to the mother and baby.

The early feminists could see quite clearly the close links between poverty, prostitution, infant mortality and maternal despair. From the early 1890s, Rose Scott lobbied the colony's politicians to support a bill that would raise the age of consent to sixteen. Her advocacy drew a storm of hostility and derision from men, who saw such a bill as posing a threat to their liberty as British subjects, and it was defeated.

In 1903, now with the added weight of the women's vote behind her, Scott lobbied politicians to support a new bill. Letters were sent to MPs of both parties asking where they stood on the issue, and women were urged to vote 'for good men and good measures' rather than be swayed by the rhetoric of party politics, which she condemned for its

'its contradictory statements ... its smoke and fire of personal abuse and savage retaliation.'[12] However the Crimes (Girls' Protection)Bill failed to pass its second reading in 1903. It failed again in 1905 and was not finally enacted as law until 1910.

Cara David, inspired by Scott's drive and dedication, started a branch of the league in Lawson, in the Blue Mountains, and planned to inform women in the district about the importance of the legislation being considered. (She also gave an address about the implications of the franchise to the Sydney University Women's Association.) The local WPEL branch met each month at the Congregational Church in Lawson and she arranged for First Class Constable Shiel to give a talk to the audience about the rights of women electors. It is to be hoped that Constable Shiel was a sympathetic speaker without the hearty patronizing manner that marked most male pronouncements about the suffrage issue and women's political rights.

There was one electoral triumph for the women's cause. The passage of the *Infants' Protection Act* in 1904 meant that an illegitimate child's father had to provide support for the child to the age of 14 or 16. Men who failed to comply could be brought to court. This legislation was of particular

AT THE FEET OF GAMALIEL.

HUSBAND : "Now, my dear, that you have got the franchise, it were well for you to know something of the rudiments of politics. First, I may tell you that there are two great parties "——

WIFE : "Two! How lovely! And have we invitations to both ?"

Women get the vote, 1902 (*The Bulletin*)

interest to Cara David. She wrote to Rose Scott asking for more details about the planned bill as she wished to discuss it with the Lawson circle.

One version of modern feminism is highly critical of the 'conservatism' of these early pioneers, condemning their exaggerated focus on maternity and 'the breeding and care of new citizens'.[13] The National Council of Women – Cara was on its executive committee from 1906 – was singled out as one of the major conservative voices. This was an umbrella group that had been formed in 1896 to offer a voice and common cause to a number of women's groups operating at the time, including the Women's Literary Society, the Sydney University Women's Association, the Womanhood Suffrage League and the Woman's Christian Temperance Union. This was a feminist network with common aspirations for reform to the laws affecting women and children, and with a desire to see a more kindly, nurturing ethos develop in society. The importance of stability and happiness in family life was a central part of their creed. One of the stated policies of the National Council of Women was for compulsory training in domestic science at all girls schools. Some modern feminists have found this especially offensive, arguing that it would have denied girls more interesting options. In the 1980s such options were taken for granted. When there was easy access to contraceptives, modern medical care, labour-saving devices in the home and free education, what middle-class woman could not be a free spirit? It was very easy to scorn their great-grandmothers who worried about poor mothering skills, the fate of illegitimate children and the vulnerability of young girls in the face of rape or seduction. There was a strong sense of women's powerlessness in the home, in the workplace and on the streets and this found expression in the kind of legal reforms feminists were seeking. Maybanke Wolstenholme, one of the chief proponents of reform, had a lifetime's bitter experiences to draw on: she knew what it was to be an abandoned wife and bereaved mother, and had struggled to gain justice for her family in a society that was still indifferent to women's needs.

But she also knew the liberating effect of education in women's lives. She saw the need for educational reform to go hand in hand with legal reform to advance the welfare of women and girls in the colony and in the young Commonwealth.

The spectre of venereal disease and its terrible legacies preoccupied many thoughtful women at the time. Until modern antibiotics brought safe and swift cure for sexually transmitted diseases, their impact on the individual, family and community was profound. But it was not an issue to be discussed in polite society. Maybanke Anderson dared to broach the topic by writing a pamphlet about it, *The Root of the Matter*. It was the first pamphlet issued by the Workers Educational Association, appearing in 1916. In the pamphlet she pointed out that since the onset of war there had been such a flood of VD outpatients that many big city hospitals now had to devote a special ward to their treatment. There were other statistics: more than half the blind persons in the United Kingdom owed their loss of sight to some form of syphilis. Deafness, paralysis and insanity followed for the man who contracted syphilis, but his partner and her offspring could suffer equally disabling and incurable disease. What was the solution? Maybanke Anderson had some practical suggestions: she felt a more honest sex education for children would help them to develop sound relationships as adults. She wanted to see higher wages for women so that they would be less driven to prostitution. She called for financial incentives to encourage early marriage and continual financial help for young families, which she thought would guarantee a more stable family life.

Cara David and many of her friends in the women's movement were strong supporters of Maybanke's ideas. When the fourth year medical students at the university called a meeting in 1916 to form a society to combat VD, Cara supported them warmly, applauding their courage in 'bursting the bonds of propriety at the Varsity'. She was to hear from David, just before the Armistice, that there were more than 6000 cases of syphilis among the women of Lille, just liberated from the Germans

– a fact that David attributed to the barbarity of the occupation forces, though in fact it was just as much an aspect of life in Allied territories.

Linked to this concern about the impact of VD was an anxiety about the racial health of the Australian population. There were fears that the best features of the Anglo-Saxon race were being diluted by 'foreigners' who had much larger families. The educated classes in the country were already beginning to use contraception to control their family size – perhaps the Davids were among their number.[14] This left the more 'feckless' to swamp the country with large numbers of offspring. Knowing as we do where debates about race and eugenics led the twentieth century, we read of these concerns with suspicion, but they were real enough to many people at the time. Cara David shared her country's antagonism towards most foreigners, especially Asians. Her husband, perhaps with a mind broadened by scientific enquiry, was always much more generous in these matters.

One of the issues which attracted the most passionate support from many early feminists related to reform of the liquor laws.

John Norton, editor of the scurrilous daily newspaper, *Truth*, coined the term 'wowser' in the 1890s to refer to the women who opposed the influence of the liquor lobby in New South Wales. It is still a powerful pejorative. Yet the women's temperance movement was in its time an effective movement for social reform, and one to which many enlightened women were passionately committed, including Cara David. What drew her to this cause? Family anecdotes suggest that Cara's own brother, Thomas Mallett, was an alcoholic in later life. He was the fisherman's son, supporting his widowed mother and four other children as a shoemaker in Southwold. At sixteen, he would have heard the village gossip about his mother and her two illegitimate children. After this, he disappears from the records. Anne Edgeworth speculates that his teenage years may have been unhappy enough to lead him to a life of addiction: he lacked the opportunities that allowed his younger sister, Cara, to escape to a new life.

When Edgeworth David wrote to his Aunt Sarah in 1893 about the christening of their first baby, Margaret, he mentioned celebrating the event with 'wine, cake and afternoon tea', and Cara kept her own home-made plum wine in the household. Beer and spirits were certainly taken as supplies on the Funafuti trip. But generally, the family avoided associations with drinking and certainly was opposed to the heavy drinking that was part of the colony's public house culture. This opposition was based to a large extent on knowledge about the damage that alcohol was causing in colonial society. Cara often expressed anger at what she saw as the undue political influence of publicans and their supporters.

Hotels were open from early in the morning until late at night and there were no restrictions on entry: children could be sent to the corner pub to purchase supplies for their parents. Alcohol was widely prescribed by doctors as a cure or panacea for all kinds of ailments. The *Australasian Nurses Journal* of 1906, the very publication that contains Cara David's piece on 'Housewifery Schools', had a report on the beneficial effects of champagne on patients suffering from prolonged convalescence. Many patients became addicts as a result of their inappropriate treatment. Addiction to opium was also very common: opium was the only painkiller for a range of incurable and common diseases, including tuberculosis. Many patent medicines, available by mail order or over the counter, had a high alcohol content and were addictive, as well as being of no therapeutic value.

For many working-class families, reliant on the weekly pay packet to make ends meet, the drinking habits of the breadwinner could bring misery and disaster to the household. A man was literally taking food out of his dependents' mouths by a drinking spree that left the family hungry and desperate for the week. Then there were the related troubles of alcohol-fuelled violence in the home and unwanted sexual attentions or rape of a woman who had no legal powers to object. She could escape with the children if she had somewhere to go, but in the

A Living Skeleton

Changed into a Healthy and Robust Child.

The trying weather of summer makes children drowsy, lifeless, and without energy. They lose appetite, their blood becomes impure, and they break out in sores.

Ayer's Sarsaparilla

Mrs. Emily Air, of Murray Park, Adelaide, So. Australia, very kindly sends us a photograph of herself and family, which we reproduce above, accompanying the same with the following testimonial:

"The trying hot weather of our summer has a very debilitating effect upon children. They run down in health, become drowsy, lose appetite, and break out in sores on the face and head.

"I have invariably found Ayer's Sarsaparilla a perfect remedy for this condition. It purifies the blood, restores the appetite, and tones up the whole system.

"One of my children only twelve month old was transformed from almost a skeleton into a healthy and robust child simply by giving it small doses of Ayer's Sarsaparilla."

Do you wonder, then, that people call it

" The World's Greatest Family Medicine "?

It is the greatest family medicine the world ever knew, good for all ages and all conditions. When you take it you get more benefit from your food, your blood becomes richer, your nerves are made stronger, and the whole system becomes filled with new life and vigor.

AYER'S Sarsaparilla

A Great Medicine for Weak Children.

Advertisement for patent medicine. Ayers Sarsparilla contained about 20% alcohol (*The Bulletin*) early 1890s there was only one female refuge in Sydney, run by the Sydney Rescue Society. It admitted 1169 women and 691 children in one month.[15]

The Woman's Christian Temperance Union (WCTU) emerged in the colonies in the 1880s, having been modelled on similar organizations in the United States. Of all the feminist groups that began at this time, the WCTU was probably the most successful in breaking down the Victorian stereotype that a woman's place was in the home. The union was firm in its support for women's suffrage and the potential for social reform that seemed possible once women had the vote. In fact its members had the confidence to claim the future as their own: they believed that 'the twentieth century [will be] pre-eminently the woman's century'.[16] The union was run entirely by women, with meetings chaired by women. Before this it was rare to hear a woman address a crowd, but during the 1890s large public gatherings were held in every state to spread temperance views. Women were the main speakers, though there were always a few sympathetic male clergy who joined the platform. While the union's long-term goal was the prohibition of the manufacture and import of alcohol, its members supported various versions of temperance. One of these was a 'local option' vote. This would be a vote in state or shire elections that allowed the ratepayers in a shire or municipality to remove licensed premises from their area by means of a majority vote. By 1911, every Australian colony had introduced 'local option' or some modified form of it on their electoral forms: an indication of the importance of this issue to voters at the time. In 1907, New South Wales held its first polls by which all residents on the electoral roll could vote to ban all licensed venues from their own region; they also had the option of voting for a 'reduction' in numbers of licensed premises in their region. No one electorate succeeded in passing the 'no licence' clause, as a 3/5 majority of votes was needed. But the numbers involved are significant: over 168,000 people voted against 'no licence' and 178,000 people voted for it. In other words, a very sizable number of New South Wales residents wanted to remove all licensed premises from their district. As it was, the 'reduction' vote was successful and as a result 292 hotel licenses across the state were revoked.[17]

While Cara David was not involved in leadership roles in the WCTU, she was sympathetic to many of the union's aims. She would have been familiar with its work and its public profile after she and David returned to Ashfield in late 1890. A Temperance Concert was held at Ashfield in December to publicize the first of the local option votes to be held as part of the municipal elections in February 1891. Undaunted by the failure to win their vote in February, the local union members organized another large public meeting on 21 February, at the Skating Rink in Summer Hill. This meeting was 'to pass resolutions in favour of petitioning Parliament on the restriction of liquor licences' in state elections. It was the persistent lobbying of MPs by groups like this that was to lead to the *Liquor (Amendment) Act* and the first local option poll in the 1907 state elections.

Cara David wrote an (undated) article called 'Women's Responsibility with regard to the Liquor Traffic' which was the written report of a public address she had given during one of the 'no-licence' campaigns before the 1910 election. In the address she outlined 'legislative, social and educational methods of fighting the dragon Intemperance'. While at times evangelistic and emotive in tone, the article also contains suggestions that have a contemporary ring and promote 'consumer rights': 'do not take patent medicines, and go to a doctor who does not prescribe alcohol as a medicine'; 'fight the advertising fiend on aesthetic as well as moral grounds. We ought to be ashamed to make money by such lies ... by Wolfe's Schnapps and Walkers Whiskey ... as now "decorate" our railway premises'. She argued for the need for women to educate themselves about the social costs of drinking: 'read up a few statistics, compare the sums spent on gaols, lunatic asylums, law-courts, police-courts ... with the revenue derived from the drink traffic, and draw your own conclusions.' She urged all women to exercise their voting rights, to be aware of the social and ethical aspects of alcoholism and to raise their children in a healthy environment as free as possible of artificial stimulants and addictions.

Cara was always a persuasive and lively speaker and she lent her support to the movement with a talk in Bowral, in the Southern Highlands, in May 1904, on the need for a local option clause at the next state elections. While Rose Scott insisted that women vote for issues rather than parties, it was inevitable that many women in the WCTU were suspicious of the new Labor Party, which had come to be identified as the party allied to liquor interests.

Generally, the Liberal candidates seemed to be more sympathetic to the women's cause. The Labor Premier, William Holman, was to become the bête noir of the New South Wales temperance movement during the Great War for his opposition to their aims. Cara David was to assume a prominent political role in the movement during those years.

8   Antarctic Mission

The Anglo-Irish adventurer and merchant seaman, Ernest Shackleton, had been a member of Captain Robert Scott's 1901/02 expedition to the South Pole. Using sledges for their journey, Scott's party had broached the Great Ice Barrier and penetrated far south onto the high polar plateau, but they did not reach the Pole. Shackleton was determined to return to the Antarctic and claim this prize himself. In 1907, he began raising private funds for a new expedition, to sail to the Antarctic from New Zealand in January 1908.

When Edgeworth David heard of Shackleton's plans he offered his support, using his influence in Sydney to raise funds for the expedition. He also wrote to Shackleton, asking to accompany the expedition on their ship, the *Nimrod*, travelling south from Lyttleton in New Zealand with the party and back with the ship in the university long vacation. He received news of acceptance in September 1907. Shackleton himself was no scientist: his main ambition was to reach the Pole. But he understood the importance of scientific support for the venture and had no doubt about the significance of the South Magnetic Pole for future geophysical research. So he was very happy to have a scientist of David's stature and international reputation attached to his expedition.

As preparations continued, David approached Prime Minister Alfred Deakin and was able to secure a subscription from the Australian government of £5000. These extra funds enabled Shackleton to add a number of Australians to his team, including David, and the young Douglas Mawson, previously one of David's students at Sydney University and by then a lecturer at the University of Adelaide. The understanding was that Mawson would stay for the whole expedition, wintering over at their base camp and then taking part in the summer journeys in 1908. Professor David would help get base camp established and then return in the expedition ship to New Zealand in time for the new university year in 1908.

Edgeworth David boarded the SS *Wimmera* in Sydney on 20 December 1907. He was already forty-nine years old, a respected university professor and public figure, of an age when most men would have been setting their sights on a few more years at the desk and then an honourable retirement. David's farewell to his family was an emotional one, as his letters reveal, but they also contain hints that he

Family portrait, 1910

was preparing for a much fuller involvement with Shackleton's team than he had first intended or revealed to his wife. He had already written to Shackleton, asking for permission to accompany any motor or pony sledge trip that might establish depots on the ice before the *Nimrod* left to return to Australia. He dropped hints to Cara that must have worried her, delegating to her all financial affairs such as taxes, insurance and university fees for the children, with the ominous advice, 'I am telling you of these extra expenses ahead in case, by any chance, of my accidental detention in Antarctica'. On 6 January, while the *Nimrod* was being towed by the New Zealand ship *Koonya* through horrendously rough seas towards the pack ice, David penned a decisive letter to Cara:

> I must tell you at once of an offer that Lieutenant Shackleton has just made to me. He has pressed me very strongly to remain with him in his winter quarters for the whole of this year … Although he has not definitely promised to take me with him all the way to the South Pole, he has promised, if I stay on, to take me with him as far as he can, and to the Pole if possible.

David knew that Shackleton did not have the funds to pay for his staying on with the expedition as a full-time member, but he wrote to Cara in a spirit of ingenuous optimism, 'we ought not to be out of pocket financially … I do not think that under the circumstances [the University Senate] will give me the sack.' (Shackleton had agreed to pay for a replacement for David during his absence from the university.)

This letter, along with others that were delivered to Cara at Woodford after the *Koonya* returned to New Zealand, was to trigger an emotional crisis for her. The coming year would prove to be a watershed in her life.

It is clear from all the written evidence that she loved David deeply; but perhaps she saw now that his heroic virtues came at a cost, to his family's peace of mind and to his own welfare. As Cara had written to Ned Touche, she had long ago realized that she must let her husband go his own way, and that she would rarely be able to follow him over that 'illimitable ocean' where he journeyed as a scientist. But now she faced the likelihood of losing him forever. For the next year there would be no news of the party. The silence and their isolation would be absolute. There must have been times when Cara felt both bitter and resentful during the long months of David's absence, feeling that his love and commitment to her had been sacrificed for a larger, grander cause, one in which women and families could play no part. To the impartial observer it seems clear that David was less than honest in his dealings with Cara. How tempted he must have been by the chance to do extended research and exploration in that ice-bound environment; the study of ice and glaciation had been an absorbing interest of his since student days. In the series of letters he wrote to Cara as the *Nimrod* journeyed towards the ice barrier, David deliberately down-played the dangers of wintering over and any doubts about his fitness for the task: he turned fifty in January 1908. He was also anxious to justify his decision as a rational and purposeful one:

> I am afraid, darling, it will be a long time for you and the dear children to wait, and I know what a sacrifice I am asking you to make. I hope you won't think me very selfish ... [but] it seems almost wicked to spend so much time and risk so much ... to get down to the Antarctic and then to come back after a stay of only a few days.

He assured her of Shackleton's trust in him as the scientific leader of the party, and wasn't averse to using a little sly flattery. Shackleton 'read *Funafuti* [while] coming from Australia to New Zealand and told me he was very much interested in it'. When he expressed anxiety about how the family would cope with his extended absence, Shackleton retorted (and this was relayed to Cara), 'Your wife's a sport, she'll do anything like that'. One can read into these letters David's attempt to reassure his wife but they also served to cast his decision in a positive light, perhaps easing his conscience in the process.

Cara was an experienced and efficient housekeeper and manager of family finances, but she must have been exasperated by David's casual approach to these matters. What would happen if the university saw David's extended absence as a breach of contract? Their savings, after the failure of the Queensland venture, were minimal, and while they had properties in the Blue Mountains, Sydney and Newcastle, none of these were very profitable and the St Marys land, especially, was a source of constant worry to Cara. There were rates to be paid, insurance premiums, income tax, university fees for Molly and Billy and annual subscriptions to the numerous scientific bodies to which David belonged, as well as their commitments to a number of charities. For much of David's fifteen-month absence, Cara stayed up at Woodford, immersing herself in the day-to-day demands of the garden, the orchard and the bush dwelling. Her involvement with a number of women's

Dr Michell, Margaret, Cara, Billy, Molly and Mrs Attride the housekeeper, during David's absence in the Antarctic (NLA MS 8890)

groups still commanded her loyalty but as the year wore on she had less and less emotional energy to give to them and resigned from any work that required leadership on her part. Her involvement with the Women's Club, a place that must have given her a lot of enjoyment, was put on hold and she resigned from the committee.

In 1908, their son Billy had begun a degree in medicine at the university, boarding during term at St Pauls College. In September 1908, Cara decided to withdraw him from the college at the end of the year, jotting down ('to send to Twed') her reasons for doing so on the back of an envelope. College fees were expensive, and there were always hidden extras, mainly involving sport. In fact Cara dismissed the college culture as being 'all sport and sideshows' and Billy was being easily distracted from his studies. Cara decided it would be much better for him to share lodgings with David in 1909 and be 'under his father's influence'.[1] Strains that were to appear in the father–son relationship were perhaps already in evidence by this time.

Cara wrote to Touche after David's safe return, about the 'awful loneliness and horror of those [fifteen] months ... That long silence during the Antarctic trip very nearly killed me. I do a fair day's work but nothing like I used to.' She sought religious consolation, 'turn[ing] for comfort to the one who alone is able to give the peace that the world cannot give'. Her private anguish was expressed in insomnia and a range of physical ailments.

What Cara endured over those months was kept very much within her family. David's experiences, on the other hand, became widely known to the Australian public and he was hailed as a popular hero on his return home. The Antarctic journey would be the great adventure of David's life but one that would test him to his physical and psychological limits.

Shackleton's base camp was set up and a hut built at Cape Royds on Ross Island in McMurdo Sound, the area from which Scott had set out on his 1902 expedition to the Pole. In March 1908, before the long Antarctic winter set in, Shackleton directed David to attempt a climb of Mount Erebus, an active volcano that towered above their camp at Cape Royds. The summit party consisted of Edgeworth David, Douglas Mawson and a Scottish doctor, Alistair Mackay, with three other men in the support team. The expedition took six and a half days and was accomplished without major incident, though the men's lack of suitable mountaineering equipment caused some problems on that difficult and dangerous terrain.

After the long winter in the hut had passed, plans were set afoot for the major expeditions of the summer. David would lead Mawson and Mackay on the northern journey to the South Magnetic Pole, while Shackleton himself would be leading the southern party of four men in an attempt to reach the South Geographic Pole. Shackleton's instructions to the northern party were to make a general geological survey of the coast as they journeyed north-west from Cape Royds, to take magnetic observations at every suitable point with a view to determining the position of the South Magnetic Pole, and, if time allowed, to try to reach the Pole itself. On their return journey they were to prospect for minerals of economic value in the western mountains.

Raymond Priestley, the young English geologist on the expedition, summarized David's achievement in these words: 'Standing far above the rest of the expedition intellectually, physically he met men half his age and twice his apparent strength on equal terms'.[2] David's companions, Douglas Mawson and Alistair Mackay, were both in their mid-twenties and very fit young men, though Mackay was troubled with mood disorders and tendencies to violence which were to have an impact on the other men.

The journey of these three men to the vicinity of the South Magnetic Pole, the hardships and dangers they encountered, and their very near abandonment to death on the ice, form one of the great epic stories of Antarctic discovery. But it was a story that was to be overshadowed by other dramatic events that soon followed: Robert Scott's fatal journey of 1912 and Mawson's own 1913 expedition, Shackleton's trip in the *Endurance* in 1916 and then the Great War.

Setting out from Cape Royds on 5 October 1908, the Northern party faced a circuitous route around the coastline of McMurdo Sound, hauling two sledges over the precarious and unreliable sea-ice that at any moment could break off and sweep them out to sea. The heavily laden sledges carrying all their gear, provisions and geological specimens had to be hauled in relays, the three men hauling one sledge for, say, one mile and then going back for the second sledge. This effectively tripled the actual distance they walked and meant that they soon had to go on to half-rations to preserve supplies and catch seals and penguins to supplement their diet. The second stage of their journey involved finding a route through the heavily crevassed and broken terrain of the Drygalski Ice Tongue to the Larsen Glacier and then up onto the polar plateau. Then there would follow a further 250 miles of sledging over steadily rising ground to locate the South Magnetic Pole at about 7000 feet.[3]

That the three men were able to achieve this goal under the most extreme conditions and stresses is a tribute both to their individual powers of endurance and to David's leadership. There were strains aplenty, with all three sleeping in the one tent, cooking and sharing food and labouring onwards with the heavy sledge in an increasingly weakened and desperate condition. On 16 January, they reached what was judged to be the vicinity of the South Magnetic Pole. The ice-rimmed beards and haggard eyes that stare at us from the photograph they took (David pulling the string on Mawson's camera) suggest something of the ordeal they had been through to get to this point ... and now they faced the prospect of an even more terrible return journey. Rations were running low and they were all in a considerably weakened state, especially David, who'd just turned fifty-one. The *Nimrod* was expected back in McMurdo Sound on 15 January. After loading all the winter stores and collecting Shackleton's Southern party by 1 February, it was to steam west along the coast looking for a signal from David's party. Very conscious that meeting this rendezvous was their only guarantee of survival, the three men pushed on. On reaching the edge of the plateau they made a fateful decision. Instead of retracing their outward route down a passage next to the Larsen Glacier, they decided to descend steeply to the coast over the glacier itself, through heavily crevassed ice. This nightmare journey drew on their last reserves of strength. Pushing on with only a few hours sleep, suffering from frostbite, snow-blindness, malnutrition and an increasing weight of despair, the three men finally reached the coast on 4 February and set up their tent on a small knoll of ice within sight of the sea. It was there that they heard a loud report and rushed from their tent to see the *Nimrod* steaming straight towards them.

All of the men in Shackleton's expedition returned alive. Shackleton's own team got within ninety miles of the South Geographic Pole but turned back after realizing that their provisions were insufficient to get them to the Pole and safely back to base. Their delay in arriving back at Cape Royds meant that they were collected on 4 March after David's party had been rescued. With all the expeditioners safe on board, the *Nimrod* headed straight back to New Zealand before the approaching winter pack ice hemmed them in. On arriving at Lyttelton in New Zealand David immediately sailed for Sydney, while Shackleton and the rest of his party stayed on in New Zealand for some further weeks before heading for receptions and lecture tours in Australia.

David came back to Australia to be feted by the general public and the academic world. His unauthorized absence from the university was forgotten in the general jubilation and excitement that greeted his return. The fifty-one-year-old professor who sailed into Sydney at dawn on 30 March was white-haired and weather-beaten, with a slight stoop and ill-fitting clothes. Yet there was around him an aura of great achievement, attracting the attention of news-hungry journalists, the general public and hero-worshipping students. His name and the expedition had been kept firmly in the public eye through thirteen articles appearing in the *Daily Telegraph* between 21 March and 4 April 1908, describing the voyage south of the *Nimrod* and the landing and setting up of the expedition. David had written the articles and sent them to Cara on the returning *Nimrod*, with instructions to edit them as required and ensure their copyrighted publication.

Cara's daughter, Margaret, was sitting with her sewing on the verandah at Tyn-y-Coed when the housekeeper brought up a telegram reporting news of the sighting of the *Nimrod* off Stuart Island near New Zealand. No further news was available. Margaret broke the news to Cara as gently as possible, stroking her mother's forehead and fearing that she would faint. She tried her best to reassure her: *of course* it would be good news, everyone would be all right …

A second telegram arrived with news of the whole company's safe arrival at Stuart Island. With that, Margaret felt a crushing weight roll from her heart. The *Evening News* that night proclaimed the expedition had been a great success, but Margaret knew that it was 'all moonshine, and just said for effect … personally I don't care as long as I get my Dad back'.

David's three children were there at the wharf to greet their father on the morning of 30 March, but Cara could not bear to face such a reunion in public. Instead, David's colleague, Professor Pollock, drove David and the children to the Maidens' home in the Botanic Gardens where the reunion took place. That afternoon a large audience, including 600 cheering undergraduates, greeted David at a lunch-time reception at the Great Hall of the university. On the evening of 30 March, David travelled with his family to Woodford, where they were met with flags, bunting and Chinese lanterns and an enthusiastic crowd of locals. After listening to a speech by the president of the Blue Mountains Shire Council, Mr Waterhouse, the family climbed into a carriage which the young men of the local boarding school, Woodford Academy, pulled the last stage to the professor's house. After all this excitement the family was grateful for a quiet evening by the fire. Margaret once again heard her beloved father reading Dickens to them all, and was held spellbound by his tales of the expedition. The following day it was back to the city for an official welcome at the Town Hall, where there was standing room only and thousands gathered outside to catch a glimpse of the explorer.

To David's relief, the University Senate chose to ignore the technicalities of his extended and unauthorized absence, and he was soon back at work at his untidy desk, deep into the usual hectic round of lectures and public advocacy of the many causes he cared about. He was soon in great demand as a public speaker, enthralling audiences with his narrative and series of lantern slides about the Antarctic trip. For a brief time in 1910, David was patron of the newly formed Ashfield District Camera Club established for amateur photographers.[4] He attended club lectures when he was able but had to resign from the position when he went to England later that year. The young *Nimrod* geologist, Raymond Priestley, had been seconded to the university to work with David writing up the scientific results of the expedition. He

recalled David's undimmed energy: after working, often till after midnight, the professor would leave his office and scale the university's six foot fence, placing his folded coat on top of it and 'over he would go like a two-year-old', going back to sleep at Priestley's rooms in Forest Lodge opposite the university.[5]

The journey left its scars on the adventurer. Margaret, examining a pair of her father's thick felt mittens one day, found them stained with blood inside. She had noticed with dismay how clumsy her father had become with his hands and

Ambrose with the professor at Tyn-y-Coed

fingers, and how stiff and battered they looked. She knew that this was the legacy of those terrible months of frostbite and struggle, as the three men dragged a sledge to the Magnetic Pole and back.

When David returned from the Antarctic he was given one of the Siberian Husky dogs which had been bred for sledge work on the trip. The country's quarantine laws were discreetly flouted in order for him to bring the dog to Sydney. Ambrose proved a great favourite with the family. Margaret called him 'the most fascinating, lovable dog I've ever known'. Molly confessed that 'taking him for walks was a strenuous business, as he pulled at his leash with same vigour that he applied to his sledge harness'. Missing the comforting warmth of his fellow huskies huddled together at night, Ambrose would get noisily lonely and Margaret found herself sleeping out on the verandah at Tyn-y-Coed to keep the sociable animal company. Ambrose died of distemper not long after coming to live with the family: coming from the pristine Antarctic, he had no resistance to the local germs.

At Tyn-y-Coed, Cara once more found herself playing hostess to visitors: on one occasion the crew of the *Nimrod* came to Woodford in two booked carriages and were accommodated.

There was a postscript to David's Antarctic journey. In May 1911, a small and ill-equipped Japanese ship arrived in Sydney. The *Kainan Maru*, on a private expedition under the command of Lieutenant Nobu Shirase, had planned to sail down to the Antarctic and make an attempt to reach the Pole. They arrived too late in the season to make landfall on the Antarctic continent and the expedition had to retreat north to Sydney. There they were received with either indifference or undisguised suspicion: Japanese imperial designs in the Pacific region were already a talking point in the newspapers and few people were willing to extend a helping hand to the group. David visited them on board their boat, giving them a sympathetic hearing and bringing his influence to bear in their acquisition of stores, maps and other necessities. He also gave Shirase a copy of his own expedition notes, an act of remarkable generosity when one considers the feverish nationalism of the times in relation to Antarctica. Shirase was greatly moved by David's kindly attentions. In his parting letter to the professor he wrote, 'Whatever may be the fate of our enterprise, we shall never forget you'. The expedition left Sydney in November 1911, heading once more for the southern continent. However, the party was to have limited success, making only a brief excursion inland on the ice before turning for home.

On their departure from Sydney, Shirase had presented David with a gift: a Samurai sword, crafted in the seventeenth century by the master sword maker Kaneyasu. It is likely that David was the only Westerner ever to be honoured with such a gift, whose historic and cultural significance for its people was profound. Cara kept the sword wrapped in a cloth, hidden away in a cupboard. Neither she nor David probably realized the full significance of the gift, though David exchanged an annual Christmas letter with his Japanese colleague from then on.

9   The War Years, Australia

The next few years were ones where Cara assumed a public role as Mrs David, wife of a distinguished professor and renowned Antarctic explorer. She was in demand as guest at girls' school speech days, the opening of charity fetes and other worthwhile community events. She was also expected to accompany her husband to vice-regal receptions, university functions and the opening of scientific conferences. It would be misleading to see this as Cara's assumption of a new and conservative public persona. She confessed to her daughters that she did not enjoy formal social gatherings and certainly despised the snobbery and pretension often associated with 'the top people'.[1] Cara always seemed to be most herself in the company of like-minded women, working on a common task with shared enthusiasms and commitment. The Women's Club, her friendship with Louisa Macdonald and Maybanke Wolstenholme, the Sydney University Women's Association, her reading circles and her community groups in Lawson and Woodford were the focus of her loyalties in those years.

After David returned from the Antarctic, he boarded during the week at Ashfield with the Misses Dove who ran a school there. Billy, in his last year of medical school, stayed with him, as well as Molly who was acting as secretary for her father. Cara David preferred the peace

Woodford: Cara with friends, Billy at rear

and quiet of Woodford, though she still travelled down regularly to the city for meetings. No doubt Cara's decision to live up at Woodford while David was in Sydney created much chat among other academic wives at the university, but Cara David was never one to take much notice of gossip.

During these years before the war, Cara resumed her involvement with the 'no-licence' campaign on behalf of the Woman's Christian Temperance Union. In the winter of 1910, she arranged a fortnight's lecturing tour and gave twenty-one lectures in western New South Wales, in Dubbo, Condobolin, Bathurst and Orange in the lead-up to the election in December that year.

In late 1913, David, Cara and Molly made a brief trip to the United Kingdom. For David there were many professional and scientific matters to attend to. He had to finalize publication in England of the geology volume of the Antarctic expedition that he had written in conjunction with Raymond Priestley. And as president of the

Australasian Association for the Advancement of Science, David had a major role to play in organizing an important international conference which was to take place in Australia in 1914. Since the 1880s, the British Association for the Advancement of Science (BAAS) had been the pre-eminent gathering of scientists in the English-speaking world. Meetings had been held in other countries in the British Empire, but now that Australia was receiving recognition on the world stage it was felt the time was ripe for the next BAAS gathering to be staged in Australia. In 1910, the High Commissioner, George Reid, offered to hold the next BAAS meeting in Australia, and planning got under way for what was to be a massive administrative and logistical exercise. It was hoped that the 1914 BAAS Australian meeting would 'prove a great event in the history of Imperial unity'.

For Cara and Molly, the trip had a different focus. Cara's elder daughter, Margaret, had married Keverall (Bill) McIntyre in 1909 and the young couple was now living in Edinburgh where Bill was studying to become a doctor. Cara and Molly travelled to Edinburgh for a reunion with their beloved Margaret and with Bill, spending a brief holiday getting to know the two little McIntyre children, three-year-old Peggy and Archie, the baby. Cara also visited her old college at Chelsea and would have found much to interest her after an absence of over thirty years. Her former principal, John Faunthorpe, had retired by that stage but Cara had continued to write to him.[2] Cara also visited a camp in the New Forest, organized by the newly formed Guides Association. She was to look back on it as the happiest time she had spent in England; it may have inspired her later interest and involvement in the Australian Girl Guides movement.

The family were back home by December 1913. By then, international rivalries and tensions were making their presence felt in the young commonwealth. Professor David, with his generous view of the humanizing role of science and exploration, tried his best to rise above the intolerant spirit that was abroad.

In the very month that war was to be declared, David was busy helping organize the BAAS conference, which was to take place in a number of cities across Australia. While the success of the conference helped reaffirm Australia's rising position in the scientific world, its significance for the general public was masked by the news of the European war. An eminent German geologist, Albrecht Pencke, was one of the visiting scientists: this was at a time when anti-German feeling was already running high in Australia. David's noted courtesy and public stature was evident in his acknowledgment of this man as a famous scientist, at a public reception in the town of Maitland.[3]

Cara David, however, identified with the strong anti-German sentiment of many in the community once the war had started. She spoke publicly in support of disenfranchising all those of German origin and the firing of all those employed in the country who had some connection with Germany. Dorette MacCallum, the wife of their family friend and David's university associate Mungo MacCallum, had been born in Germany and Cara had unkind things to say about her during the war. Dorette MacCallum had been a loyal supporter of the National Council of Women and the Ashfield Infants Home, so Cara's animosity towards her was hardly justified. Perhaps there was a clash of personalities or, on Cara's side, a case of her fiery patriotism getting in the way of good sense.[4]

After war was declared, most Australians were swept up in a fever of patriotic excitement. Women rushed to offer their services to the cause at the same time as their menfolk were crowding into the recruiting offices. The Women's Club in Sydney turned its headquarters over to the Red Cross as a collection centre. Everywhere, women and girls were knitting socks and balaclavas for the troops. Cara and Molly took their knitting with them to the theatre one June evening in 1915, feeling very guilty at spending the money 'when the Belgians were starving'. At Tyn-y-Coed, Cara held weekly classes for local girls who could not knit, with up to ten young women sometimes turning up. Taking some friends to Blackheath one day, she hired a trap and pony and drove out to the popular tourist spot of Govett's Leap where the women sat for an hour enjoying the glorious views down into the Grose Valley, 'our knitting in hand of course'.[5]

The summer months of early 1915 saw heatwaves across the state, and in late January a frightful dust storm spread from the west, carrying topsoil from country denuded by drought, overgrazing and rabbits. The interior of Tyn-y-Coed was covered in dust blown from beyond Wagga, 300 miles away. Cara mourned the wreck of her garden, with the melons, cucumbers and pumpkins burnt beyond recall. She rose at dawn in the hot weather to do household chores and cooking; days were spent making jam from the plums that were plentiful that year despite the drought, and from blackberries growing wild in paddocks and gullies. There always seemed to be people staying in the house and she had no regular servant help by then. David brought colleagues up from the university; their friend, Mary Dove, the schoolteacher from Ashfield, came to stay; and for a few months Cara welcomed into her home a young friend, Olive Docker, and her two babies, while Olive's husband was battling to establish a medical practice in the north-west township of Trangie. Molly helped with the cooking but seemed to be often in poor health and low spirits once the hot weather began and sometimes retreated to her bed for the day.

As the wife of Professor David and an active presence herself in Woodford, Cara was often called upon on public occasions, to chair local community meetings and to address women's groups. In a letter to Margaret, she described spending a hot and unhappy afternoon at Springwood where she had been asked to open a charitable Bazaar. It was a ferociously hot day and the small, unventilated corrugated-iron shed was 'crammed full of perspiring people in fancy dress trying to sing patriotic songs and sell one useless trifles in aid of the Belgian funds'. It was the droll humour of the event that Cara really remembered; she had broken a tooth at afternoon tea and had to deliver her address while trying to hold on both to the remnant tooth and her dignity.

She also had commitments in the city. There were regular three-hour train trips to Sydney for shopping for the homestead, and she was involved at that stage in helping assess candidates for the Australian Nurses Training Scheme: there had been a rush of candidates for the scheme once war began, and the assessment board met for long hours to interview candidates and read references.

In April 1915, the Davids rented a newly built suite of rooms in the T&G Building in Elizabeth Street, opposite Hyde Park. There were so many calls on their time it seemed necessary to be based in Sydney while the war lasted. David more or less suspended his university research program for the duration of the war but his professorial duties continued; he also took on the drilling of recruits for the University Rifle Club and was engaged in a round of recruiting speeches in Sydney as temporary New South Wales president of the Universal Service League.

As news of the growing number of casualties on Gallipoli filtered back to Australia, it was clear that hospital and rehabilitation services would be stretched to capacity, so the Davids decided to offer Tyn-y-Coed to the Red Cross as a rest home for wounded soldiers. In true wartime fashion, the directive from above came with little notice and a degree of urgency. In August 1915, the Red Cross called 'and asked for Tyn-y-Coed in three days' time'. Cara asked for a week's grace: she was exhausted from a new campaigning effort involving early closing of hotels. In late August, she hurried back to Woodford with Molly to prepare the cottage for its new residents. She had already arranged with local tradesmen for a new bathroom and a wider verandah to be built at Tyn-y-Coed and a small cottage, Carinyah, was being erected on the property where the Davids could stay. At this stage Cara was hoping that a competent full-time matron would be appointed to run the home.

The villagers were enthusiastic about the project, excited at this opportunity to be part of the great drama unfolding in Europe. There were offers to collect firewood, take the washing away, help in the kitchen, donate milk and vegetables, groceries and money. The boys from Woodford Academy made a flagstaff and erected it to fly the Union Jack and the Red Cross flag while the soldiers were in residence. Up to a dozen soldiers at a time could be accommodated at the home, the Red Cross giving precedence to nerves, malaria and rheumatism cases. Cara commented dryly that she feared the villagers would not be so excited once they realized that the men bore no evidence of battle wounds. Soldiers were generally allowed to stay for one month's convalescence and then returned to Sydney so others could have a chance to stay at the rest home.

The soldiers arrived in ones or twos on the Sydney train over the next few months, and each received a down-to-earth scrutiny from Cara. One was 'a nice boy with nerves after the shock of a mine exploding under him'; one, an Irishman, 'with breakdown from over-training in Egypt'. Another was 'a low Londoner, bold and impudent with a nameless ailment in his knee. I think it is malingeritis myself.' The Londoner had blown his deferred pay in a week's drinking spree and arrived at Woodford cold and famished. Cara was blunt about his chances. 'He's a rotter and we shall have to get rid of him I fear.' Another new soldier she met at the station who was 'palpably drunk' aroused her pity: 'Poor wretch, he seems decent enough'.

A housekeeper, Mrs Vinden, was appointed and arrived with her three daughters. Cara, for want of a better arrangement, took over the duties of matron herself. At first all went smoothly, while donations of fresh vegetables poured in and the hens and cows were providing plenty of eggs and milk. Then the heatwaves of early summer brought bushfires to the district, the animals went off producing and the supply of vegetables dried up. Mrs Vinden and her three 'capable but bad-tempered' daughters found it hard to cope with these emergencies and ended up creating such a negative atmosphere that Cara had to dismiss them. After they left she found to her dismay that they taken quite a few of the family's favourite 'read-aloud' books which Cara had left in the home for the men.

Olive Docker agreed to leave her children with her husband in Trangie and come up to Woodford as matron in mid-December till Cara could find a full-time resident for the job. As well three members of the Voluntary Aid Detachment (VAD) came up from Sydney to help. Their contributions were a mixed blessing to Cara.[79] One 'little VAD girl' was a source of great irritation to Cara, cluttering up the main bedroom with her clothes and makeup and never clearing up after herself. Once the hot weather began in earnest, with westerly winds blowing over the mountains and above-century temperatures, the girls wilted and were 'slack', as her diary recorded tersely. For Molly David, the rest home provided a new and purposeful project. She and a local friend, Isobel Houison, became reliable and hardworking members of the rest home staff.

In November 1915, Woodford took part in a welcome to one of the Coo-ee recruitment marches that were taking place throughout the New South Wales countryside. The men from Gilgandra marched down to Lawson in time for 'sacred songs' (it was a Sunday). On Monday morning they were nearing Woodford where a cheering crowd welcomed them. Ladies served cake and lemonade and they were greeted by the local councillor, Gustavus Waterhouse. Some of the wounded soldiers from Tyn-y-Coed had been brought up to the main road to add their greetings. The Gilgandra men finished their march two days later, at Ashfield.

The months leading up to Christmas 1915 saw Cara taking on yet another public commitment, one that evolved into the Women's National Movement (WNM). This was a concerted effort by feminists to work with temperance groups to extend the 'no-licence' battle and bring in legislation to close hotels at 6 pm. In August 1915, the WNM collected a petition of 144,600 signatures on a sheet over two miles long, and on 26 August their president, Cara David, led a procession of forty cars, accompanied by the Musicians Union Band, up Macquarie Street to Parliament House to present the petition in favour of early closing of hotels.

Throughout August, September and October, Cara spoke to a wide range of community gatherings on this issue. She addressed an audience of fifty mothers in the slums of Newtown on the need to restrict their men's access to licensed premises. In early December she travelled out west for a week, to Bathurst and Lithgow. On 7 December, she addressed a crowd of men and their wives at the Trades Hall at Lithgow, home to the state's small arms factory. Then there were meetings in the Blue Mountains townships as well as throughout Sydney. Balancing these speaking commitments with the need to supervise the soldiers home meant a frantic pace of life and Cara found herself leaning heavily on Molly as a backup at the home. Her colleague from Hurlstone days, Miss Nicholls, helped out while Cara was away. The workload left Cara with persistent symptoms of stress and fatigue. She complained in her diary of 'this terrible pressure and "crawling" in my head' but dismissed it as a 'nuisance'. Her robust spirit kept her going but there were many times of bad temper and intolerance of others during those trying days. Her diary over the hot summer was a terse record of the battle. 'January 10, 1916. A shocking day and very weary – inclined to grouse.'

From mid-September 1915, Cara faced a new source of anxiety. David had quietly enlisted in the Australian Imperial Forces and been appointed major in a newly formed Mining Battalion: his commission was formally gazetted on 28 October. The Australian Mining Battalion was the first Australia-wide group of servicemen to be put together, rather than being a state-based affair like the other regiments. The men – 'a dour, nuggety lot' according to David – were recruited from across the states, from settlements like Cloncurry, Mount Lyell and Kalgoorlie, and included miners, sewer workers and engineers. A large number of David's former students became officers in the battalion.

David was excited at the challenge of helping form this new body and the chance of a lifetime it presented for him 'to get to the other side'. University leave was granted and his colleague, Leo Cotton, a Quaker and a pacifist, took over the reins of the Geology Department during his absence. (Cara muttered darkly to her family at this arrangement.)

David's friends, family and colleagues received the news of David's enlistment with a mixture of admiration and disbelief. At fifty-seven years of age, David was the one of the oldest men to volunteer. Margaret wrote a loving letter from Edinburgh to her mother, the news invoking in her 'pride in him, and sorrow for you'. Cara, too, was proud of his decision even as she knew what this new absence would mean for her after enduring the long Antarctic separation.

In December, David was transferred to the AIF training camp at Casula near Liverpool. He spent his days in physical drill, giving lectures to the men and officers on the geology they might expect to find on the battlefront and travelling to Victoria to test designs for drilling equipment. His visits to Woodford were few and far between. Generally he caught the last train from Casula, arriving after midnight at Woodford. Sometimes, exhausted, he fell asleep on the train and missed his stop, having to walk the six miles back from Lawson.

As Christmas 1915 approached, Cara was hoping David would be free to join them for a last celebration before embarking for overseas in the new year. She was determined to give the men a festive day that would lift everyone's spirits. She and Molly spent a day shopping in Sydney for gifts, chiefly for the soldiers. 'Molly wanted a pistol for a Christmas present – a nice peaceful Christ-like thing. I bought Dad a pocket book and a boot-cleaning outfit as he was using his handkerchiefs with Kiwi tan polish for his boots, gaiters and leather belts.' (Edgeworth David was well-known for his absent-minded dress sense.) They bought pocket-books for three of the soldiers, a Brownie camera for another and a pair of hairbrushes for another, as well as a cheap little toy for each man 'to try and raise a laugh as the Christmas season has made them all depressed'.

On Christmas Eve, Cara was expecting David on the late night train from Casula. She was resigned to spending Christmas Day fully occupied looking after the men as Olive Docker had asked for leave for the day to join her family in Sydney. 'Of course I said yes, though it meant working at the home all day instead of having a quiet day with Dad, perhaps our last – but there never is any time for that sort of sentiment now.' Waiting up till after the last train pulled out from Woodford at 11.30, Cara left a lamp burning in the cottage and with low spirits retreated to a cold bed.

Christmas Day dawned bright and cool, a welcome change after the fires that had been threatening the mountains. Molly and Cara were kept busy decorating the verandah with a blaze of gaudy paper decorations, making beds, emptying the slops, peeling potatoes and preparing the turkey. The soldiers had great fun over their comic gifts, though the mood of the day was inevitably darkened by the news they'd just heard of the evacuation of Gallipoli. Her mind full of the thoughts of 'those dear dead boys', and deeply disappointed that David hadn't been able to get leave, Cara found herself unexpectedly weepy and emotional. She felt like one of their boys, Private Rutland, whose nervous condition meant he would burst into tears at the slightest provocation.

She tried to stay cheerful for the sake of the men. With Molly's help a splendid feast was prepared. There was turkey and sausages, ham and green peas, baked potatoes, plum pudding and mince pies, and junket and stewed fruit for those not well enough for rich fare. The Red Cross sent chocolates, cigarettes and cigars. After dinner Cara helped clear away and tidied the dining room ready for tea, then went back to snatch a few hours sleep at Carinyah. She was woken by a heavy step on the verandah and the dear familiarity of David's voice. It was late afternoon on Christmas Day: he had just come up from town having had orders to test machinery and working till late on Christmas Eve.

There were further brief visits to Woodford before the battalion embarked on 20 February. On New Years Eve, David brought Captain John Davis to stay for a few days. Davis had been first officer on the *Nimrod* and after the Antarctic expedition became a lifelong friend of David. Sunday 2 January had been declared a National Day of Prayer and Humiliation and accordingly there was a large gathering at the local Woodford church. Cara and David were there with Molly and Isobel Houison, Olive Docker and Captain Davis. Six of the soldiers also turned up. This was partly an expression of their respect for the professor, who used to drop in to the home for a yarn in the evenings and to read them some of Kipling's poems. Cara admitted that the men didn't like church 'but they always roll up when Dad goes'. She noted on other occasions that 'they are not a pious lot and are very forthright in their views if the minister is comic or boring'.

There was little time for Cara to miss David in the frantic days of work as the new year advanced. She admitted to being well enough to work hard and she found that work was the 'best palliative for loneliness'.

In September 1915, Thomas Brown, a Labor member and temperance reformer, had secured the adoption by the NSW Legislative Assembly of a resolution to advance closing hours of licensed premises from 11 pm to 9 pm. Premier Holman, swayed by the advice of the publicans' organization, opposed the move and even resisted suggestions that a 9 pm closing should be brought in temporarily as a prudent war-time measure. In addition, he began using the contemptuous term 'wowser' to describe his opponents, and this served to harden temperance opposition to

Convalescent soldier, Tyn-y-Coed (NLA MS 8890)

his leadership and to the Labor Party generally. When a by-election was held in Parramatta in early December, the Liberal candidate, a strong temperance reformer, won the seat by a large majority.

On 14 February 1916, a riot among the soldiers at Casula training camp, provoked by an extension of training hours, saw men loot the hotels and shops at Liverpool and then take possession of the trains into Central Railway Station. There a group of about thirty soldiers, most of them drunk, attacked a military guard, turning a fire hose against them. Ultimately shots were fired, one soldier was killed and nine wounded. The federal authorities, acting under the *War Precautions Act*, ordered the closing of Sydney hotels at 6 pm until further notice.

This was not only a setback to Holman's prestige but showed him clearly the force of public opinion on the question. He decided to hold a referendum in mid-1916 to put the closing hour of hotels before the public.

The Women's National Movement under Cara David campaigned hard for months before the referendum. In December 1915, they submitted a petition to the King, duly forwarded by the state governor, asking for his help in the campaign to limit the sale of liquor in their state. The *Daily Telegraph*, always seeking a chance to undermine Holman's leadership, threw its editorial support behind the women's movement. The paper published a copy of the petition in full and followed this with a letter from Cara David demanding a personal apology from Mr Holman for slanderous remarks made by him in the Legislative Assembly. Holman had committed the tactical error of condemning the women's movement as unpatriotic and motivated by hysteria. He found a formidable public opponent in Cara whose patriotic credentials were impeccable and whose husband's enlistment had received wide and favourable publicity throughout the state. 'Mrs David attacks the Premier,' announced the *Telegraph* while covering a state by-election in January 1916 in the Sydney suburb of Drummoyne.[7] Cara had been invited to speak there in support of an independent candidate, Walter Bentley, a strong temperance candidate.

Cara used the occasion to address the crowded Masonic Hall with a no-nonsense and fiery condemnation of publicans, party politics and the 'shirkers' who had failed to enlist.[8] The secretary of the state branch of the Woman's Christian Temperance Union, Miss Eva Bowes, also took up arms against Holman, and in a letter published in the *Telegraph* she reminded the Premier of the power of the women's vote which was going to make itself felt in the next election.[9]

In mid March, Cara left with a Woodford friend, Mrs Blain, for a lecturing tour of the Northern Rivers district in support of the coming referendum. In her absence from Tyn-y-Coed, one of the soldiers, Private Cartwright, was to look after the property and garden. The tour took them by train and motor car to Tenterfield, Lismore and Murwillumbah, Grafton and Casino and back via Hexham near Maitland. The regional newspapers covered the tour with varying degrees of support, their views shaped by local issues and personalities. For many people the coming 'liquor referendum' was one more instance of the meddling power of the state at work. The *Grafton Argus* condemned the teetotal party in the town, accusing them of hypocrisy: the editor's bitterness was accentuated by the knowledge that the teetotallers were giving their patronage to the rival paper, the *Daily Examiner.* The *Argus* called on the teetotal party to 'wake up' to the fact that the *Examiner*'s major shareholder was also the largest owner of hotel properties on the North Coast. In spite of these local hostilities, the *Argus* devoted a polite column to Cara David's visit, though it made only cursory mention of the referendum which was the point of her visit.[10] Its rival, the *Daily Examiner*, gave a close-packed three columns of coverage to Cara's afternoon and evening address, describing the aims of the Women's National Movement and quoting her at length: 'we have serious reasons for spending our time as we are doing now. We ask ... women to study up the liquor traffic question. Use your eyes and your sense, then decide the question for yourselves.'[11]

The *Casino and Kyogle Courier*, quoting the *Tenterfield Star*, saw the referendum as the work of 'extreme killjoys' and an infuriating waste of tax payers' money (the campaign was to cost £25,000). It argued that 6 o'clock closing would bring unrelieved gloom to country town evenings, where the public house was 'one of the very few meeting places for companionable men'. Nevertheless the paper, conscious of the power of the Edgeworth David name, assured its readers that Mrs David's lecture 'would prove an intellectual treat'.[12] A large crowd of women attended her afternoon address and there was another large mixed audience in the Masonic Hall that evening.

Cara's travelling companion on the train back to Sydney was Henry Archdall, Dean of the Church of England at Newcastle. In spite of her fatigue Cara was excited by this encounter and by Archdall's views on the need for a new life and spirit in the church; he felt institutional Christianity was failing them. Given Cara's own continuing search for an authentic faith, it is not surprising that his views would have found a sympathetic hearing, even while her mind was racing ahead to the work awaiting her in Sydney.

The New South Wales referendum for which she campaigned was a resounding success for the temperance cause. The poll, held on 10 June 1916, had a very large majority voting for 6 o'clock closing of hotels. Cara, and the women with whom she worked, were exultant. It seemed to them to have a larger significance than just the curbing of the liquor trade. They felt that for the first time in the history of the state the weight of the women's vote had really counted, and their campaigning had had a direct bearing on legislation. The Women's National Movement presented Cara with an illuminated address of thanks. It was signed by many whose names are now part of the feminist story in NSW, among them Jessie Street, Annie Golding and Mary Booth.

With the benefit of hindsight, more recent historians have noted that the success of the referendum was due in part to the powerful patriotism of the times and the overwhelming public support of the war effort. There was a very strong case to be made for a more sober and

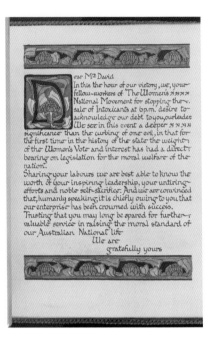

WNM testimonial (NLA MS 8890)

healthy population which would be fitter for military service and more ready to win the war. Many people were impressed by the story that King George V had given up alcohol until the war was over. They also heard that the sale of alcohol had been restricted in most of the Allied countries: Russia, France, England and Canada. The campaigning material on the issue appealed to women's wish to support the troops, win the war and do their bit for King and Empire. In fact the Women's National Movement made clear that 'national efficiency' was their main goal. These currents united in a powerful move that saw the legislation enacted.

There was to be more campaigning later in the year, but for a while Cara could return to the mountains and attend to the work at the convalescent home. On 3 September 1916, Woodford celebrated the anniversary of the opening of Tyn-y-Coed as a rest and convalescent home. During the year nearly a hundred men had been treated there for a variety of conditions; many of them we would now call psychological casualties. The village was proud of the home and took an interest in what was going on there, although Cara did note that people were getting tired of subscribing cash: in September 1916 she had to apply to the Red Cross for £50 to carry out running repairs on the building. But it was still her proud reflection that for a year the home had not used a penny of public funds. Her own careful budgeting allowed Cara the 'wicked extravagance' of the purchase of a new car, a Dodge. She persuaded Molly that she must learn to drive it and was able to report to Margaret that by August 1916, 'Molly has now qualified (at an engineers' workshop, among a lot of rough boys who have been very kind to her) as a chauffeur.' Cara, ever resourceful and keen to make a success of the home, felt it was important for the men's recovery for them to be able to go on 'jaunts' to some of the famous beauty spots nearby. The car, which Molly named Cuthbert, served admirably for this purpose, though the real reason for its purchase was to transport wounded or disabled soldiers to Tyn-y-Coed from the railway station. There was one car in the village, owned by Gustavus Waterhouse, but Cara was incensed to learn that he would not allow soldiers to travel

Cuthbert, with Molly at the wheel

in it. His strict Methodism irritated her: his family was critical of her harvesting vegetables on the Sabbath, and was shocked that the soldiers played ping-pong instead of going to church. Cara noted caustically, seeing the Waterhouse family head off to Tasmania for a holiday, that 'some folk don't seem to know when there's a war on'.[13]

As spring weather came to the mountains, Australians were hearing of the terrible casualties their sons had suffered in the battles along the Somme. No fewer than three boys from the tiny village at Woodford had been killed during August. The war was over for the men at the convalescent home, though as Cara noted, very few of them would ever enjoy a full restoration to health. 'Most of them are to be more or less sufferers for life, but they have very much improved, that is something.' Scholars since that time have established more clearly the cost of the war to that generation of men and its terrible legacy of alcoholism, chronic physical and mental disability and personal breakdown. At the time there was just a vague and troubled sense that the men would never be quite themselves again. One local man, returning to convalesce at Tyn-y-Coed, suffered a relapse from shell shock at church one Sunday.

Nevertheless, there were plenty of good times at the home: the men enjoyed tennis with the local people, picnics and swims down at Mabel's Pool, card games in the evening and of course the jaunts with Molly in Cuthbert. Cara found that the men who came to stay soon settled in 'and we get to like them very much before they leave'. A few marriages took place in the village as the men got to know some of the local girls who visited the home socially or worked part-time in the kitchen.

In mid-October, Cara set out on another lecture tour to the New England area. This tour had strong political overtones. She had been asked by the Universal Service League, who knew her reputation as a popular and effective speaker, to undertake some campaigning in support of the federal referendum on conscription which was to be held on 28 October. The voting public was to be asked to agree to legislation which allowed the government to send conscripted men overseas as reinforcements for the depleted battalions serving on the Western Front.

It is difficult to read her campaigning speeches now. Their ideas and content and the triumphalist note they sounded are too profoundly at odds with a twenty-first-century understanding of the war. Cara David reminded her listeners that Britain was waging the war with 'honour and justice' in defence of Belgian neutrality and to defeat Germany's plans for colonial expansion. Australians, urged on 'by the thrill of patriotism', recognized their moral obligation to support the Mother Country in return for a hundred years of safety and prosperity provided by the Imperial navy. She urged a 'Yes' vote in the referendum as a reflection of the debt owed to their Imperial leaders and to the men serving and dying in the trenches. What mother or father in the audience, their sons serving on the Western Front, could not see the reasonableness of these arguments? Alternative views were hard to come by in rural Australia, unless one subscribed to the *Australian Worker* or the *Catholic Voice*.[14] Every major newspaper supported the 'Yes' campaign, with large advertisements and favourable editorials for the referendum having a prominent place in the papers. All the Protestant churches sanctified the cause from the pulpit and by their role on recruiting platforms, farewells to the troops and in other public gatherings.

The 'liquor referendum' may have aroused heated arguments within communities but it could not match the deep bitterness and sense of social and class division evident during the conscription debate. The controversy accentuated longstanding religious differences. Most Irish Catholics, under the leadership of their outspoken archbishop, Dr Daniel Mannix, opposed conscription, while those of Protestant stock, most of them of English stock or born in England remained loyal to King and Country. The New England papers reinforced a pro-conscription message, but many country people were undoubtedly worried about a national call-up and the threat it would pose to productivity. Who would run the farms if all the able-bodied men were in uniform? Cara's address to such a group on 23 October at the Narrabri Town Hall was reported at length in the *North Western Courier*. At times it was 'rather boisterous' and at one stage an interjector was ordered by police to leave the hall. In the same edition of the paper, the National Referendum Council inserted a blustering condemnation of rural opponents of conscription, calling them 'puerile and inane' and assuring landholders that the Prime Minister would not needlessly call to arms 'the sturdy yeomen who are the backbone of our national life'.[15]

Cara David finished her speaking campaign on 26 October at Raymond Terrace in the Hunter Valley, 'where everyone was full of affectionate enquiries about Dad'. The next day she reached Woodford in a state of nervous and physical exhaustion. She was worn out by the constant travel and demands on her time, days on end when she had been 'carried round like a parcel and turned on like a gramophone'. Her own sturdy patriotism and practical grasp on life meant that she saw the issues of the war in black and white: there was a job to be done, in which all her family were engaged, and her own strong sense of family and community duty meant that she would devote her considerable energies to helping the war effort as long as was needed. At least there was little sense of martyrdom or self-righteousness in Cara's record of those days. A dry and self-effacing sense of humour kept her going, as in this account of a meeting in the early-closing debate: 'being a swagger crowd and C. of E. [Church of England] only twenty women there. However I gave the same old jaw and got off in time to catch the 6.30 train without a meal again.'

On referendum day, Molly decorated Cuthbert with red, white and blue streamers and a Union Jack, plus the purple colours of the Mining Battalion, and drove all the 'Yes' supporters to the polling station. By this stage Cara's thoughts were miles away. While on tour she had received a cable from the Defence Department in Melbourne informing her that on 25 September Major David had been wounded as the result of a fall down a deep well on Vimy Ridge. He had fractured ribs, a ruptured urethra and a scalp wound, and after some days in No. 7 Stationary Hospital near Boulogne he had been transferred to a private hospital in London. Further cables from London told her that David was convalescing well and this heartening news buoyed her up for the remainder of the lecture tour. With news that David was to have sick leave and a pass to visit his daughter in Edinburgh, Cara decided that she and Molly should also try to join their extended family. Thus a new phase in her wartime life began.

10   The War Years, Abroad

While Cara's energies were directed to events on the home front, her thoughts turned increasingly to England and the battlefields across the channel. Many of her Woodford hours were taken up with spinning – she had arranged for Margaret to send her a spinning wheel from the Hebrides – and the wool was knitted into numerous pairs of socks to send to her menfolk for the European winter.

In October 1914 her son Billy, recently graduated in medicine from the University of Sydney, went to Melbourne to enlist with the Royal Australian Medical Corps. While cooling his heels there, waiting for a commission that didn't eventuate, Bill decided he would travel to England and seek a place in a British medical unit. There is no record of his reasons for doing this, but later evidence suggests it was a gesture of independence on his part. He wanted to get away from the Edgeworth David name which, with its expectations of high achievement and valour, lay heavily on the shoulders of a twenty-four-year-old just out of university. He signed up as a surgeon on the SS *Shropshire* and travelled to England. There he was sent to a military hospital at Tadworth in Surrey. But he had come to England for active service, not hospital work, and was relieved to be starting regimental work in early 1915 with the 39th Infantry Brigade. Later that year he transferred to the 6th Cameron Highlanders and by September 1915 had arrived with his battalion in France.

Margaret's husband, Bill McIntyre, had completed his medical degree in Edinburgh in June 1915. Commissioned soon after as a lieutenant, he was posted in November 1915 to Salonica as transport officer with an ambulance unit. Margaret was to stay with her two young children in Edinburgh, where she had made some close friends.

David's own war had begun with his embarkation on the *Ulysses* in Sydney in February 1916. He travelled with the Australian Mining Battalion to Marseilles and from there to Hazebrouck, in north-eastern France. There the men discovered that the battalion was to be broken up into three separate companies, which were to join the tunnelling units already established by British, Canadian and New Zealand companies.[1] The men would be reporting directly to General R.N. Harvey, the British Controller of Mines for the whole of the British Expeditionary Force on the Western Front. The British front, extending from Le Cheer in the north to Givenchy in the south, was at the very centre of the war effort by then and urgent tunnelling under the German lines had been in operation for months. Within a week of their arrival at Hazebrouck, the Australians had started mining operations in the front line near Armentières.

The decision to disband the battalion meant that the headquarters staff was now redundant. Their Commanding Officer, Colonel Albert Fewtrell, was transferred to the AIF Pioneer Battalion. Captain James Pollock, Professor of Physics at Sydney University, was appointed as officer commanding the Mine Rescue and Mine Listening School attached to the 2nd Army. He was responsible for training the men as 'listeners', using apparatus that he had helped to design to foil German countermining measures.

The British were unsure how to place David. His reputation as a world-class geologist had preceded him, but at that stage of the war there was little recognition of the role that expert geological advice could play in advancing the Allied war effort and he was not assigned a specific role. So for the first month or two of his war David had the freedom to travel independently around the front line, familiarizing himself with the geology of the area and getting to know the commanding officers. It soon became clear that his specialized and practical knowledge would prove invaluable and he was appointed Geological Adviser to General Harvey.[2] This commission required a great deal of travel in all kinds of weather over the undulating chalk plateau of Picardy, in the region of the Somme, and through the heavy clays of the Ypres Salient in Belgium. In both these regions, David was able to advise on such aspects as provision of water for troops and horses, location of dugouts and the nature of the surface and underground soils and rocks that would aid the building of defensive and attacking structures like trenches and tunnels. By the summer of 1916, the British had already put in place a grand scheme to lay deep underground mines under the ridge overlooking the city of Ypres, an area strongly held by the Germans. David was to be heavily involved in the planning for this operation in 1917.

Before then, David found his commission brought 'much adventure and hard work', though censorship restricted the details he could provide of his travels in his letters to Cara and his family. He did share with her his pride in 'young Woodward', one of the officers in No. 1 Mining Company, who was awarded the Military Cross for his work in crossing to German lines and destroying an enemy post and its machine gun emplacement.[3]

David wrote affectionate and entertaining letters to his daughters about life at headquarters, about the French villages and their inhabitants and the beauties of the French countryside in spring and summer. He composed a little cartoon story about two French kittens and their adventures in escaping from 'le Boche' into the Allied trenches, and sent this in a letter (in French) to his grandchildren in

Edinburgh, Peggy and Archie McIntyre. An early letter to Cara, in May 1916, conveyed his affection for the tunnellers and also his gift for penning a humorous story: 'The miners are beginning to slightly elevate the shoulders and turn the palms of their hands outwards and downwards at an angle of 45 degrees to make the hopelessness of their case (chiefly thirst) more apparent to out brave allies.'[4]

Later letters to Cara conveyed the challenge and danger of the operations that the tunnellers were engaged in and the difficult and claustrophobic conditions under which they worked: crawling along underground tunnels lit only by flickering candles, whose dimming light warned of 'bad air'; the nerve-racking race to lay explosives knowing the Germans were preparing their own mines in galleries a few feet away. There were also the more conventional hazards of trench warfare where work in trenches and dugouts was constantly and often fatally interrupted by German shells and Minenwerfer bombs.

It was while engaged on his duties as Geological Advisor that David suffered the accident that nearly ended his life. Investigating water levels in the chalk, he was being lowered down a deep well on Vimy Ridge when the windlass broke and he plummeted down about seventy feet to the hard rock of the dry well. Conscious the whole time, David wondered at finding himself not only still alive but free to move his arms and legs. He was able to call for help and after a quarter of an hour a doctor was lowered down to inspect him. The doctor bound up the gash on his head and was able to fix him to the rope again, to be slowly and painfully pulled to the surface. He was taken by field ambulance to a casualty clearing station and thence to hospital near Boulogne. By 8 October he was in a comfortable private hospital in London, his scalp wound and fractured rib healing well and the partly ruptured urethra joining up. His cable to Cara reassured her that he was recovering 'splendidly' and was hoping to be back at the front in three weeks' time, by early November. Meanwhile, he obtained a pass to visit his daughter in Edinburgh. Cara was heartened by this news.

Margaret had given her mother a much fuller account of David's accident than his cable had provided, and it was clear that he had had a near-miraculous escape from death. His fall down the well had slammed him at an oblique angle into the rock and so his spine had not been smashed to pieces as it would have if the fall had been vertical. Billy David reported to Margaret, after visiting his father at the casualty clearing station, that 'the old dad is made of indiarubber and steel, and has the heart of a lion'.

It now seemed essential to Cara that she travel to England, where she could be near Margaret and her young family and closer to her husband and son. David had already suggested that she join Margaret in Edinburgh for the duration of the war. Fighting off her aversion to sea travel, Cara started making plans for the journey. Arrangements were made for the Red Cross to take over the running of the convalescent home. After convincing the authorities that they had David's permission to leave Australia and that their income tax had been paid, Cara booked their passage. On 18 January 1917, she and Molly left Sydney on SS *Niagara*, accompanied by Molly's young friend, Isobel Houison. They planned to travel from Vancouver across Canada and then board a British ship at Halifax for the Atlantic crossing. The United States was still neutral and therefore it would have been much safer to travel on an American ship, but the fervently patriotic Cara would have none of this. In spite of the growing submarine menace, they would cross the Atlantic on a British ship or die in the attempt! However, soon after the women arrived in Halifax the British government issued a new regulation: owing to the extreme submarine danger, no women were to be allowed on British ships crossing the Atlantic. The other women passengers on the *Niagara* immediately travelled down to New York and thence across to England but Cara dug her heels in. 'We are going to fight the Canadian government to try and get leave to go from Halifax,' she wrote to Margaret. Questions of economy played a part in this decision as well. Life on the American continent proved to be extremely expensive, and a trip to New York would cost nearly £30. There were dark references in her letters to the profiteering around her: there were 'people in fat billets making money out of the war … the wives and mothers of soldiers are of no account'.

Stranded in Halifax, money became a pressing problem for the three women. They had enough for travelling expenses, but Cara's savings had been transferred to a bank in Edinburgh. Margaret, who had permission to draw on her mother's account, received urgent requests for money to tide them over. Molly and Isobel looked around for work, scanning the 'situations vacant' in the Halifax newspapers. They applied for one post where a doctor's household required a cook and a chauffeur and went along hopefully to the interview. The doctor's wife, sympathetic to their plight and very willing to help them, was in the end unable to offer them a place. She explained that conservative Halifax was not yet ready for women chauffeurs, and that to employ one would mean her husband losing not only his practice but his reputation.

The women were advised to travel to New Glasgow, a small town in Nova Scotia where several munitions factories were operating and work should be easier to come by. There Molly and Isobel found work in a factory, cutting and turning the metal for eighteen-pounder shells. Their pay packets kept them going from week to week, topped

Munitions factory. Molly at rear on right

up by whatever money David could transfer to them and a £50 draft from
Billy. Cara kept frugal house for the three of them in rented rooms. She
shopped and cooked for the household, trying her best to provide warm
and nourishing meals. To buoy her spirits she put photographs of Margaret
and her young family on the mantelpiece: she wondered if the little boy,
Archie, had developed 'a pronounced Scotch accent'. Keeping busy as
always, she cut out and sewed a number of warm nightgowns to send to
Margaret, enhancing these utilitarian gifts with delicate embroidery. Spring
was coming to gentler climates but in Nova Scotia the brutal Canadian
winter still lingered. The washing froze stiff on the line and their main
outlay of money was for shoe repairs and to buy galoshes for their tramps
through the icy slush on the roads. 'The climate is awful,' Cara wrote to her
daughter. 'Edinburgh is a sunny land compared to it.' She struggled with
episodes of ill-health: persistent colds brought on by the bitter climate and
a serious case of blood poisoning from an infected tooth.

At the end of April, the shell factory closed suddenly. Government
inspectors had found that faulty shells were being passed by the
manager, and sabotage was suspected. Molly and Isobel were out of

Canada: Cara and friends

work for over three weeks and the three women were restless and discontented. Cara had to wire Margaret urgently for more money. (However she was still in sufficient command of the family finances to organize David's affairs: she directed Margaret to pay an extra £50 into his London account as he was overdrawn by £47.) She confessed to her daughter that it was a scary experience to find oneself 'without means in a strange country'.

In late May, the girls obtained work in another factory. Striking workers had left the machines idle and the management decided to employ women for the first time in the hope of breaking the strike. Molly found it a depressing and alarming experience on their first morning at work to be booed by the line of strikers drawn up at the factory gates, though later experiences in wartime England were to give her new insights into the struggles working-class people were facing.

Snowbound in Canada. Cara with Molly and Isobel

The women manned the machines for a week before the strikers went back to work. Molly had enjoyed her role there and her post on a magnificent 'turret' machine which swung round on a pivot, bringing various tools into operation on the shells. After the men returned to work, the women were given dull, shell-inspecting jobs which involved a lot of just 'hanging about' and dodging the spittle of the men who were all inveterate tobacco chewers.

David did what he could

to press their case among influential friends but at the same time he dreaded the thought of his wife and daughter embarking on the voyage to England. His letters to Margaret through the winter and spring of 1917 reveal his deep worries about the submarine menace: he seemed almost convinced that their ship would be targeted if they attempted to cross the Atlantic and he thought it best if necessary that they return to Australia. During February he wrote nearly every day to Margaret, seeking news of the travellers and urging her to cable Cara in Canada and implore her to stay put. David found his eldest daughter to be a calm reference point when so much around him was in frantic disarray: she was loving, reliable, and even, in David's eyes, heroic as she coped with wartime conditions and a young family with her own man away at the front. David came increasingly to confide in her and rely on her judgment as misunderstandings arose in his correspondence with Cara, misunderstandings that were to cause unusual strains in their relationship. Correspondence at the time was always going to be plagued by difficulties: letters and parcels to troops often went astray in wartime Europe and much mail was also destroyed in torpedo attacks on Allied ships. But David's main concern, and one that preyed on his mind for months, was that Cara had failed to acknowledge his report of an incident that seemed to him to convey much of the pathos and pity of the war.

In July 1916, David and his men were in the front line at Ploegsteert, south of Ypres. They were drilling to test soil and rock conditions for sinking inclined shafts for the tunnellers. The lines were being heavily strafed by the Germans and a number of large shells fell near their dugout. A Royal Fusilier sentry, 'a mere boy', ran to them to report that he had been blown from his post by a shell explosion. Nevertheless he refused to leave his post until given orders to do so. David raced off to find his commanding officer and they returned to rescue the lad, pulling him from his post just before another huge shell hit the trench.

The young boy, collapsing with shell shock, was comforted by David, who 'patted him like a child and told him that he was a brave lad not to have deserted his post'.

For some reason Cara did not comment on this incident, which David saw as 'one of my best efforts made during this war'. Her failure to respond weighed on his mind, especially as he lay in hospital recovering from his fall. Cara in turn, upbraided him for giving her only sketchy details of his accident. Their usual closeness was disrupted by misunderstandings, fatigue, illness and anxiety and the strains that great distance imposed on the relationship. In his low and dispirited state, David began to feel that he would somehow be to blame if anything happened to them on the trip to England; that he should never have suggested that they make the journey.

February 1917 was a dark month for David. He returned to the front in November 1916 having been given a clean bill of health, though in fact the internal injuries he had received in his fall would return to plague him severely after the war. He was fifty-nine years old. After the comfort of the London hospital and the joy of a brief two-day reunion with Margaret in Edinburgh, the return to what he described as the 'scarred and tortured earth' of the Western Front would have been difficult for even the most sanguine of men. David found the cold particularly trying; the winter of 1916/1917 in France was the most severe in living memory. Like most men at the front, he kept his letters as brisk and laconic as he could. He wrote to Margaret that the February days were full of 'very strenuous work up and down the line, with heavy strafing by the Boche'. It was only while lying in the peace and quiet of the London hospital that he had allowed stronger images to intrude. He had written then to Margaret about his relief at being away from 'the five months of noise and dirt and squalor and horror of the Western Front'. So little space separated the front line from the peace of England; this made the contrast between the two the harder to bear.

David had another brief period of two weeks leave in March 1917 purchasing new scientific equipment. He enjoyed a few days with Margaret and her children in Edinburgh, and his son Bill was also able to get leave to join them. On 16 March he saw Bill off on the train for the front. David's loneliness after the parting was made greater by his knowledge of 'the terrible battles' yet to come in France and Belgium.

The months of early summer in 1917 were marked by the final preparations for the great mining offensive which was to see a series of deep tunnels dug under the Messines Ridge to the south-east of the city of Ypres. Over a period of almost a year in conditions of great secrecy, the Allied forces had driven twenty-two tunnels under the German lines along a front of about ten miles. They were to be exploded as a preliminary to a mass attack on the German lines on the morning of 7 June. David was heavily involved in preparing one of the mines in this series and he reported the success of the operation to Margaret: 'Every one of our mines went up at zero hour (3.10 am) and there wasn't 15-second interval between the time of the explosion of the first and that of the last. It was far and away the biggest thing in military mining the world has ever seen.'[5] He added a proud note that 'Hill 60 that is described as going up in dust was undermined almost entirely by our Australian miners'.

At the end of June, he had the sad task of attending the funeral of one of their officers. The family's young friend, Major Leslie Coulter, commanding officer of No. 3 Tunnelling Company, had been shot through the head after an attack on a German dugout. In late June, David received a welcome parcel from Canada: cake, dried fruit and some knitted socks. With his thankyou letter to Cara he enclosed a dried cornflower from the summer harvest fields. He had to admit ruefully that the cake hadn't survived the journey: the socks had yet to appear 'from under a mess of cake crumbs'. He addressed Cara as 'darling little Mootie', which was always the family's term of endearment for her.

In mid-June 1917, Cara and Molly had received the welcome news that their case had been reconsidered and they were to be allowed to travel to England after all. Relieved to be on the move at last, they packed their bags, caught a train to Montreal and there boarded a British ship. Their trip across the Atlantic was remarkably trouble-free and they landed at Bristol on 9 July. The next day they were reunited with Margaret and her family in Edinburgh. David, getting leave, caught the all-night train from Kings Cross to Edinburgh, sustained by a cup of hot tea at York. He arrived in Edinburgh early on 12 July, to be reunited with 'dear Mootie' at the top of the stairs at 76 Thirlstone Road, Margaret's flat.

The next week was a glorious interlude to the war for David and his wife and daughters. Edinburgh turned on an unusual spell of warm and sunny weather to welcome him and the days were spent in leisurely family gatherings, enjoying the simple pleasures so missed in 'the dirt and squalor and horror' of life at the front. Supper was taken with Margaret and Mootie 'chez Les McIntyres' (Margaret's parents-in-law who were staying in Edinburgh); he took Mootie and his daughters to a picture show, *Disraeli*; there were gatherings for afternoon tea with friends and strolls in the Edinburgh parklands. On 18 July, David kissed his two grandchildren goodbye and made his farewells to Mootie and his daughters at Waverly station. He caught the 10 pm train to London and after some work at the Geological Survey Office he arrived at Boulogne on 21 July.

Back in Edinburgh, Molly decided to go to London to join the Women's Auxiliary Army

Molly in WAAC uniform (NLA MS 8890)

Corps (WAAC). Her friend, Isobel Houison, had already found work as an inspector at an aircraft factory. In October, Molly, accompanied by Mootie, caught the train to London, a city by then under attack from a new kind of warfare. People from the inner city slums crowded into the Tube each evening in fear of air raids; the streets round Piccadilly Circus were littered with broken glass after a bomb dropped in such a raid.

Cara herself was determined to find a constructive job in Edinburgh to keep busy and to aid the war effort. She found a flat in Thirlstone Road, which would be her base while she looked around for work. The flat looked towards the Castle and the quiet rural surrounds of St Margaret's Convent. From there she could see the oats being harvested as autumn set in. She showed Peggy and Archie how the oats were gathered in 'stooks' and set out to dry in the sun. Their grandfather described his own surroundings in a letter to seven-year-old Peggy: from his headquarters he too had a rural vista and used to watch the local children coming to gather the last of the summer grass and take it home for their rabbits. How they longed, this older couple, to offer their grandchildren a version of life that would survive the war.

Margaret had made many good friends in Edinburgh. Among them were Ned Touche and his family, who had moved north from London before the war. Margaret and her family and Cara spent Christmas 1917 with the Touche household. Margaret's Christmas gift to her father was a pair of fur motoring gloves, which he received with much gratitude: they were perfect for the long snowy journeys he was making up and down the line. The fast and efficient British postal service meant that it was easy to send creature comforts to the troops in France. Sweets, special cakes and luxury items could be ordered from Fortnum & Mason, who did a roaring trade in gift assortments for the front during the war. The London papers arrived in the trenches only a day late and officers could continue to receive their subscriptions to *The Tatler* and *Punch*. Books, too, were easily accessible through the postal service and helped many men endure the boredom of static trench warfare. David had asked Margaret in May 1917 'to kindly forward me Kipling's latest book' and his son Bill had also written with requests. He asked for 'Gibbon's *Decline and Fall*, Virgil's *Bucolics* and *Georgics* in Latin, Book III of Horace's *Odes*, a Latin dictionary, a good history of England and Kipling's booklet on France at War'. That he could ask for these so unselfconsciously suggests that it was not an unusual list for a bookish officer at the time.

Bill David had not had an easy war. In September 1915, he had taken part in what historians would call the Battle of Loos. Loos was a small coal-mining town over the Belgium border, an area held by the Germans. It was the site of the first large-scale attack by the Allies on entrenched German lines and was to result in 60,000 British casualties with no ground gained in the end. The assault was to be preceded by the release of gas, but in the event the wind drove the gas back over the British infantry, many of whom were poisoned. The Cameron Highlanders, in another section of the line, kept moving forward under heavy fire and eventually gained their objective, Hill 70, capturing prisoners in the process, but at a heavy cost. Bill, writing to his sister in Edinburgh after the event, saw plenty of the horror and suffering of that day. Organizing stretcher bearers from the rear after the advance, he combed no-man's land for survivors. Everywhere dying and shattered men were calling out for help, but many had to be left as all the stretchers were already in use. The next day, advancing with his battalion, Bill reached a small wood on Hill 70 and set up a regimental aid post, barely sheltered from the hail of lead and shrapnel raking their site from the numerous fortified villages beyond Hill 70. There he tended the wounded through a long night of heavy rain and constant shrapnel attack.

Forced to retire through lack of reinforcements, Bill's Highlander division had over 6000 killed, gassed or wounded in the attack. The Battle of Loos was officially ended in October after renewed offensives by both German and British forces failed.[6]

The operation had begun on 25 September, the very date in 1916 of David's near-fatal accident at Vimy which was just a few miles to the south. This date had a poignant significance for David thereafter and was noted in his diary as the day he and his son had both had 'deliverance from death'.

Bill, patriotic to the core, put a fine gloss on the operation. 'I was proud to be with a Scotch regiment and was ashamed of the English, who by the way seem to be getting nearly all the credit for what we did. Still, it's no use grousing.' Like many of the men, he was gassed but was dismissive of the effects of gas: 'with respirators it soon passes off'.

Billy was back with his division in the trenches in November 1915. 'This part of the trenches is absolute hell,' he wrote to Margaret. 'Mud up to your knees, feet soaking all the time and sore.' During his weeks behind the lines he was doing medical work with the local villagers. He was given a little ring by a grateful French girl after he cured her brother of pneumonia. He also wore a little medal of St Christopher, another thankyou gift for his work. By early 1916, Bill would have served a year with the British Expeditionary Force.

He suffered minor effects from the gassing but there was to be a toll of further physical damage as the months proceeded. In the winter of 1916, he had time in hospital with 'trench fever'; he also had a bout of appendicitis. He was to suffer yet again from the effects of gas in August 1916, which he admitted was 'very unpleasant' when one was out on all-night vigils over mangled bodies. He spent yet another week in hospital in July 1917 recuperating from the effects of gas.

In early August 1917, shortly after the travellers arrived from Canada, the family received a telegram from the War Office. Bill David had been wounded in action. A large German shell had killed four men in his battalion instantly and Bill David, blown head over heels by the blast, had a shell splinter pierce his rib cage. His father, back at headquarters after his leave, tried frantically to discover his whereabouts. General Harvey lent David his Rolls-Royce and he set off on a hunt over northern France in search of Bill, finally locating him at a hospital in Rouen, where the two men had an emotional reunion. David was able to report to Cara after the hospital visit that he was 'recovering comfortably'.

From the French hospital Bill was transferred to London to convalesce. Margaret hoped that he would then come to Edinburgh where she could keep a sisterly eye on him. However, Bill knew that the cold, damp climate of the north would not help his recovery: he was still coughing up blood from the shell splinter near his lung. He opted for a convalescent hospital at Torquay on the South Coast.

While convalescing in hospital at Torquay, Bill was made much of by one of the voluntary aid workers, a young woman named Marjorie Aynsley. She was twenty-one years old. Bill had had no previous experience of women apart from university flirtations and was naïve and young for his age. Behind him lay two years of the horror of the Western Front. It comes as no surprise that he asked Marjorie to marry him.

All accounts of the young Bill David suggest he was a sensitive boy, and a bit of a loner. His two sisters were very close in age and friendship and Bill never quite made a trio with them. Boarding school from the age of eight must have cut him off to some extent from full participation in family life; and his father was absent for significant periods of time during his childhood and adolescence. In 1906, Cara confessed to Touche, 'Billy is a very quiet boy – too quiet for a boy of 16. He is so tall that he can't scamper round with boys, and so he has few chums and a rather quiet, studious life – friendly with girls though!' A family photograph taken at Woodford shows a tall, gangly, serious lad: chosen for the rowing team at his college but no good at other team sports apparently. His letters to his beloved Mootie show that he was very fond of his mother but there were tensions between father and son. In later life Bill confessed to his niece, Anne Edgeworth, that his feelings for his father had soured after he had been thrashed for some misdemeanour, a punishment that Bill considered unjust. (As David was universally considered to be the gentlest of men, he may only have applied the rod as a conscientious Victorian father was expected to.) The great stresses and heightened emotions of wartime threw father and son closer together, as they sought each other out in the chaos of wartime France. Early in 1916, Bill had borrowed a motor bike and tore along the back roads to David's headquarters, where they 'had a speechless hug and a long yarn about life in general'.[7]

In the early, jubilant days of the war, in Australia David had rejoiced in his son's adventures. Hearing in early September 1915 that the Highlanders had moved to France and would shortly be going into action, David wrote to Bill of his excitement at hearing 'that your men were just due for the trenches and that you were within range of the shells. How I wish I were with you!' He confessed to Bill that his job on the recruiting platform was made much more convincing now that he had a son on active service.

If Bill felt the weight of family expectation as a burden, he knew that enlisting overseas would be a chance for him to carve his own identity. He disowned his father's full name and always signed himself as plain 'Bill David', leaving out the significant 'Edgeworth'. (The Edgeworths, David's maternal ancestors, had had an influential pedigree in Ireland and Scotland.) Bill's father was hurt and annoyed by this omission: he confided to Cara that he felt it showed a lack of due pride in the family name. However, on hearing in January 1918 that his son was to be married, he expressed devout hopes for the future happiness of 'our dear splendid Loos-Somme-Arras-Ypres hero's life'. Later generations see the sad irony of invoking those names to bless a marriage.

Bill and Marjorie's wedding was to take place in Torquay in March 1918, after which Bill would be reporting for duty as a medical officer in a local military hospital. Mercifully his days in the trenches were over. Both Cara and David had hoped fervently that after two years work in the front line as a medical officer for his battalion, Bill would be entitled to seek some other, less dangerous line of war service. His latest injury was thus a blessing in disguise.

Marjorie Aynsley was clearly from a very different social background to Bill David. Her father had managed an earthenware and pottery factory in Staffordshire. He is not mentioned as being present at his daughter's wedding though there are later references to both parents coming to live with Marjorie and Bill in London. Marjorie's younger sister, Phyllis, lived in London where Molly David made her acquaintance in October 1917 through a mutual friend. Molly took Phyllis out to dinner from time to time, partly, no doubt, to satisfy her curiosity about the family her brother was marrying into. Molly heard from her friend that Marjorie was very fond of Bill 'even if she did powder her pretty little nose' (horrible thought to the austere David women!) Second-hand reports came through of Marjorie's temperamental nature: she had stormed out of one hospital where she was doing voluntary work because of an argument about hairstyles. Bill confessed later to his father that some of Marjorie's family had been 'four bottle men' – dreadful news for a temperance sympathizer to hear. Still, the family hoped for the best from this unexpected liaison and gave all the support they could to the wedding. Cara and David's present to the couple was £50 of war bonds.

David obtained four days' special leave from France for the wedding. Margaret and Molly joined him but Cara, laid low with mumps, was unable at the last moment to travel from Edinburgh. Perhaps she felt thankful to be absent from an occasion that would have been unbearably emotional for her. It was clear from her early worries about Margaret and her 'young man' that Cara felt possessive about her children: she acknowledged that she had been 'a jealous old woman' in interfering in Margaret's courtship. If her children married they would be lost to her to some extent, even more so if their affairs took them away overseas as had happened with the McIntyres. She must have worried intensely about Bill and his chances of surviving the war, given the maelstrom into which the Highlanders were constantly being thrown. She also worried, more mundanely, about his future prospects. She had had hopes, back in Australia, of his marriage to a local girl, Dot Paton, the daughter of a Blackheath doctor, but nothing had eventuated. Now there was to be an unexpected wartime wedding in England, with none of the dear associations with home, family or friends that Cara valued … and the very real prospect that after the war her son would never return to Australia. Cara had to rely on her husband's careful account of the wedding day to get some impression of Bill's new wife. He sat down and wrote her a long letter immediately after the wedding.

David had met Marjorie, Phyllis and their mother in the evening before the wedding at a Torquay hotel. His diary noted, 'Very favourably impressed'.[8] The wedding day was gloriously fine and David drove Marjorie and her mother to the nice old church for the marriage service. The small wedding party had lunch at the hotel, then Bill and Marjorie left for Dartmouth on their honeymoon. David put Margaret and Molly on the train for Plymouth and then he returned to France.

In Scotland, Cara took on the management of a hostel at Kirkcudbright in the Highlands. Young women who enlisted in the Women's Land Army came here to gather the sphagnum moss that grew in abundance on the moors. This work was classified as 'essential war work' because the moss had a vital medical role to play as a dressing for wounds on the Western Front: its antiseptic and absorbent properties had been known in folk medicine since the Middle Ages.

Molly joined her family in Scotland in February 1918. All UK based WAACs were to be transferred to the Women's Legion Motor Drivers, another army organization employing women drivers. Molly arranged to be transferred to Edinburgh, where she could 'live out'; in fact she was able to be billeted with Margaret in Thirlstone Road. She felt a strong need to be nearer her sister as the war dragged on with no end in sight.

In July, Cara took a room for a week for herself and Margaret and the children at a temperance hotel at Dunblane, a quiet old cathedral town noted for its lovely river valley. This was an austere wartime holiday

– Cara reminded her daughter to bring her sugar and butter rations and her ration books – and the four of them would share a room: 'tell the babes they must be very good here and not jump on beds or scratch furniture'. They spent most of the days out walking with the children and playing in the local parks. Then in August it was back to the hostel where the land army was gathering in 300 bags of moss, racing to finish before the autumn rains arrived. In France, David was busier than ever, having been appointed Chief Geologist of the British Expeditionary Force. Bill McIntyre was still in Salonika, in a nightmarish world of malarial heat and dust, conscious of the 'awful butchery' this war had become.

As the war drew to a close David was approached by the University of Wales, offering him the position of principal. He explained to Mootie that he would not dream of accepting the position, feeling honour-bound to carry on the teaching at Sydney University and to complete the writing of a geology of Australia. At a more personal level, he knew that the family's health was much better in Australia and, besides, the people and places there were very dear to the family. His years in Australia had been a 'golden time', he admitted, since they corresponded to the years of his partnership with the woman he loved.[9]

The armistice was celebrated quietly in Edinburgh, without the frenzy witnessed in the streets of London. The Davids had all survived more or less intact, saved as a family from the deep tragedies that left their mark on so many of their friends. The Spanish influenza which had already caused a terrifying death toll in Europe that year passed them by, though the family in Edinburgh certainly suffered from one strain of the virus before the war's end.

The family embarked together for home in March 1919. Cara and Molly travelled down from Scotland and joined David on the *Eurypides* at Portland on 3 March. With them on the ship were Douglas Mawson and John Davis from Antarctic days, James Pollock from the tunnellers and 550 troops.

It was a trying voyage for Cara. She suffered inevitably from seasickness and hated the days at sea. David confessed in a letter to Touche that she would probably never make another voyage to Europe and would have to resign herself to a permanent separation from her son, who 'would probably settle in the old country'. As well, there was the heartache of leaving Margaret and her young family in Edinburgh. David and Cara had made clear to Margaret and Bill that they would not interfere in decisions about their future, though they both lived in hope that the young couple would decide to move back to Australia. David's personal diaries of the voyage show that his wife, in her depression, was both grumpy and irrational at times: 'she resents the sea'. Going ashore at Colombo, Cara was accidentally bruised in the leg and knocked on her head by the local boys manning the boat and she cursed them vigorously, commenting loudly about 'the unfitness of the dark races to survive'.

They arrived in Sydney on 25 April 1919, to a city already feeling the impact of the influenza epidemic. People still gathered to commemorate the Gallipoli landing in a service at the Domain, but all attendants were to be masked and the march through the city streets was cancelled. Theatres, restaurants and racecourses were closed and the hospitals were stretched to capacity with influenza victims. Schools, closed since the summer holidays, were converted into makeshift hospitals.

Nevertheless there was a joyous reception for the ship and its travellers. The returning troops received an official welcome home at the Anzac Buffet in the Domain, where the Davids were also greeted by many of their old friends from Ashfield days: among them Miss Nicholls, from Hurlstone College, and the Misses Dove, who had corresponded with them throughout the war. Molly and Cara were presented with bouquets by Jeanie Maiden and one of her daughters and went back to the Maiden residence in the gardens for afternoon tea and for a renewal of that warm family and community engagement that they had longed for during the war. One of the Maiden girls had married before the war: Gertrude Maiden was now the wife of Dr

James Paton, whom Molly had hoped to marry in earlier years. He had enlisted in 1915 but been discharged with pneumonia and entered private practice in Sydney.

11 A Public Life

The years after the war were marked by an extraordinary level of public activity by the Edgeworth Davids. By the time they returned to Australia they were both in their sixties. At that age many of their contemporaries were seeking a dignified retirement or were faced with physical ills and infirmities that limited what they could do.

Cara and David were certainly not in the peak of physical condition. David was to struggle increasingly with a painful arthritis and with the legacy of internal injuries sustained in his accident. Cara also suffered from a debilitating form of arthritis and seemed prone to severe headaches that laid her low for days at a time. Yet for David these were years of constant travel and writing in connection with his geological interests and university teaching and with public advocacy of educational and scientific matters. His wife, based permanently in Sydney from 1920, became involved with a wide range of community groups concerned especially with the education and welfare of girls and young women.

Their family had survived the war when so many had not; did they feel that they owed it to their country to repay that debt? Certainly David was conscious of the miracle of his own survival after his accident. He often expressed in both letters and his diary a profound thankfulness that life was offering him another chance and that the love affair begun in 1882 still continued with his life's partner. 'How beautiful the Earth looks and all that is in it,' he wrote to Cara after the Armistice.[1] His own sense of vocation was as strong as ever. Rejecting his father's call to embrace the Church, he had taken a very different path. For him the world of science continued to offer sufficient revelation, for he saw expressed in the natural world 'a garment worn without seam, the living garment of God'.[2] Right until his last days David retained a sense of great wonder about the high calling of science. The University Senate, conferring on him the title of Emeritus Professor at his retirement in 1924, felt that he had 'set an example of ascetic devotion to science for its own sake, and of power to combine a humanist ideal with the spirit of scientific research'.[3]

Cara was not of an introspective habit but it is clear from the range of her post-war activities that she too saw the coming years as a gift and a challenge. This was to be especially evident in her work for the Girl Guides movement.

Edgeworth David returned to Australia with a number of honours bestowed on him for his war service. He was awarded the Distinguished Service Order in 1918 and was promoted to lieutenant colonel. In September 1920, he was appointed as Knight of the British Empire (KBE). David had earlier refused the offer of a knighthood several times but in 1920 'the Governor-General practically commanded' him to accept it: it was an honour for the university and the profession of geology as well as for David himself. The couple were now known as Sir Edgeworth and Lady David.

David wrote to Margaret about his feelings: 'Personally there is no denying that I like the honour but strongly dislike the title. Why vary from the common lot of men?' He would have much preferred it to be just another set of initials after his name 'as one writes FRS' (Fellow of the Royal Society).

Lady David

Cara had always opposed titles as part of her general aversion to social snobbery. When David had received the honour of Order of the

Companion of St Michael and St George (CMG) in the NSW Honours List in 1910, she wrote to Touche that she and David had previously joked about such a title, suggesting it referred to 'Corner of George and Market Streets' or more pointedly, 'Colonial Money Grubber'.[4]

David's resumption of his university work plus his numerous other commitments meant that life was busier than ever. It became clear to both David and Cara that the regular train journeys to and from Woodford were no longer practicable for a couple who were not getting any younger but whose range of activities seemed to be expanding.

In late 1920, Cara began looking around for a home in Sydney and from October 1920, Tyn-y-Coed was rented out.[4] By this stage the Gunyah at Ashfield had been sold and in any case the Davids, attached to the bush environment at Woodford, were looking for somewhere less built up than Ashfield had become. Most professional and business people who could afford to do so were now buying land and properties in the fashionable and expensive Eastern Suburbs and lower North Shore but Cara was not interested in a 'good address'. She found what she was looking for at Hornsby, at that stage still undeveloped bush on the very outskirts of Sydney. A small weatherboard cottage,

Coringah in 2010 (Author's photo)

Coringah, looked over a few acres of bushland and sandstone to a little creek spanned by two small bridges which gave access to the road. The property was purchased and Cara promptly set about house-building operations. A carpenter added a dining room and sitting room, a study for David, a new kitchen and laundry, a bedroom and various verandahs. Water and electricity were laid on, and Cara had a septic system installed for sewerage. David's daily journey to the university took him from Hornsby station down through Ryde and over the bridge on the Parramatta River. Ever observant, he made geological notes on the journey about the cross-section of rock exposed along the railway cuttings as the train came down off the Hornsby Plateau onto the Cumberland Plain where the city lay. (The Davids always travelled to the city by second-class carriages, much to the surprise of their wealthy friends.)

Cara's community engagements continued and the range of her commitments grew wider. It is clear that she was still keen to support those without a voice or influence in the community, especially women, and to do whatever she could to raise their access to education and training. Before the war she had helped organize what we would now call a 'careers expo' but which then bore the title, 'What to do with our girls?' It was a large exhibition at the Town Hall giving advice to young women about the variety of occupations and professions that could be open them. Cara David was making her own attempts to counter the stereotyping of sex roles: on display were a variety of careers in agriculture and commercial art.[6]

Cara supported numerous projects in the years following the war. Among these was a Voluntary Workers' Cottage in south-west Sydney which could be occupied rent-free for six months. She also gave her support to help set up community networks in the suburbs where lonely women could meet, socialize and learn new skills. Cara continued to be concerned for the conditions under which domestic servants worked and in December 1919 she attended a meeting at the Town Hall to discuss the need for better wages and conditions for domestic service workers.

In Sydney, the Women's Prohibition Campaign was inaugurated in August 1920 at the Town Hall, with Cara David presiding. Her friend Dr Mary Booth also spoke. The new movement was formed by the amalgamation of the Woman's Christian Temperance Union with a number of other women's groups. The temperance movement had won some its battles during the war, when the national mood had favoured sacrifice and self-discipline in support of the wider battles being fought. Now that the war was over, many in the movement wanted to extend their campaigns and bring in total prohibition. They aimed to put pressure on state governments to hold referenda where voters would be asked whether they wished to see their state prohibit the sale and manufacture of alcohol. The *Volstead Act*, passed in America in 1920, had banned the manufacture, sale and transport of alcohol nationwide, and reports were coming through to the temperance movement in Australia of encouraging social reform in some of the states. At its 1921 annual convention, the Woman's Christian Temperance Union declared that its aim should be Australia-wide prohibition by 1925. Cara's campaign committee met throughout 1921 to discuss novel ideas to raise public awareness of the issue. She asked for volunteers to hold neighbourhood 'doorstep' meetings, to arouse discussion among women about prohibition and to convey simple facts accurately and clearly.

The New South Wales Labor Government was reluctant to move on this issue and incurred the scorn of the temperance activists. Cara David was present at another large meeting at the Town Hall in February 1921, 'condemning the government for side-stepping on the prohibition referendum'.[7]

Disillusioned with the failure of government reform on this issue, Cara turned her energies to other community-based activities where the shared enthusiasms of like-minded women carried the projects forward. One of her enduring interests in the years leading up to the war and in the decades following it was the Bush Book Club. This was the kind of imaginative project which appealed to Cara. It shared some of the ideals and philosophy of the Australasian Home Reading Union but it was aimed at – and successfully reached – a much broader range of Australians than the AHRU had been able to do. The Bush Book Club had been founded in 1909 when a few friends gathered at the Queen Victoria Club to discuss ways they could collect books to send out to remote communities and isolated stations in the bush. They had been led to do this on the suggestion of Arthur Jose, a London journalist who had travelled through New South Wales and been appalled by the loneliness and isolation of bush life.[8] This project, like many such charitable movements in the early years of the century, was initiated by socially prominent and educated women who themselves were wealthy or comfortably off but who had a strong social conscience (and who indeed were supported by a small group of sympathetic and like-minded men). In 1911, the club joined the National Council of Women and thus it became part of that broader network of groups who wanted to create a more kindly, nurturing nation. Australia was still a notably masculine society and the tone of public life was combative and individualistic. It was an age when government and policy making were decided by men; women's role in public life was marginal. So these voluntary groups were important for women, enabling them to turn their energies to a certain kind of constructive social action.

A public meeting held at the Town Hall in April 1910 had brought the new club to wider notice and it began to gather a lot of support among both men and women. Its method of operation was simple. Books and magazines were donated by the public, sorted and packed by volunteers and sent to country rail centres anywhere in New South Wales (the railways had offered free carriage). Country people who wanted to join the club paid a small subscription each year and also the cost of freight for the parcels of book sent to them from the nearest rail centre. Country libraries could also subscribe to the club. The books did not have to be returned but could be passed on from reader to reader until they were worn out.

The reach of the program is suggested in the club's 1911 report, which stated that books had been supplied to 'Barringun and Alexia, beyond Bourke, the Mission Station, Tuncurry, Booligal and Cow Creek (a small settlement in the Bathurst district)'. Supplies of illustrated papers and magazines were also sent from time to time to railway fettlers' camps and to shearing sheds. The club did not disseminate political or sectarian books: Bibles and prayer books were sent on to the Methodist Mission. Books 'of a doubtful moral nature' were discarded.

The growing success of the program and a busy round of fundraising by its supporters allowed the club to employ a paid secretary, and office and storage rooms were donated for its use in the city. Cara David was president of the Book Club for a number of years both before and after the war. Among others on the committee were Margaret Windeyer, one of the foundation librarians at the new Mitchell Library, and Dorothea Mackellar, the only daughter of the wealthy philanthropist and politician Charles Mackellar, and widely known to generations of Australians as the writer of 'My Country'.

Throughout the war years the club grew in size and influence. Mothers on lonely stations and small bush hamlets wrote of their gratitude at receiving regular parcels of books: for some women, grieving at the loss of sons or husbands, the books were their one contact with a kindlier, better world. At a remote fettlers' camp, the books were the means of bringing the fettlers' wives together so successfully that they formed a branch of the Red Cross and raised over £70 in funds before the camp was disbanded.

By 1920, Cara David was back serving on the Book Club committee as vice-president. By that stage the club was sending books and other reading matter to 716 different places in the country. Among the many groups that were ordering books were families living on the new soldier settlement schemes. Those hard years of drought and struggle in the bush were reflected in some of the letters sent to the club: 'We came from London, and we do miss the lights at night, and the buses going past the door, and the people. I shall never go back as long as we can get a living. You cannot think how pleased we were to get that last parcel of books. The dingoes killed our favourite dog last night.'[9]

A boundary rider wrote: 'I am camped out here on my own with miles of mallee scrub between me and any other camp, but your books keep the devils away at night, and as soon as I knock off work I cook my tucker and read until it gets too dark to see.'[10] Another letter came from a fossicker: 'having recently lost my faithful companion and mate, my dog … you can imagine how a parcel of reading is appreciated.'[11]

Until the 1920s, Australia was still predominantly a nation of rural dwellers: the total population of country districts and small towns still exceeded Sydney's. City people were still aware to a greater or less extent of a close connection to their rural neighbours: if nothing else, the clouds of dust that sometimes blew in to the city spoke of continuing droughts out west on land stripped bare by rabbits and over-grazing. The Bush Book Club's philosophy acknowledged the 'safer and easier life' available to city dwellers and saw its mission as stretching out 'a hand of fellowship' to those in the bush, where the companionship of books might provide their best 'solace and distraction'.

Cara David stayed a loyal supporter of the club for the rest of her life, sending in her yearly subscriptions and often giving an address at its annual general meeting. The club was not wound up until 1959, when the growth of public libraries and increased ease of communication meant a decline in demand for its services.

Another important project in which Cara became involved after the war was the Lord Mayor's Armenian Relief Fund. During the war, Turkish troops had systematically driven Armenian nationals from their homes to be slaughtered or to starve to death, and the horror of these events had become known as servicemen returned from Europe after the war. Australians who had been prisoners of war reported seeing Turkish troops armed with whips, driving women and children into cattle trucks, and the wholesale massacre of able-bodied men. After the war, thousands of children were orphaned, families left homeless and reduced to huddling like animals in caves for warmth and shelter.

An international relief effort was initiated by the United States in 1919 and Australians were drawn in to help. The NSW Lord Mayor's Relief Fund was set up in December 1918 and fundraising over the next couple of years was conducted mainly through various churches. In May 1922, Dr Lincoln Wirt, the international commissioner for the Near East Relief Fund, arrived in Australia to organize and expand Australia's relief effort. Committees throughout the country embarked on a massive campaign to collect food, clothing and funds for the Armenians, and as a result of the national appeal a first shipment of goods was sent to Europe on a Commonwealth Government steamer in September 1922. On their return to Australia many of the relief workers were invited to speak at public gatherings to explain both the enormity of the Armenian tragedy and also the scale of the humanitarian effort taking place to help the survivors.

The relief effort engaged the interest of a number of prominent women. Eleanor Mackinnon, a resident of North Sydney, had founded the world's first Junior Red Cross division, based on the idea of using young people's idealism and generosity in a wider international cause. Eleanor's Red Cross office in the city became the headquarters for the NSW Armenian Relief Fund and she also attended the monthly meetings of the Ashfield Women's branch of the fund. There she would have met Cara David and Edith Glanville, who became vice-president and honorary secretary, respectively. Cara was living in Hornsby by this stage.

Edith Glanville had been personally touched by the tragedy of the war. She and her husband had lost their elder son, Leigh, at the Gallipoli landing. In her grief she turned to community work, seeing such work as a way of building bridges of understanding between people. After the war, she became active in helping immigrants settle in Australia through the work of the New Settlers' League. In 1921, she became one of the first two women to be appointed as a Justice of the Peace in New South Wales: the other was Mrs Jessie Street. Edith became honorary secretary of the NSW Armenian Relief Fund shortly after the visit of Dr Wirt. Beginning in January 1923, Edith Glanville and Cara David set about an active speaking campaign throughout the Sydney district and beyond. They organized and spoke at public gatherings in the Blue Mountains, Bowral, Wahroonga, Manly, Wagga and Moss Vale.

Organizing the thousands of destitute Armenian children into orphanages became the main priority for the relief funds. An Australasian Orphanage was established in Beirut in November 1922. Throughout 1923 and 1924 a series of fundraising events for the orphanage was organized by Cara David. These included craft stalls for the display and sale of beautiful craft and needlework made by Armenian girls at the orphanage. The headquarters of the relief fund, which had been transferred to George Street in the city, also became a shopfront for the needlework and leather goods produced by the orphans.

In 1926, Edith Glanville was appointed as liaison officer between the League of Nations and the Near East Relief Fund and in this capacity travelled widely in the Near East to see first hand the condition of the Armenian refugees and orphans. The NSW Relief Fund wound up its operations by 1930 as all the Armenian orphans under Australian care had become capable of self-support. Edith Glanville continued her connection with the Near East, however, and travelled widely in the region in support of refugee work. In later years she and her husband fostered an Armenian orphan who came to live with them in 1937 at their home in Haberfield.

Cara David was also to travel overseas in 1926. This was on a family mission, as she was once more called upon to be near her husband.

David had retired from his professorship at Sydney University in December 1924 after thirty-three years of service. His main objective after retirement was ambitious, indeed heroic in scale: it was the publication of a comprehensive textbook on Australian geology. Around late 1914, David had signed a contract with Edward Arnold and Co. of London to write such a book: one volume on a relatively modest scale was envisaged. In fact the project was to grow to unwieldy proportions over the next decade and was still not finished at the time of David's death in 1934, when completion of the task was taken over by W.R. Browne of the Geology Department at Sydney University. In 1921, David had been given leave from the university for the specific purpose of writing the book and he set out on wide-ranging excursions to Western and Central Australia, Queensland and Tasmania in search of new material. He led another student expedition to Kosciuszko in January 1922, an area of continued fascination for him for its evidence of Australia's ice-age past. In September 1922 a gift by a private philanthropist, the tobacco magnate Sir Hugh Dixon, allowed David to be released from official university duties for two years. But numerous other commitments and diversions dogged David's path. He was still writing regular newspaper articles, giving speeches and special lectures; elected as chairman of the university's Professorial Board, he was heavily involved in the move to establish a Chair of Anthropology; and he was still active in the affairs of the Australian National Research Council and the Australasian Association for the Advancement of Science. By the time of his retirement very little progress had been made on the book.

In August 1925, David set off for what he planned to be a six-month retreat in England, a time when he could devote himself entirely to the project of organizing and completing the book. At a farewell function at the Sydney Chamber of Commerce he was presented by his friends from the university and from business and pastoral interests with a handsome cash gift to support his travel and publication of the book.

Arriving in London in January 1926, he set to work at the Geological Society rooms. But there were immediate distractions. He gave a series of lectures at University College, London, and spoke at the opening of the Scott Polar Research Institute at Cambridge – under its first Director, Frank Debenham, one of David's ex-students and a member of Scott's 1910–12 polar expedition.

In late April 1926, David suffered what seemed to be a minor stroke as he was crossing Hyde Park one day. It was the beginning of six months of ill health and a further postponement of work on the book. Doctors advised him to reduce his workload and he reluctantly accepted the fact that *The Geology of the Commonwealth of Australia* would not be finished in time for the Pan-Pacific Science Congress in Tokyo the following October. He cancelled his trip to Japan and called again for help from the family, cabling Mootie and Molly to join him in London.

They set off promptly, though their ship took a devious route. Cara chose a cargo steamer as it was cheaper than a mail steamer. On the journey it tied up for several days at Wyndham on the Cambridge Gulf, where crocodiles, attracted by the nearby meatworks, gathered in the muddy waters outside their portholes. Cara called on the small hospital and the school, and went on a drive through bonnet-high grass to visit a Chinese man who owned a flock of goats. An open-air picture show, provided for the meatworkers, was a pleasant interlude one evening.

After these adventures it was sobering to arrive in London. It was clear that Bill's and Marjorie's marriage was a terrible failure. The two of them quarrelled bitterly and constantly and Bill confessed to his mother that 'she goads me till I feel I shall murder her'. Marjorie upbraided Bill for his failure to earn a large enough salary and refused to consider moving to Australia when Bill suggested that. Their daughter, Pam, was a difficult, insecure child, given to showing off and tantrums. Bill's private practice was not flourishing but he stayed in it, and in the marriage, with a grim and resigned persistence. They had considered separating but Bill could not afford to keep two households; anything else was out of the question in post-war England, where adultery was the only grounds for divorce. Marjorie's parents were living with them at a time when new housing was in very short supply and that added extra strains to the marriage. Altogether it was a wretched situation and Cara decided she could not bear to visit Bill's house again. In her misery she wrote a heartfelt plea to Margaret in Tasmania, 'Oh my beloved people be thankful to each other – and pray for these unfortunate young people.' Relations with the Welsh side of the family were strained as well, as issues about family inheritance and David's increasingly demented sister, Ethel, rose to trouble relationships between David and his elder surviving brother, Edmund.

There was the relief of an interlude on the Continent for David, Cara and Molly shortly after they arrived. In September they visited Willie, David's favourite brother (and Cara's favourite as well) in Switzerland, where he had settled with a Swiss woman, Sunny Wolf, after returning from the Far East. The rest of David's family would have nothing to do with Willie in this irregular relationship but Cara, David and Molly seem to have warmed to Sunny, judging by correspondence that passed between them afterwards. They stayed with the couple and their dog (who only obeyed commands given in French) and the excellent French cook at their beautiful villa on the shores of Lake Nyon, and visited Byron's castle while they were there. It was David's last chance to see his brother, who died the following January.

The winter of 1926/27 was a difficult one for Molly and Cara in London. Molly suffered from the cold, damp climate and her parents dispatched her back to Australia after several periods of illness. Cara succumbed to bronchitis and influenza and painful arthritis in the hip, and reverted to a vegetarian diet in the hope of a cure. Pining for the Australian climate, she decided nonetheless to stay on with David in London to support him in getting the book finished. They took a flat

Nyon, Switzerland. Cara and Molly

on the edge of Hampstead Heath and David set about organizing his material in neat filing boxes in a valiant attempt to finish the task before time and further ill-health overtook him.

In June 1927, David took Cara, Billy and Annie Pollock (sister of his late friend and colleague James Pollock) on a brief tour of Belgium and northern France. They were part of that first wave of post-war visitors to the battlefields of the Western Front, many of whom had intense personal connections with the places visited. By 1926 the numbers visiting the region from England were high enough for Michelin to publish illustrated guides to the battlefields. The YMCA ran cheap hostels in Ypres and the French cities close to the battlefields and the Davids, in keeping with their temperance principles, may well have stayed at them rather than in local hotels.

Cara kept a scrapbook of their itinerary, including a map she drew of the route taken through all the major battle sites in the region. From Boulogne they travelled to Amiens, having secured in England the services of a car and a chauffeur. In Amiens, they visited the cathedral, still protected with sandbags nine years after the war. A long day of touring saw them also visiting the British cemetery at Delville Wood on the Somme, where 8000 men lay buried; Villers-Bretonneux and its memorial to the French (the Australian memorial was not completed until 1938); and the Ulster Memorial at Thiepval.[12] A plain wooden cross at Pozières marked the thousands of Australian dead at what C.E.W. Bean called a 'ridge more densely sown with Australian sacrifice than any other place on earth'.[13]

The following day they caught the train from Amiens to Arras, a place which had a particular interest for them because Billy had been quartered there – in an underground sewer – for a time during the war. They also visited Robespierre's house 'from where he watched executions' during the French Revolution. At Arras they visited an ossuary, whose cellars piled with skulls were the only permanent home for the unidentified war dead in France.

Then they moved north to the Ypres region, an area with so many powerful associations for David. They visited Hill 60 and its simple memorial to the Australian tunnellers. They saw the ruin of the Cloth Hall at Ypres and observed the rebuilding of the cathedral. They had their photograph taken by the scaffolding of the unfinished monument of the Menin Gate. The memorial was to be unveiled the following month, and would soon become an eloquent symbol of the nation's mourning with the completion of Will Longstaff's painting and its ghost-like apparitions of the dead. The following day they travelled south through Belgium to Loos. There they visited the Chalk Pit Farm, the site of Bill's dressing station on the night of 26 September 1915, and Vimy Ridge, scene of David's near-fatal accident.

Then it was back to England to resume work. But by the time they left England in late October 1927, the book was still in draft form only; it had become a logistical and managerial nightmare, an unwieldy mass of information without clear structure or definition. David enlisted the help of other contributors, finally admitting that it would be impossible for him to cover the whole range of subject matter. The new Professor of Geography at Sydney University, Griffith Taylor, prepared a chapter for the project, only to be faced with the need to rewrite much of his material after David mislaid part of Taylor's manuscript.

David himself continued to spread his effort, devoting time to a geological map and accompanying notes which were planned to be components of the larger book. In fact they were the only parts of the original project that David was to see published in his lifetime. The huge *Geological Map* (1931) and its *Explanatory Notes* (1932) were published to universal acclaim. They were printed in time for the ANZAAS meeting held in Sydney in August 1932, where many scientists were lavish in their praise of this monumental work, the most detailed map of its kind ever published. It was praised by colleagues as 'wonderfully illuminating'. Sir John Flett, Director of the Geological Survey of Great Britain, was quoted as saying, 'I do not know a finer map of such a wide expanse of country depicted geologically on such a scale. It is not only a scientific triumph, but very satisfactory also from a cartographic and aesthetic standpoint.'[14]

During those years of intense work for David, his wife took on a prominent public role in the Girl Guides. For many educated people at that time, hopes for a better society had faded under the impact of the Great War. Cara David's response was to turn towards the young and the promise that they embodied for the future. She had known the liberating power of education herself and was determined to help young girls gain access to a wide range of opportunities. Always a lover of an active, outdoor life, Cara became involved in the Girl Guides Association in Sydney from 1922. Her involvement with this movement shows us her continuing zest for life well into her later years. It also reveals quite clearly that she was loved and widely honoured by those who knew her in the movement.

Robert Baden-Powell founded the Boy Scouts Association in

England after his return from the South African War, where he had noticed the poor level of bushcraft and general fitness of the men serving in the ranks. In 1907, he held a camp to train schoolboys to 'be prepared' to meet all the challenges life might throw at them. The Scouting movement aimed to develop in boys the habits of observation, obedience and self-reliance, teaching them skills and services useful to others and helpful for their own development. The first Scouting rally, held at the Crystal Palace in London in 1909, attracted 11,000 Boy Scouts – and also a few girls who wanted to join the movement. In 1910, Baden Powell decided to set up a separate movement for girls, calling it Girl Guides. The values and laws of the movement were similar to those of the Scouts. Guides promised to do their best to be cheerful, loyal and trustworthy citizens, to be helpful to others, to care for the natural world, to be adventurous and physically active and ready to have a go at mastering a whole range of challenging skills and activities. Being true to the spirit of its time, both Scouts and Guides emphasized the need for loyalty to the King, and all members were expected to belong to some religious body and attend its services.

The Girl Guides started in New South Wales in August 1910, with similar groups starting in Tasmania and Victoria but going into recess during the war. In September 1921, twenty-three girls 'made their promise' at Government House in the presence of their first Commissioner, the Governor's wife, Dame Margaret Davidson. Cara David began work with the movement as a Division Commissioner in the Northern Suburbs of Sydney in 1922. In 1928, with the resignation of the then Commissioner, Lady Cullen, Cara (known by then as Lady David) was chosen for the position of State Commissioner and Chairwoman of the Executive Council of the movement.

Cara was an ideal choice for such a position. She had proved to be a natural leader from her early days in the colony: educated, adventurous and self-confident, with a gift for public speaking and for capably running committees. She held progressive views on diet, nutrition

Chief Commissioner Cara David with friends

and outdoor exercise, and shared in the awakening recognition among some Australians that their country was a unique and beautiful place in which to live. She valued self-reliance and believed that all in a community needed to make some contribution to society. Above all, she had a proven record of commitment to education for young women.

In 1931, an anonymous benefactor offered the Guides association twenty acres of bushland at Turramurra, on the condition that the site was to be named in honour of his mother, Mary Everard. He was identified after his death as Donald Frederick Milne. It was an attractive gift and a beautiful piece of land but the executive saw the drawbacks of establishing a training camp there. The site had no running water, no electricity or telephone, and was reached by rough, unmade roads. However, Cara David had both the vision and the determination to advance the project. It was largely due to her that the decision was made to accept the donation. Perhaps her own pioneering experience of establishing a home on a few acres in Woodford gave her the confidence to say 'yes' to this gift.

The following year brought further challenges. The adjoining property, Glengarry, was for sale and was a very appealing piece of real estate. It would provide another twenty acres of land for the training camp, in a magnificent location, with city water laid on and three buildings ready for use. The bush overlooked Ku-ring-gai Chase, which is part of the remnant coastal sandstone bush of pre-white settlement, too rugged even now to be overtaken by suburban development.

The decision to go ahead with a major property purchase would have been a very difficult one for the Guides executive to make, and for Cara especially, who knew what a risk it would be for the organization to be in debt at such a time, in the midst of the Great Depression. A gift from the Walter and Eliza Hall Trust helped and that money, together with the association's own funds, made the purchase possible. The funds were raised at least in part by voluntary efforts among the branches. An enormous 'badge display' was held at the Sydney retail store, Mark Foys, in May 1933 and ran for a week. It was entitled 'See What Girl Guides Can Do'. There were continuous demonstrations of some of the skills and hobbies which Guides were pursuing, and these ranged from spinning and weaving to lace-making, cooking and the mastery of Braille. The public paid to enter and the funds raised during the week enabled the mortgage on Glengarry to be discharged. The professor of course had supported his wife throughout the project, and was often seen at the Glengarry site: he chose a suitable area where the creek running through the property could be dammed to make a splendid swimming pool.

Glengarry was officially dedicated on 21 October 1933, on a bright spring day enlivened by a tempering breeze and the scent of wildflowers. Hundreds of Guides, Rangers and Brownies trekked from

Turramurra station along Bobbin Head Road and down the rough track that led to the property. The dedication ceremony, with its mix of orthodox Christian rites and older symbolism, bore the imprint of Cara David's own eclectic approach to religion. Two of the children scattered corn on the camp site, as a symbol of Growth and Plenty; then salt, symbolizing Truth and Friendship. Lastly, oil was poured on the site as a symbol of Peace and Goodwill. A Prayer of Dedication was read to the 'Great Maker of the Universe' followed by the Lord's Prayer and the singing of the National Anthem. Like her husband, Cara saw the natural world as a great teacher of the young, and her own deepest sentiments seemed to be expressions of that Deism which David also accepted. Both of them, however, were also quite comfortable voicing orthodox Christian beliefs on public occasions.

In her address to the gathering, Cara expressed thankfulness and pride that the property had been fully paid for before the dedication took place. She reminded the listening girls of the need to avoid indebtedness, which she saw as a form of slavery, her words coloured by the sentiments of the time: 'We do not mind being servants; service is part of our work, but we do object to being slaves, because we are Britons'. She expressed gratitude for the beautiful expanse of native bushland now under their care (and which was soon to become a bird sanctuary). After the dedication service, Cara David spread her arms wide. 'Go now,' she told the girls, 'and enjoy your beautiful property.'[15]

A further ceremony took place at Glengarry the following winter, when Cara opened a set of gates that had been erected at the front of the property in appreciation of a past Guide leader, Margaret Radford, who was leaving the movement to join an Anglican religious order. Again the ceremony had Cara's particular stamp on it, as she drew attention to the gates as symbolic of the life choices young people needed to make, choosing 'kindliness and laughter … the spirit of life and adventure'. On a more pragmatic note, she reminded the listening Guides of the need to 'have other interests beside Guiding … a knowledge of the world and of social life and the work other people are doing in the world'.[16]

Cara David was nearly eighty years old when she handed in her resignation from the role of commissioner in 1938. Yet until the end she was still actively leading the movement despite increasing pain from arthritis and other infirmities that had crept up on her. She attended camps across the state every year and in 1933 she pitched her tent along with the younger staff and the girls at the All-Australia camp at Jamberoo. In December that year she went on a motor trip right around the coast from Sydney to Adelaide and back, visiting branches along the way. Generally she spent about three days every week on Guides business, and when not involved with that still did a considerable amount of domestic work and gardening at Coringah, their Hornsby home, getting up at first light in the summer to put in two or three hours in the garden. In late 1937, she wrote a letter to all the Guides groups encouraging them to get involved in the project planned for the state's 150th anniversary in 1938. This was to be a tree-planting project, with each branch exhorted to organize the planting of suitable trees in their own community. Cara kept a close watch on this project, providing practical horticultural advice to many groups. In April 1938, she helped plant an avenue of oaks at Milton Road, Turramurra, near the training camp. The trees had all been donated by the retail merchant, Anthony Horderns.

In 1934, Cara David was given the award of the Silver Fish, the highest honour which could be bestowed by the Imperial Headquarters of the Guides. In January 1937, she was invited to a gathering of senior Guides (known as Rangers) at Glengarry, where she was surprised and delighted to find a sundial had been created in her honour with the initials CMD inscribed on it.

The NSW Guides journal, *The Waratah*, contains many references to the positive influence of Cara David on many of its members. It refers to her gift of humour, her empathy with young people and her commitment: 'all the rich fruits of her life's experiences are given to the movement'.[17] There are glimpses in the journal of joyous events that she shared in at the Glengarry campsite. In November 1934, a Sunday service on 'a glorious afternoon of wind and sun' saw Cara David preside with prayers and an address on the Guide Law: appropriately, considering her life's history, the talk was about caring for the 'sisterhood' of guides irrespective of their race or religion. In the evening a campfire was lit – an early 'Christmas tree fire' – and the group sang carols in that bushland setting. 'A cloudless sky, a brilliant moon and a high wind, songs and good fellowship ... What more could we ask of life?' enthused the editor.[18] The high spirits of the young people gathered round her must have caused Cara David moments of poignant grief: her husband of forty-nine years had died just two months before this.

12   Loss. Cara's Later Years

Edgeworth David died in harness, working on his great project right to the end. After his retirement in 1924, he had been able to retain his room at the university to continue work on *The Geology of the Commonwealth of Australia*. As his arthritis, spreading from the damaged hip throughout his body, became increasingly painful, he could no longer walk the half mile to Hornsby station and Molly would drive him to Waitara station, where a quicker trip to the city was now possible over the newly completed Harbour Bridge.

On Monday 20 August 1934, David set out on his accustomed journey. From the city he took a tram along Parramatta Road to the university, but alighting at the usual stop, he fell. Struggling to his feet and claiming to be unhurt, he climbed the stairs to his room and collapsed. He was taken to the nearby Prince Alfred Hospital, where he was to die eight days later.

The record of those last days is preserved for us in a series of letters which Margaret McIntyre wrote to her husband. She was not to be present at her father's death, reaching Sydney the day after he died. Arriving in Melbourne from Tasmania early on Tuesday 28 August, she was told it was doubtful that he would live through the day. While passing the anxious hours that day waiting for the night train to Sydney, she learnt that her father had died: the front page of an evening paper, glimpsed in a man's hand in the street, had a photo of Edgeworth David's 'smiling face' – and the news of his death.

Margaret arrived too late to say goodbye to her father, but David was nevertheless surrounded in his last days by a close and loving family. Margaret's eldest son, Archie, was in his final year of undergraduate Medicine at the university. Just twenty-one years old, he took on responsibility for family decisions surrounding his grandfather's final days and stayed with him constantly during the last thirty-six hours, feeding him and administering oxygen. Archie decided not to immediately summon his mother from Launceston as David was lapsing in and out of consciousness and he thought it would be very distressing for her to watch her father as he struggled increasingly with breathing problems. After she did reach Sydney, Archie gave her a full account of her father's last days, which she wrote down in detail for Bill. Archie marvelled at the courage of this frail old man, keeping his sense of humour and his courtesy right to the end. Captain Evans of the *Nimrod* came to visit him on the Saturday, and David, whose mind had begun to wander a little, was so thrilled that his strength and clarity of mind came back and he talked at length and in accurate detail with Evans about Raymond Priestley, his co-worker during the Antarctic mission and afterwards.

Cara – Mootie to Margaret and Archie – was there of course during those days at the hospital, but in her anxiety and grief she found herself taking directions from her grandson, who seemed to have an understanding of what was wanted that belied his youth. He was present with Molly and Mootie when David spoke to them for the last time. David had been more or less unconscious all Monday, but in the afternoon opened his eyes wide. In Margaret's words to Bill:

Archie said it shook him to see that sudden bright intense gaze.

[Father] looked full at Mootie and said 'Bless you!' to her – it was a great comfort to her. Later that evening he rallied for a minute or two, and looking at Mootie, gasped out 'Are you all right?' and she said yes, and he turned his head to Arch, and said 'are you all right?' and when they asked him how he was feeling, he said very clearly and emphatically, 'Everything is all right' – after that he lapsed into unconsciousness and didn't speak again.

If the family's grief was private, their sense of loss contained and expressed within the close family circle, nevertheless the wider community wanted to be able to share in a more public expression of mourning at the death of this most loved and revered Australian. David was given a state funeral by the Commonwealth and State governments at St Andrew's Cathedral, next to Sydney's Town Hall, on Thursday 30 August 1934. The funeral procession led from the cathedral down Sydney's main thoroughfare of George Street to the Harbour Bridge, the streets lined with the largest crowd ever seen in Sydney for such an occasion. A second, military service was conducted at the Northern Suburbs Crematorium in Ryde, David's coffin draped with the tunnellers' flag which his company had carried to Flanders in 1916. Chopin's 'passionately tragic funeral march' and the traditional muffled drums accompanied the coffin on the last half mile of its journey.

Margaret was anxious about how her mother would stand up to the strain of such a public occasion, whose very solemnity and orchestrated ritual seemed to emphasize the extent of her loss. However, she was able to report to Bill that Mootie was 'really wonderful and keeping up well' and that the 'beautiful service and princely honours done [to Father] helped her a lot'. Margaret felt that her father would have loved the dignity of the occasion; she knew that 'it was a fitting end to his wonderful life'.

Public obituaries and tributes, local, national and international, flooded in, reflecting the affection and reverence which David had inspired and his eminent stature as a scientist, teacher, explorer and soldier. Mootie treasured them all, both the personal letters of sympathy and the newspaper cuttings which she collected in a scrapbook. Some of the tributes expressed in a very personal way the kind of man she had lost. Raymond Priestley, honouring in later life his friend and mentor, recalled David's gentle nature: 'what a peach of a father and a grandfather he must have been! He returned from preaching at the local church in the Blue Mountains to keep a family of hairless young mice by feeding them warm water dropped from a camel hair's brush.'[1] A former geology student recalled university excursions with the eminent professor, who took off his hat 'to ask the way of a little bare-legged, bareheaded, ragged country girl'. Dorothy Taylor, former student of David, paid for a stained-glass window to be built in Mosman Congregational Church, bearing the words 'Beloved

The central window dedicated to Edgeworth David, Mosman Uniting (formerly Congregational) Church (Author's photo)

Teacher and Worker in Science'.[2] Miners from Maitland wrote their tributes to him, and the Tunnellers also, who continued to meet for a reunion every June. David had been with them a few months before his death when they had gathered at the Cenotaph in their yearly act of remembrance. Bent almost double by rheumatism and leaning on two sticks, David had still gathered the strength to stand upright and in his beautiful voice recite 'For the Fallen'.

The family treasured their own memories. Billy had not returned to Australia since the war, caught up as he was with his own troubles, but he must have been conscious of the great gap his father's death had caused in the family's life. He had seen very little of his father after leaving university but in their last years together father and son for the first time found common ground in the horror and comradeship of the war. For Margaret, 'so close in soul' to David, the sight in the hallway at Hornsby of his old felt hat was almost more than she could bear, summoning up so clearly the father she remembered.

Margaret's younger daughter, fourteen-year-old Anne, wrote a gravely worded letter to her grandmother: 'I am proud to be a person that has his blood in my veins'. Anne later distilled her childhood memories into poetry:

> ... an old man
> with white hair and a limp and a strong
> young voice full of poems and a seven-year-old
> small girl with fat legs beside him, spellbound
> at his tales filled
> with penguins, seals and storms in a cold white
> country where it was always light
> in summer, always cold ...[3]

Cara David decreed that there was to be no period of official mourning for her husband, and after a few weeks of rest in the privacy of her home she was back working at her Girl Guides duties. A campaign got under way by the Sydney newspaper, *Truth* – much to Cara's indignation– reporting that Edgeworth David's widow had been left with few resources and that the government should create a special life pension for her. 'I will *not* go on the dole!' was her response to this suggestion.

Life inevitably narrowed as her physical mobility declined. After David's death, Cara found the solitude of Coringah too much to bear; after about six months the house was let and she moved into an upstairs bedroom in the house further up the slope which had been built for their unmarried daughter, Molly. Before Cara moved she decided that she must still have a workroom of her own where she could follow her hobbies of spinning, weaving, bookbinding and pottery-making, and so for the last time in her life she started building operations. 'The Growlery', a detached flat to the rear of Molly's house, was built by a capable carpenter as a comfortable retreat for Cara who, in her eighties, still retained a great deal of physical and intellectual energy. She still made all the jam for the household and also the wholemeal bread, a tradition of skilful 'housewifery' that would be carried on by her daughters and granddaughter, Anne. Molly recalled coming into her workroom one day to find her mother stirring marmalade with one hand and holding a volume of Shakespeare in the other. She had just finished reading a novel about Richard III and was looking up Shakespeare's version to compare the two.

With the coming of war Molly and Mootie did what they could on the home front while living quietly in Hornsby. Mootie, increasingly immobilized by arthritis in the hip, continued to be an assiduous supporter of the Girl Guides Association and knitted items for them to sell at their shop in Parramatta. Letters to friends and family became a lifeline. She was especially close to Archie McIntyre and his artist wife, Anne. She confessed to Archie that 'I don't appreciate this slowing down and weakness. After such a busy life it is a trying experience. I lie about and knit and read and think and pray – no use to anyone.'

On other days she saw her life in a different perspective, warmed by memories of the past. Receiving a postcard picture of the chapel at Whitelands College from an old friend of those years, Mootie wrote back, 'it's pleasant to look back on the hard work I had in the Chelsea days – but I'm not anxious to re-live it. My varied life gives me heaps to think about now that I must soon leave it – and it is on the whole pleasant thinking.' [4]

When war broke out, Billy David enlisted in England as a doctor in one of the administrative arms as he was too old for overseas service. The job was no sinecure: he had plenty of experience of bombing raids and V2s in the course of his duties around England. By that stage Billy had left Marjorie and his daughter, who was now grown up and earning her own living. Determined to move back to Australia, he had first to see out the war years in England and the requirements of his war service to qualify for a pension. Receiving his discharge at the end of the war, he returned to Australia in time for his mother's ninetieth birthday party. He planned to set up house with his sister and mother in Hornsby. Inevitably, there was discord. In the thirty years he'd been away, Billy David had changed from a tall and reserved young man to a large, stout, bald individual with a rather overbearing voice and manner, developed when trying to cope with the disharmony and deep unhappiness that marked his family life. Anne Edgeworth recalled her uncle as having a bluff 'club room' manner and holding very conservative opinions which he defended loudly. Underneath this manner she found him to be an affectionate and generous individual whom she was able to turn to from time to time for advice and help.

It soon became clear to Cara David that the house-sharing by the three of them would not work. She offered Billy his own house, one of the properties that she had acquired over the years as investments for the family. Haldane was a house on the bank of Tarban Creek at Hunters Hill, a quiet and leafy peninsula jutting out into the western reaches of the harbour. Billy set himself up there and found work as a consultant specialist at Repatriation House in the city until he retired in the 1960s. A woman who lived in the vicinity recalls travelling home as a student in the 1950s on an evening ferry, when Dr David would be met at the wharf by a cheerful bus driver. Somewhat the worse for drink, the doctor would be helped on the bus and dropped off at his residence.[5] Billy still made a weekly visit to Hornsby to have dinner with his sister, washed up the dishes for her and then caught a taxi home.

The Davids, all three of them enmeshed in the small domestic dramas involved in getting along, were to face together a great trial in 1948, when Margaret McIntyre was killed in a plane crash on her way back to Sydney from Brisbane.

For Cara, life closed in even more after her daughter's death. Still mentally alert, her physical strength had declined to the point where with two arthritic hips she could no longer come downstairs to her workroom. Instead she would travel down the passage from her bedroom to the northern balcony where she retired for the day to a bed in a sheltered corner, looking out over the treetops and open sky to what was still a suburb of bird life and plenty of bushland. She still knitted and enjoyed what she called a 'pretty love story' – one which, as her daughter noted with amusement, meant to her generation one that had no mention of sex in it. Something of the spirit and wit that had marked the younger Cara David was still present in the ninety-four-year-old woman who wrote this letter to an English friend:

I can still read and write and knit and as Molly says my tongue is in quite good order. So you can see I'm not calling for pity … I'm afraid this is a jerky and tiresome letter – you'll be a saint and make allowances for a chattering old bird who is of course left alone for a fair amount … here endeth a wail!!![6]

Cara David died on Christmas Day 1951. According to Molly's

account of her last hours, her mother's passing seems to have been in the end one of acceptance, and a consciousness of love given and received. She breathed the name 'Tweddy', the term of endearment she had always used for David but had not uttered since the time of his death. Then she spoke Margaret's name and said slowly, with a light of happiness in her eyes, 'I think I know now ...' The next day her breathing became laboured. She 'suddenly became physically aware that the last enemy was at hand, and told me with fear in her eyes that she was dying'. The young family doctor, seeing her distress, put her under sedation. Billy David, Molly and Margaret's husband, Bill, were with her when she died the following day.

Mootie, to those who loved her, had been at the very centre of their family life. Molly found that, with her passing, 'all strength and stability seemed to leave my life'. David was the storyteller, the romantic weaver of tales with a gift for language and history: he brought alive for his children the rich imaginative world of poetry and literature and inspired them to believe in a world where great and honourable deeds were still possible. But their mother was the practical, energetic manager around whom home life revolved: she organized the parties, the welcome meals for visitors, the network of women who gathered to learn knitting from her during the war. It was Cara who gathered friends around her to plan the speeches, letterboxing and demonstrations that marked her wide involvement with feminist causes. She was the one who planned extensions to their dwellings, who laid out orchards and vegetable gardens. Till her very last years she was happy to stand in front of a crowd and inspire them to take up a cause worth living for. In the later years, this was essentially the Guides movement. 'What a warm-hearted, out-going person she was! And how quick to help lame dogs over stiles!' Molly wrote in later years. Molly could appreciate the contrast in temperaments and outlook between her parents and gives an account of an evening at home, when David was reading poetry to the children. After a moving rendition of Tennyson's 'Crossing the Bar' and in the contemplative silence that followed, Mootie, who disapproved of the display of emotion, pondered out loud, 'I think I shall make a potato pie for supper out of the cold lamb'.

Cara and Archie, 1940s

Part 2: Margaret

13   Youth

Margaret, the first born, was her father's favourite child. '[You] are so like him in mind and soul,' wrote Cara to her daughter during the war years. In her adult years there was a great physical likeness also, in voice, face and manner. A Tunnelling officer who visited the family after David's death looked intently at Margaret and said, 'As long as *you* live there will always be a living image of him'.

David was absent for many of his children's infant years and must have missed out on many of the formative and endearing moments of their babyhood and childhood. One tender interaction with the young Margaret is recorded in a letter to his Aunt Sarah after they had first moved into the Gunyah and before David's work took the family back to Maitland in 1890. While still frantically busy with fieldwork that saw him travelling up and down the colony, David snatched treasured days at home with his wife and young child: drawing animals for little Margaret, singing her to sleep and playing with her in the garden at Ashfield. He wrote to his aunt that Margaret

goes toddling about the house with her feet set wide apart to ensure her balance, and follows her mother all about the house like a little floppy haired puppy, and imitates all she does and says. She was

Margaret Edgeworth David (NLA MS 8890)

grubbing with her little fingers in the dry earth of one of the flower beds. I said, not thinking she would understand, 'Madgie, bring some earth and put it down Daddy's neck' and the little monkey at once got a handful and toddled up to me where I was lying on the grass and poured the handful of dust over my head.

From her childhood Margaret seems to have been a calm and capable individual, with a degree of self-possession that her younger, more insecure sister never attained. When she was about thirteen, and in her mother's absence, she organized her younger siblings into a 'bucket brigade' to put out a fire that had broken out in the kitchen at Tyn-y-Coed. Molly recalled that Margaret as a child had a strong sense of justice, 'laying out the school bully, a boy older than herself' at the small 'dame school' they attended near Ashfield for a brief time. When she was about fourteen, Margaret gave evidence before a magistrate at Katoomba police court. The two sisters had been horrified witnesses to an act of animal cruelty when they came across a thin, underfed horse, straining to pull a cart out of a shallow ditch, being beaten by two men with lengths of barbed wire. The girls galloped home to report this incident and were later summoned to the station as witnesses. On Margaret's evidence the men were convicted and punished.

Most of the girls' schooling was done at home under the tutelage of their Scottish governess, Miss Wilson, who was with the family for seven years from 1896 until Margaret started university. They learnt to read and write while young, in a household full of books. Their father read them the classic European folk stories, translating from the German as he went along. Margaret later recalled a gift of *The Arabian Nights* on her ninth birthday from Aunt Sarah while the family was visiting England. She read the book straight through in a fortnight. Learning poetry by heart was an accepted and treasured part of their childhood schooling. In 1917, David wrote to his daughter from the Western Front, enclosing a daffodil he had picked outside the ramparts of an old fortress which was serving as General Headquarters. He recalled Wordsworth's 'Daffodils', 'which you used to recite so sweetly when quite a little girl with your charming variant "tossing their heads in sparkly dance". That was in the dear old days of the Gunyah, long ago.'

The girls' education was impressively thorough and allowed them both to sit for and pass the University of Sydney's matriculation exams at the same time, when Margaret was seventeen, Molly fifteen.

The David girls, Tyn-y-Coed (NLA MS 8890)

The initial plan had been for Margaret to study medicine. There is no record as to why she changed to the Faculty of Arts. David and Cara would have known only too well the pressures that female undergraduates had to cope with in the medical faculty at that time, and may have persuaded their daughter to change her mind. Margaret graduated with a Bachelor of Arts degree at the end of 1906, having majored in English, History and Palaeontology with units in Chemistry and Physics.

Margaret at Tyn-y-Coed (NLA MS 8890)

She met her future husband, William Keverall (Bill) McIntyre when they were both undergraduates. McIntyre was a student in the Department of Mining and Metallurgy. He also graduated at the end of 1906 with second-class honours in Metallurgy and shared Professor Liversidge's Prize for Practical Metallurgy and Assaying.

Cara, hearing word of her daughter's new interest, was not impressed. Perhaps she found the young undergraduate too

Margaret's graduation, 1907

cocky; not good enough for her daughter. Letters written from Woodford had a hearty tone that did not quite conceal the painful anxiety underneath. 'Take my advice and don't monopolize all that young man's recreation time … I like him so much except when I think of him as a prospective son-in-law. If you are not sensible enough to get over this romance you'll have to go away from a real beast of a mother-in-law.' She called herself, 'Your loving though cantankerous Mum'. Margaret confessed in a letter to Bill in November 1906 that her mother had 'done everything in her power, till very lately, to set me against you … she was very afraid of my making a mistake'. Cara herself acknowledged to Margaret that her own 'ghastly, brutal candour' had got in the way and led her to say and write hurtful and critical things about the young man. Perhaps her negativity was due in part to not having a husband at home to consult about a topic that weighed so heavily on her heart.

From May till November of that year, David was travelling

abroad, initially to India, England and the United States and then to the international geological congress in Mexico. It was an exciting and intellectually stimulating trip for David and placed him firmly in the forefront of international geology with a paper he delivered at the congress. Margaret reported that her father, returning in early November 1906, was 'chock full of stories and adventures' about his trip. Conscious of her mother's disapproval of Bill, Margaret waited anxiously for her beloved father's impression of the young man. However, '[all] my apprehensions vanished when I saw his angelic old face again and I nearly wept with joy at having him back.' David arranged an interview with Bill, in the accepted way, to learn his future intentions. The young man was no callow, youthful undergraduate: he was five years older than Margaret and had seen service in the South African War, having enlisted as a nineteen-year-old with the Tasmanian Bushmen contingent in 1900. After returning from South Africa, Bill worked as a junior hand at the Beaconsfield goldmine in northern Tasmania before moving to Sydney to do a three-year Bachelor of Engineering course. He was hoping to establish himself in the mining profession and marry Margaret once he could offer her some economic security. The parents agreed to a formal engagement in January 1907, before Bill left to take up a job as mining assayer at Waratah in north-west Tasmania.

Cara seems to have recognized in her daughter a determination and a strength of spirit that she came to admire. Certainly Cara seems to have made her peace with Bill after this, and in fact she was quick to defend the couple when an acquaintance asked her whether she 'would allow her daughter to marry on less than £300 a year'. Cara's retort was spirited and heart-felt: 'I'd let her marry him on 2½ pence a week if she had grit enough to do it!'

During the two years that were to pass before their marriage, Margaret and Bill were to see each other only once. David's Antarctic adventure intervened and affected the lives of the whole family.

Edgeworth David with Molly, Margaret and group, on a mine excursion in Tasmania. Bill McIntyre second from right, next to Molly

After her graduation, Margaret was planning to do a nursing course at her mother's suggestion: no doubt Cara, anxious for her daughters to have other options than an early marriage and 'domestic slavery' (as she termed it), saw nursing as a useful and worthwhile career. However, after David's departure for the south in December 1907, Margaret cancelled the nursing plans and came up to stay with her mother at Tyn-y-Coed for much of 1908. The twenty-one-year-old was acutely aware of her mother's state of mind and the loneliness and distress she was experiencing. A letter Margaret wrote to her father gave poignant expression to these worries but was remarkably free of self-pity. Written at the end of 1908, the letter was to be taken by the *Nimrod* as it sailed to meet the men after their year on the ice:

Daddy dear, we will be so thankful to have you back again, you have made a big blank in our lives this year, and I do hope you won't go away again for such a long time – it has been a great strain on poor

Mootie, and we have been very anxious about her several times. Your letter [about not returning] came as a great shock to all of us, I have never seen anyone in such terrible grief as Mother was that day. She has been very ill on and off: insomnia, kidney trouble and nervous collapse … It really has been a big responsibility this year Daddy and sometimes I've felt it was very heavy for my shoulders.

Unwilling to leave her mother for any length of time, Margaret refused an invitation from Bill's family to spend Christmas 1908 with them in Tasmania. The only time she saw her fiancé before the wedding was for two weeks in June 1909, when she travelled down to stay in Tasmania at Waratah with Dr Faulkner and his wife, a couple who had befriended the young mining engineer and welcomed his fiancée into their home. She planned to stay with Bill's parents at Kaoota, near Hobart, for a few days on the way home.

The wedding took place in Sydney on 28 September 1909. The David family moved temporarily to Ashfield from Tyn-y-Coed in June 1909 to prepare for the event and the McIntyres travelled up from Tasmania. It was to be a fairly formal affair. Mrs McIntyre, from a prominent Hobart family and wife of a Tasmanian High Court judge, warned Margaret that 'dress *must* be considered'. Given the professor's well-known disregard for sartorial elegance and Cara's own aversion to costly display, it is likely that the David parents presented a proud but modest face to the world that day. Margaret's gown of soft white silk had been hand-embroidered by her mother and the groom wore his Boer War medals on his evening coat. The ceremony took place at the old stone church of St John's which was just across the road from the Gunyah. Cara's friends, in a nod to one of her main botanical interests, had decorated the church with spring wattle. The parents hosted a reception at the Gunyah after the ceremony.

After the wedding, the McIntyres left to take up married life in the remote tin mining settlement of Waratah below the tin mines of Mount

Group at Kaoota. Bill McIntyre's brother, Allan, with his son Keverall, Edgeworth David, John McIntyre, Molly and Margaret standing (NLA MS 8890)

Bischoff, an area of north-west Tasmania where the forests are mired in eighty inches of annual rain.

In its boom years in the late 1880s, Mount Bischoff was the world's richest tin mining operation. Tin had been discovered in 1871 in this wild and heavily timbered region of the state and from the start of production in 1875 the mine paid huge dividends to its shareholders. Very early after his arrival in New South Wales in 1882, the young Edgeworth David had noted in his diary, 'Bischoff Mine, Tasmania. Lode 30 foot wide contains 45% of tinstone!! Jumbo shares more than 100 times their original value.'[1] A town, named Waratah after the abundant wildflowers that bloomed in the region during its brief summer, sprang up at the south-eastern base of the mountain, which soon became scarred by open-cut workings and denuded of its tall timber. At the height of its prosperity, Waratah had several hundred houses, about fifteen shops, a post office and bank, a school, a town hall and school of arts and three hotels (one a temperance hotel). When Margaret and Bill arrived there were well over 2000 people living in the district, with the mine's workforce estimated at about 1000.

Mount Bischoff provided a career opening for a young mining graduate and it wasn't long before Bill earned his mine manager's certificate and a greater level of responsibility on the job. Wilhelm Kayser, the manager of the Mount Bischoff mines, oversaw the operations and the township, introducing modern milling technology and better processing of the ore. As the virtual manager of the whole town and the major employer, Kayser lived with his family in comfort in a gracious timber house with wide verandahs and a pretty garden. With a constant eye on the need for good dividends to the shareholders, Kayser would not tolerate slackness or inefficiency. Unionism was non-existent and men could be sacked for lateness to work. While newcomers flocked there for work, the conditions on the job were primitive and dangerous. Men on the open-cut mines worked for nine hours, with a half-hour break for 'crib' (lunch), in the teeth of bitterly cold south-westerlies and driving snowfalls. No wet-weather gear was provided by the management; the men had to provide their own. While most of the work was open-cut mining, underground reserves of tin on the seemingly inexhaustible Brown Face of the mountain were being tapped by an adit, or tunnel, which would eventually bore right through the mountain. Men worked in pairs underground, one to drill holes while the powder monkey laid the sticks of gelignite. After diving for cover during the explosion, the men returned to the rock face to dig out the broken rock, which was loaded into hoppers to be taken down on an aerial ropeway to the crushing mill. The perils of setting and detonating dynamite in close quarters were increased tenfold by the fact that the men worked by candlelight, even into the twentieth century. 'Miners' disease' (either silicosis or tuberculosis caused by dust in the lungs) was prevalent. Terrible accidents were common and the miners' families had to cope with a brutal climate and poor sanitation, with outbreaks of diphtheria and typhoid carrying off young and vulnerable children.

Nevertheless, for hardy and resourceful families the place held much promise: there was a strong community life and a great wilderness at their doorstep where men and boys enjoyed the chance to go hunting, fishing and camping. No doubt many of the men earned high wages that set them up for the future in more settled regions of the state.

The Davids and their daughter expected that Bill's stay at Mount Bischoff would be relatively brief. Planning their life together, Margaret was glad to hear that a five-roomed cottage had been found for them in the township. She looked forward to making curtains but 'we don't want to get any furniture worth mentioning, even if we have to stay at Mount Bischoff a while after we're married'. She enquired hopefully as to whether Bill was reading *The Australian Mining Standard*, where a range of jobs might be on offer.

By the autumn of 1910, Margaret was pregnant, with the baby expected at the end of the year.

Anxious to see how her daughter was faring, Cara took a ferry across Bass Strait in September 1910. It would have been a rough trip. A boat travelled round the coast to the port of Burnie and from there a company train snaked up through the mountains and over the deep river gorges to Waratah. What Cara saw of the township can hardly have reassured her. Row after row of miners' cottages faced each other across the muddy roads. The cottages were slab timber, their shingle roofs high-pitched to keep them waterproof and to disperse the winter snows. At least timber was plentiful in the nearby forests and every cottage kept its indoor fires burning during the day, sending spirals of wood smoke into the still air. Burnt skeletons of great trees, victims of past bushfires, stood between the town and the southern face of the mountain which was scarred raw with mullock heaps and marked by dirty patches of snow that lay for months after the winter. Well beyond the settlement the dark wet forests of the Tasmanian highlands began.

The hours were marked by the wail of the siren summoning men to work in the morning and by the noise of the stamper batteries breaking up the ore in the works below the town. During her visit, Cara must have reflected on her own pioneering days of marriage to a mining surveyor and the muggy warmth and sunlit spaces of the Hunter Valley where she camped with David. What a benign place it would have seemed in contrast to this desolate southern landscape.

The baby girl was born on 22 October 1910, shortly after Cara had returned to Sydney. David left for England in early December; he was taking his Antarctic lectures to England during the university long vacation to raise funds for a planned new expedition, to be led by Douglas Mawson. Molly was accompanying him to see something of 'Home'.

The news from Tasmania frightened Cara: Margaret was dangerously ill with puerperal fever after an incompetent doctor delivered her baby at Mount Bischoff. The McIntyres' kindly friend, Dr Faulkner, had retired from medical practice in 1909, after ten years of service to the mining community that had earned him the love and respect of the locals. The new doctor may have been a locum. Most babies in the town were delivered at home with a midwife in attendance; Margaret and her baby might well have been in better hands with one of these experienced local women.

Cara rushed south again straight away and arranged for Margaret and the baby to come back with her to Sydney to convalesce under her care. Bill came too of course. 'How we had to work and fight together to save Margot [her pet name for her daughter],' she recalled. Peggy, her first grandchild, always had a special place in her heart after this. Perhaps those vigils by her daughter's bedside also drew Cara closer to her son-in-law, as they both nursed the young woman who was so central to their happiness. Her letters to Bill after this certainly suggest a warm relationship.

David returned from England in March 1911 to find his wife 'quite broken down with anxiety' from the days and nights of nursing.

The Davids were horrified at the risks their eldest child was running at Mount Bischoff. Before the marriage they had sounded out the possibility of work for Bill in England, asking Ned Touche whether he knew 'of any good billets knocking about your way for such a young fellow to start on'. By 1911, mining jobs were few and far between in Australia due to labour unrest. Accordingly Cara and David persuaded Bill to accept a loan of money from them and travel to Edinburgh to undertake a medical degree.[2] Cara explained this decision in a letter to Touche. 'My ... son-in-law has always preferred medicine to mining but had drifted into mining through casual circumstances. A mining engineer has either to leave his wife much alone or take her to unhealthy and sordid and miserable townships ... I would rather have a strong daughter in Edinburgh than a frail one here.'

14 Scotland

Margaret, Bill and the baby were to leave by the *Orontes* on 10 June 1911. A Sydney doctor had warned that Margaret had used up all her strength in fighting the obstetric crisis and needed to live for a couple of years in 'a cold bracing climate': this was a common prescription among doctors at the time for any number of medical conditions. Edinburgh was to prove a friendly and invigorating place for the family to live.

By September they were settled in a flat in Marchmont Street in central Edinburgh, with Molly there to help them settle in. Margaret told her mother that they were charmed by the gracious old city. She felt in better health than she had for a year, having put on weight and regained a hearty appetite. She assured her mother that this was partly due to the healthy diet the family was following, based on whole grains, vegetables and fresh fish. She described the simple but wholesome food that at that time formed the basis of the Scottish diet: lovely oatcakes and scones, a rich variety and abundance of fresh fish, plenty of dried and fresh vegetables. But fruit, she confessed, was very expensive and most cuts of meat were only for the wealthy. She was convinced that they'd be able to live quite cheaply: the children's clothing, of course, would be made at home, and knitting, darning and 'making do' were skills she'd learnt from her mother.[1] Their little daughter, Peggy, was proving a source of delight and fascination to the young parents and Margaret pleaded with 'dear Gran' to try her best to come for a visit, possibly accompanying Billy on an undergraduate trip that Christmas. This was not to happen, but Molly stayed with her sister until her return to Australia in early 1912. The Davids' old friend, Ned Touche, lived in Edinburgh with his wife, Sally, and their infant son, John, and they were to prove a great support to the young Australian couple.

Bill had before him the challenge of a four-year medical degree at the University of Edinburgh, renowned worldwide for the excellence of its medical school. They would not be easy years: the family budget was tight as they were living on their allowance from the Davids and on their few savings. By the next year, Margaret was pregnant again: the baby boy, Archibald McIntyre, was born on 1 May 1913. There must have been many broken nights and anxious days as the infants went through the usual range of childhood fevers and maladies. Bill had to juggle the claims of family life and study, with lectures and laboratory work, a heavy reading program and practical experience in a dispensary in an Edinburgh slum area. There would have been little time left over for helping his wife with child-rearing. Yet both husband and wife were to look back on those four years with pride and affection as some of the best years of their life, sustained as they were by love, hard work and good friends.

Most of our knowledge of the McIntyres' life in Scotland comes from the letters Margaret wrote to her family during those years. They provide a picture of a loving and hopeful family life upon which the coming of war left its inevitable mark. The shock and disillusion with which later generations were to view the Great War inevitably colours the way we read this material. Margaret's letters are full of delight in her growing children, pride in her husband's work and strong affection for her Australian family whose fortunes she was to follow closely. The letters are also expressions of the loyalties, idealism and prejudices of the late Edwardian age, one where war aims and official propaganda were accepted wholeheartedly, where religious sentiments found expression in the service of militarism and where the enemy was demonized and dismissed from considerations of pity.

When war broke out, Bill was tempted to enlist straight away as a private; his own loyalties to the Empire ran deep, as his service in the South African War had shown. But that would have meant abandoning his medical course and, with it, the promises he had made to his wife and her family, and the deep obligation he felt to the Davids for their financial and moral support. Instead, he promptly joined an Officer Training Corps attached to the university and began training at weekends with them. He was soon promoted to sergeant major. By early 1915, the end of his studies was in sight: he planned to sit for the final exams in June that year, though he confessed to Margaret that the amount of reading to be got through for his exams appalled him.

The months leading up to June were a stressful time for the family. Bill's long hours at the books gave him badly inflamed eyes which he needed to rest completely for a week, time he could ill spare before the finals. Margaret spent the evenings after the babies were put to bed reading aloud to him from his textbooks in the hope that the material would be retained. An added pressure on the family was the need to find new living quarters as the lease on their flat ran out at the end of May. After packing up the flat, Margaret took a small cottage at Elie, a village in Fife on the east coast, for the month of June while Bill stayed in Edinburgh for the exams. They had made good friends with a Presbyterian elder and his wife and family, the Ritchies, who kindly took Bill into their home for the month and looked after him like a son. Bill came to stay at Elie after his exams were over, the first holiday he had had for four years.

Neither of them expected him to pass the finals in June. First came the written exams and then the formidable hurdle of the clinical exams and interrogation by the departmental heads. The last clinical exam was on 17 June, which Margaret spent with the two infants at Elie, on a glorious sunny day with skylarks singing their hearts out in the nearby fields. The war was never far away though, with destroyers moving constantly up and down the Forth Estuary in search of German submarines. Billy David spent four days with his sister at Elie before his embarkation for France with his division on 21 June.

Bill passed all his written exams with second-class honours in Medicine and Surgery. The family's delight and relief was shared by the Davids, who cabled a letter of congratulation as soon as they heard. As her husband returned home with the results of his clinical exams, Margaret dared not look up from her knitting for fear of what she might read in his face. 'How does Dr Keverall McIntyre sound to you?' were his welcoming words.

Margaret expressed her relief and gratitude in a letter to Mootie, glad that her parents had not only suggested this undertaking but given them the means to carry it out. Bill wrote Mootie his own letter of thanks. 'When I think of the narrowing stuffy life in a mining township, I am truly grateful to you and the Professor.' He gave his promise to pay back the loan in full if he survived the war.

The graduation ceremony took place at the university in July. Margaret was able to travel to Edinburgh from the coast for the ceremony, leaving her children in the care of Ned and Sally Touche who had taken a large country house at Elie for the summer.

Then the serious business of the war took over. Bill travelled to London to receive his commission as a lieutenant in the Royal Army Medical Corps, then returned to Edinburgh to organize the OTC training camp. In August, the family moved to Wiltshire, to a small village on the edge of Salisbury Plain where Bill would be based at England's second biggest military encampment. The young family moved into a small but comfortable boarding house with upstairs rooms and their own dining facilities. Margaret was relieved to know she would not have to cope with two lively infants in a public dining room under the gaze of the other middle-aged residents of the house.

The midsummer days were muggy and enervating after the cooler climate of the north. Bill came over from his camp in the evenings if he was off-duty, but the weeks must have passed in a sad and lonely blur for Margaret, knowing the separation that was coming and with no family close by. Bill arranged an outing for his family as the day for departure drew nearer. A nearby public house was to send their motor car and driver to collect his wife and the children and take them for a trip to Stonehenge. Margaret, entranced by the spectacle and drama of the site, wrote home at length about it with illustrations of the stone circles. 'I longed to have an intelligent grown-up to discuss it with,' she confessed to Mootie. She was determined that when Bill left she would take the children back to Edinburgh where there were good friends and a purposeful community life. Meanwhile, she walked with Peggy and the baby's pram out along the country lanes as often as she could but discovered that it was 'not done' for an officer's wife to be seen in such a humble activity. Consequently, she wrote to Mootie, she had secured the services of a local girl to push Archie's pram. It was not the first or the last time that the David daughters were to find themselves out of step with English society. [2]

The war was everywhere. Recruiting posters covered every public wall; every day Margaret saw soldiers out on route marches along the dusty lanes, Red Cross motorcars going about their business and often a string of forty or fifty great transport vehicles lumbering down the road. Bill was the transport officer for the 80th Field Ambulance, overseeing transport wagons, fifty-five mules and horses plus the ambulances and men. It would be his responsibility to get them all safely to France. Another of his tasks was to teach the men in his unit to ride and handle horses: very few had any experience of this kind before they enlisted.

On 24 August, the directive finally came from the War Office: the 78th, 79th and 80th Field Ambulances were to join the 26th Division at Sutton Veny, a small village some twenty-one miles away. From there, after a review by the King, they would get ready for transport to Southampton and embarkation. Margaret took the children over to the railway line and they watched and waved as the long train chugged noisily past with its load of carriages, horseboxes and flat trucks on its way to Sutton Veny. Bill, hanging out the carriage window, waved until the three little figures disappeared from view.

'My old man and I intend to hang on to one another as long as we can,' Margaret assured Mootie, and with this in mind Bill arranged rooms for the family in a boarding house in the village. Margaret found she had the company there of Mrs Johnson, the wife of Bill's commanding officer, an Irishman for whom Bill had a great deal of respect. Benjamin Johnson had been in a German prison camp for six months and was still brusque and nervy at times. His wife, having no children to console her, dreaded the prospect of another separation. Her husband, unable to bear the idea of an emotional parting in public, refused to let her come up to the station when the division left for Southampton.

The families attached to the 26th Division, hundreds of them, had gathered at Sutton Veny to spend the last few days with their menfolk. They would all have known that this might be a final separation and most made their farewells in private. Bill asked Margaret to come down to the station at 8.30 in the evening for a brief farewell before the train pulled out. A young officer ran to meet her as she walked down to the station, entreating her to hurry as the train was moving off early. He ran with her along the line and across some low platforms to where the train was being shunted back to a siding. Mercifully, there was a delay – another truck load of mules to pick up. A hot mug of cocoa handed up to Bill at the train window and a brief clasping of hands was all that time allowed. Then the train was moving off into the summer evening, the railway lines lit by the glare of a fire burning near the tracks. The men on the train were singing. Margaret could not hear the words of the song but the grave and mournful melody drifted back to her on the wind.

The next day, with all her luggage and the two children, Margaret set out for Wales where she was to stay for a few weeks in her father's family home. Battling through the families crowding the station that hot midsummer day, she was glad that Bill had purchased first-class tickets for the three of them to Bristol. A brief stop at Bristol station to toilet and feed the children and then they caught the train to Cardiff. They arrived at Llandaff by taxi at six that evening. Margaret's nerves were on edge. She would have heard of the unpredictable temper of Aunt Ethel, and to make matters worse six-year-old Peggy was uncooperative and wilful, unsettled after months of boarding house life and the drama of the last few days. Archie was 'a perfect angel', however, and after a few days Aunt Ethel declared herself charmed by the young family. There was also a brief visit to Uncle Edmund and his wife and children who lived nearby.

By October, Margaret was settled in new lodgings, in a third-storey flat on Thirlstone Road, not far from their previous lodgings and close to the centre of Edinburgh. She wrote joyfully to her 'beloved Fambly' about its virtues. It was a roomy flat, its sense of space enhanced by the sunny southern aspect and the lovely view of the Pentland Hills. There was a sitting/dining room, three bedrooms, kitchen and bathroom, and the flat had the advantage of plenty of storage space and solid, old-fashioned furniture. There was a big nursery into which the sun poured that autumn and warmed their bodies and spirits. The children lived there, except when they were taken on their daily walks. Sally Touche had secured a maid for them, twenty-one-year-old Lizzie, who was inexperienced in domestic matters but keen to learn and who soon settled into the routine of getting up to light the fire, make porridge and help with the daily chores. Perhaps Lizzie's cooking efforts were not always successful: Margaret received a note from their neighbour in Thirlstone Road complaining that porridge had been thrown over the shrubbery in her front garden.

Margaret wrote to her mother of Bill's movements. By that stage he had been five weeks in France, based in a village not far from Villers-Bretonneux. It was a place inhabited by black-clothed widows and old men. 'God only knows the appalling grief and mental suffering of Europe during this war,' he wrote to Margaret.[3] Even the village children seemed subdued, with very little of the high spirits and larking about that he remembered from his own childhood days. The autumn weather turned rainy, cold and bleak while they were there, though his men had roomy barns to shelter in and he knew that conditions would have been infinitely worse for them in the trenches. Everyone expected that the division would soon be leaving for Egypt or the Mediterranean, and Bill was kept busy as transport officer seeing to provisions and equipment for the horses and mules. He tried his best to find shelter for all his animals, knowing the sickness and disability that would result if they were left on picket lines out in the wet and cold. He wrote to Margaret about the pitiful sight of other units' horses, standing all day in lines up to their knees in mud.

By 21 November, the division was on its way south to Marseilles, where they would embark for Greece. German and Bulgarian troops were expected to invade the country via the mountain ranges near Thessalonika (Salonika) once winter was over.

The journey that took them south by train from Amiens was nerve-racking and incident-filled. Bill wrote to Margaret about it as the train lumbered slowly through the darkened landscape. He sat wrapped in his overcoat and muffler in the freezing railway carriage, the stub of a candle flickering at his elbow. As transport officer he had responsibility for 50 trucks, 240 mules, 100 ambulance corps men, 13 ambulances and transport wagons. At one stage when they stopped, a mule, made violent by colic, had to be dragged out of its truck where it was endangering the other animals and their minders, and hauled up a gangway into a carriage of its own.

It was also Bill's job to deal with the French railway officials and guards who seemed to be singularly uncooperative. The officers had been given the times and places where the train would stop to take on water, and Bill arranged for the cooks to boil up tea for the men at one of the longer stops. The train, without warning, started pulling out early, and Bill had to yell to the men to race after the departing train and jump on board. Men who had been using the latrines were racing and yelling frantically while pulling up their trousers; the two cooks, bent over their steaming pots, did not even hear the summons and had to be left behind to catch a later train. Bill fumed to Margaret that his greatest frustration was his lack of demotic French with which to curse the French guards and their railway system.

The 26th Division's move to Salonika was delayed by submarine activity in the Mediterranean and they spent frustrating weeks at Marseilles, in a huge encampment at the city racecourse. Cold westerly winds – the dreaded Mistral – blew sand and dust through the camp. The men were bored to distraction and headed when they could for the fleshpots of the port city. The possibility of disease in that large encampment was also a constant worry for the medical staff. Bill told Margaret he had made himself a calico inner sheet as protection against the lice that lived in his woollen sleeping bag. Christmas was a bleak and lonely time, with photographs and gift parcels from home but only the morose presence of fellow officers to enliven the day. Bill reflected on the good fortune of earlier generations: his father and grandfather had lived out their full lives in peacetime.

The division finally left Marseilles on 9 January 1916, sailing towards Greece on a voyage where they were kept on high alert for submarines. A week later they had unloaded all the animals and set up camp on a great bare plain to the north of Salonika. It was bitterly cold in that mountainous region, the ring of hills around the town white with snow. The steep hills and gullies to the north were stony and treeless, with just a feeble cover of grass and heather. This was to be the range over which invasion was expected in the coming months and the division was holding one of the main defence lines into Salonika. Bill was to be based in this region for the remainder of the war.

Margaret knew that the division's transfer to the east meant that she would probably not see Bill again before the end of the war. Heartsick and lonely, she kept reminding herself that there were hundreds of thousands of women all over the world with these same anxieties, some with much worse troubles than hers. But she craved the comfort of her family nevertheless. 'I do wish you and Molly could come over and be with me while Dad [Bill] is away – there is plenty of room in this flat,' she wrote to Mootie. Later she rebuked herself for trying to persuade the two women to give up their commitment to running the soldiers' home at Woodford. Her father wrote from France to his 'dearest little daughter. Your old Dad does feel for you and your dear old man very deeply. It is hard, hard for young hearts to be parted so long.'

Margaret was befriended by kindly families, warm-hearted if somewhat austere Scottish Presbyterians who invited her into their homes and to Sunday services. Her friend, Dr Kelman, welcomed her into their church and Mrs Kelman asked Margaret along to a weekly church sewing circle, an offer she took up gratefully once she had a reliable girl to stay with the children. The Kelmans also invited her to help set up an Overseas Club for the many Anzacs on leave in Edinburgh. Margaret leapt at the chance to enjoy some adult company, to be of use to the war effort and to be involved in community activities.

The Ritchies were another Presbyterian family connected to the church. Their daughter, Ella, who was serving as a volunteer nurse at a nearby convalescent home for soldiers, became one of Margaret's close friends. Another in the circle was Dorothy Crerer, who lived near Thirlstone Road with her widowed mother and sister. Her friends invited Margaret to 'Shakespeare evenings' where they would have play readings in improvised costumes, followed by a convivial supper. Margaret played Romeo to Dorothy's Juliet, whom three-year-old

Archie called 'Jewelette'. Henceforth this became Margaret's lasting term of endearment for her friend.

Christmas 1915 offered few reasons for celebration to families touched by the war. Women put their efforts into comforts for the men abroad: Christmas parcels stuffed with hand-knitted socks and mittens, chocolate, stationery, cartons of cigarettes and sweets and copies of the popular weekly or monthly magazines. Margaret's Christmas box for Bill included a jar of New Zealand honey and a large plum pudding for him to share with his men. She wrote to Mootie of the collaborative effort this had been, with the children 'helping' to make the pudding and getting covered in flour in the process. Their mother allowed them

Peggy and Archie, Edinburgh 1916 (NLA MS 8890)

to drop little silver-plated novelties into the mixture which was then stirred in a giant basin and boiled for eleven hours. Peggy was ill the next day after she and her little brother, finding themselves alone in the kitchen, had made up a concoction of baking powder, sugar and mustard powder and eaten it.

By early 1916, Margaret had settled into life in the city, sharing with thousands of other wives the need to keep busy and purposeful for the sake of the children. 'I love Edinburgh and it suits the kiddies so well,' she wrote to Mootie. The young maid, Lizzie, was very fond of the children, caring for them on the evenings when Margaret had community work and taking them for their afternoon walks. Margaret spent Saturday evenings at the convalescent home where Ella Ritchie worked, mending and darning clothes for the soldiers. Her fondness for the theatre and play acting saw Margaret deciding to 'get up little plays', involving the men in their production, and these proved very popular. During the week there were evenings on duty at the Overseas Club and during the day she had also taken on a garden project. Not having a garden herself, Margaret took over the croquet lawn at the Ritchies and planted peas there once the winter snows of 1916 had melted. There were also times for relaxation with her friends, enjoying afternoon tea in the city with Ella on her day off, and attending a lecture on 'English wild birds' with Sally Touche.

Bill's letters home at this time, during the dreary months of inaction at Salonika, were full of intense longing to be with his wife and children again. The Macedonian front was stationary and quiet throughout 1916, though work proceeded constantly on communications and defences. Bill told Margaret that he spent a lot of time building himself a small dugout near his tent, and also helping organize boxing matches. But the men could not help wondering what cause they were serving in this stagnant campaign, when there seemed such an urgent need for experienced troops on the Western Front and in Palestine. Their main enemy was the weather, with heavy rains often turning the camps into a muddy quagmire and wintry blizzards blowing down the tents. The summer months brought ferocious heat and mosquitoes, with malaria claiming increasing numbers of victims as the war dragged on.

In December 1916, with so little activity on the front, there was a chance for leave and Bill, together with twelve other ranks, left for a month in England. Dorothy Crerer offered to stay with the children so that husband and wife could go away for a week to the country. They shared with each other dreams for their future together after the war: a combined farm and poultry run somewhere in the Tasmanian countryside and a 'not too exacting' medical practice for Bill; a carefree, open-air life for their young children.

At the end of January 1917, Benjamin Johnson went on leave to England and Bill took over temporary command of the unit. He also put his energies into designing and constructing a lightweight wheeled stretcher, which could be attached to a pair of light shafts and pulled by a mule down the steep and rocky mountain tracks along which the wounded would have to be evacuated.

The 26th Division was involved in attacks along their northern line in April and May 1917, with great losses sustained, and the three field ambulances with their mobile stretchers found themselves at work at last evacuating the wounded. The campaign was to culminate in September 1918 with an attack along the entire Bulgarian front and a successful drive forward to the frontier.

By that stage Johnson was suffering from influenza so Bill, by now Major McIntyre, was in charge of the 80th Field Ambulance as it moved north and crossed the Serbian–Bulgarian boundary. This region, on the edge of the dying Austro-Hungarian Empire, was a scene of desolation in the bitter autumn weather. Wounded Bulgarian soldiers, left behind in the panic of retreat, lay abandoned on the roads or huddled in ruined villages, their wounds septic and gangrenous from neglect. The sick and wounded – British, Greeks and Bulgarians – were loaded onto empty motor lorries lined with straw and evacuated to the nearest casualty clearing stations. Much of the ambulance unit's work at this time involved treating the large numbers of men sick with dysentery and influenza.

Hostilities ceased on 30 September with a rout of the enemy, the capture of prisoners and guns and a Serbian advance on the capital, Sofia. But peace brought little change to the work of the ambulance units, which spent the next weeks treating sick and wounded British prisoners of war. Major McIntyre had leave to England on 2 January 1919, effectively the end of the war for him. Benjamin Johnson stayed two more months in Macedonia, battling to control an outbreak of typhus amongst a war-ravaged and weakened civilian population. In London, there were honours and formalities for Bill, including a presentation at Buckingham Palace of the Military Cross and the Greek Cross of the Redeemer for his work with the ambulance unit in this campaign.

In Edinburgh, Margaret had been sustained through her husband's long absence by the needs of her young family and by friendships and purposeful work. In 1917, she began a course of driving lessons at a city garage with her friend Dorothy Crerer. Margaret knew that this skill would prove very useful after the war when her husband might have a country practice. The war had changed the face of work, especially in English cities: there were women tram conductors in London and many women in the services were driving trucks and other vehicles. Others – in trousers! – were to be seen cleaning windows and running delivery vans.

Driving lessons took up four mornings a week, and then Margaret had the chance to try out her skills on a family friend's big Humber (with their chauffeur along as apprehensive passenger). She and Dorothy took the big car for a spin on the country roads, having first to crank the starter motor into action. They were thrilled by the novel sense of freedom and excitement that that race through the quiet countryside provided.

Dorothy joined Ella Ritchie in voluntary work at a convalescent home in Edinburgh, but in the summer of 1917 she applied to work at a hostel in the Highlands supervising 'land army' girls. (Cara David was to join her there as a hostel 'mother'.) It was hard physical labour, out on the moors in the summer heat, digging up the moss and hauling the full sacks about a quarter of a mile down to the collection points. Dorothy revelled in the grandeur of the Highland landscape and in the sense of companionship and purpose this work provided. In truth it was a kind of escape for her from the loneliness and anxiety the war had brought. Her twenty-year-old brother, Alistair, had been dangerously wounded at the Somme in 1916 and was facing a slow recovery with a shattered thigh in a London hospital.

The friendship between Dorothy Crerer and Margaret was to be a lifelong one, sustained through letters though they were never to meet again after the war. Years later, when Dorothy was dying of cancer, she wrote to Margaret in Launceston, 'I know you will never forget me, for you are in my very bones'.

15   Launceston

Margaret and Bill had planned to stay on in Edinburgh after the war: in fact Bill bought a medical practice there in 1919. The plan was short-lived as he came down with an attack of malaria and a severe respiratory infection and was advised to move permanently to a milder climate. In October 1920, the family returned to Tasmania, to Launceston, where Bill bought another practice from Dr Gustave Hogg, renting Dr Hogg's home and surgery in Brisbane Street and later forming a partnership with Dr Hogg's son, Tim. The leafy parks and solid Victorian buildings of the city centre brought Edinburgh to mind, as did the fog and grey winter rains drifting in from the Tamar River estuary. However, the suburbs that reached north and south from the city centre were more typically Australian: weatherboard cottages and utilitarian backyards. Launceston was to be the family's home for years to come, and the story of the McIntyres forms part of the memories of many of that generation who grew up there.

The early years were taken up with children: their third child, Annabel (Anne), was born in 1921 and David McIntyre was born in 1925. With the security of an established and growing practice, Bill was able to build a comfortable family home in 1933, in Carnarvon Street, on the heights above the city. A secretary was employed in the surgery, which relieved Margaret of this role, one often taken on by the doctor's wife in those times.

Margaret became involved in the city's community life while her children were still young. She had her own car and a maid was employed who cooked and cleaned for the household. Her son, David McIntyre, maintains that there was never a sense that the children were neglected, and in fact their home became the centre for many of their mother's activities.

In 1927, Margaret helped found the Launceston Players, an enthusiastic group of local people with a love of the theatre. The group staged regular productions – plays by George Bernard Shaw, Noel Coward and Oscar Wilde – in various venues around the city including the ABC radio studios, the Kings Hall, the National Theatre and the Princess Theatre. Margaret was often the director. The productions brought a sense of excitement and occasion to this provincial city and were always well attended; ticket sales benefited local bodies like the Baby Health Centre, the hospitals and the Red Cross. In Sydney in August 1947, the Launceston Players won the British Drama League Competition for the best one-act play, with a performance of *The Man of Destiny* by G.B. Shaw. Margaret's daughter, Anne, by then a young woman with her own passionate love of the theatre, was one of the cast; her mother was the director. Margaret also wrote and presented a popular series of lectures for the Players and other interested people on such topics as 'Women Dramatists' and 'Women Writers'. These two talks were reproduced in two instalments in the local paper, the *Launceston Examiner*: an indication of the influence this intelligent and active woman had in what was a conservative provincial city.

Other organizations claimed Margaret's loyalties as well. From 1925, she was president of the Launceston Girl Guides Association, a position she was to hold for the next five years, taking on in 1930 the role of District Commissioner. Margaret found in the Scouts and Guides movement an expression of that ambitious, purposeful activity that marked her parents' own lifelong projects. She talked of the Guides movement as a 'chain of gold' encircling the world and uniting the youth of all nations, from a range of cultures and religions. Part of its appeal for Margaret – her mother's daughter – would surely have been the high ethical calling it represented while it remained independent of any one religious institution.

By 1940, the world was again at war. In that year, Margaret was appointed State Chief Commissioner and oversaw a wide range of guiding activities connected to the war effort. Young women and girls spent their holidays working with the Land Army, raising funds for the War Chest or the Red Cross. The summer holidays saw many young guides attending a month's 'fruit picking camp', helping local farmers harvest the cherry crop. They also collected clean newsprint for reuse, maintained vegetable gardens for families whose menfolk were away, and washed bottles for recycling. It was not all hard work; the girls enjoyed overnight pack walks into the hills near Launceston, had swimming carnivals and learnt lifesaving skills. At home and at their group meetings they sewed garments for Europe's evacuated children now staying in Britain.

The Guide International Service (GIS) had been set up in 1942 by the British Guides movement in conjunction with Olga Malkowska, the founder of the Polish Girl Guides. The service aimed to bring relief and support to families in Europe once the war had been won, and with this end in view training of relief workers and fundraising got under way in England. Malkowska, an outstanding intellectual and activist and a revered figure in modern Polish history, had fled to England after the Nazi invasion and was working with orphaned refugee children in London. As State Commissioner in Tasmania, Margaret knew of her work and was very keen to see Tasmanians support the GIS, which she saw as a way to strengthen a feeling of solidarity among young Australians with their sisters in the devastated lands of Europe. One of Margaret's Guides colleagues, Gwen Hesketh, had been training with the GIS in Australia since 1943. In April 1945, she sailed from Sydney and joined a relief team entering Germany in June, working among Displaced Persons in camps there until 1952. In 1946, a GIS team of highly qualified guides left Australia for Malaya where they provided medical care for thousands of local people who had been abandoned and isolated since the Japanese invasion.

Inspiring stories emerged from Europe of the role of leadership that young guides and scouts had played in some occupied communities. Margaret, addressing her state's members at the end of the war, hoped that many of the girls who had been serving their country in wartime might now with equal zeal become young architects for a new world. Her leadership was recognized with the award in 1947 of Guiding's highest honour, the Silver Fish, an award also given to her mother.

In 1942, the Invermay Youth Club was opened in an industrial area of North Launceston to provide creative and interesting activities for boys and girls between fourteen and eighteen, adolescents who did not belong to any other community groups and who were already being seen as alienated or rootless. The club was soon attracting large numbers of young people and continued to do so throughout the war. Margaret was one of the club founders. She also began the Launceston Youth Players and encouraged the youth club members to be involved in the productions – some of which were staged first in the living room at 10 Carnarvon Street and then won awards in state drama festivals. (There are still a few elderly people living in the town who were involved in these productions.)

In 1946, Tasmania was the first Australian state to raise the school leaving age from fourteen to sixteen. Traditional high schools catered for academic pupils and there were private schools for those whose parents could afford to send them there. Now the state was faced with the need to cater for students who would previously have gone early into the workforce. Margaret McIntyre was one of a group of prominent Launceston citizens who formed the Launceston Progressive Education

Group (PEG) as the war drew to a close, to draw up plans for a new type of community school for these adolescents. The group urged the state government to secure a large tract of land, some of it native bushland, within easy reach of the city and develop on it a decentralized school that would function as a model community.

It is clear from a number of articles she wrote that Margaret McIntyre was one of the driving forces behind this scheme and that it was an expression of that idealism she inherited from her parents. She thought of education as a doorway to a richer, more meaningful life for all citizens, not just a training to prepare the young for work as efficient but isolated units in an economic system. Participation in community life was the very essence of a true democracy, so the school hoped to put in place a form of self-government that would see all its students learning 'how to live with others in a truly democratic fashion'. The children would be given academic and technical education but the school would also contain a dairy, poultry runs, a farm and a domestic arts centre, and would cater for a wide variety of cultural interests with facilities for visual education, music and drama, a school choir and orchestra.

The school curriculum, as Margaret McIntyre envisaged it, would include the teaching of a broad 'social history' that moved beyond narrowly nationalist themes. The school's ethical base was to be 'the broad principles of Christianity only – nothing sectarian or dogmatic'. It would of course be coeducational and thus hopefully pave the way for a greater participation of women in social and political life in the state.

David McIntyre recalls a book that was part of the household when he was growing up, a book he believes had a profound effect on his mother. *The Socialist Sixth of the World* had been published in England in 1939 by Victor Gollancz of the Left Book Club. It was written by the Dean of Canterbury, Hewlett Johnson, who had visited Stalinist Russia and was trying to understand the vast social experiment taking place there. Dismayed by the increasingly ruthless nature of capitalist society, he believed he found in Russia a genuine alternative way of life. The book glossed over the authoritarian aspects of Stalinist Russia but praised the great social advances that had been made possible in an organized Socialist state.[1]

Johnson's themes appealed to Margaret McIntyre, especially the early parts of his book which laid out a blueprint for a just society. This was one where men and women had equal status; where everyone, whatever their ability, had access to productive work and opportunities for constructive leisure; and where everyone could receive a good education and security in sickness and old age. She saw the community school as embodying many of these socialist ideals.

The state government, impressed by the PEG's submissions, made 179 acres of land available for the school's foundation on the Newnham Hall estate to the north of the city. In February 1948, the school, which became known as the G.V. Brooks Community School, was opened by the District Education Officer in the presence of the staff and pupils, who had come from all the Launceston state primary schools to begin their high school life here.[2] These were the students who had not passed the entrance exams to go on to the traditional high schools, but who formed the 70 percent or so of non-academic children, and who would become some of the workers, voters, parents and citizens of post-war Tasmania.

G.V. Brooks School, under its first, enlightened headmaster, Richard Whitford, became something of an educational and social laboratory. It embodied the post-war desire for radical social change and for the creation of a more democratic, generous and public-spirited community. Whitford was given a great deal of freedom by the Education Department to experiment with the curriculum and management of the school. There was to be no corporal punishment, itself an innovation in those years, and the school motto was an Aboriginal expression meaning 'everybody work, everybody help'.

The school was often in the news over the next decade as politicians, academics and foreign visitors were taken to inspect its airy classrooms and thriving vegetable plots and to see the students at work behind tractors and machinery on the productive farm. The children featured positively in the local papers with their wins in the Launceston drama and music festivals and their active participation in area sports carnivals.

How much of the idealism of the school's founders was realized? A former Launceston schoolgirl recalls that in the early 1960s, the grammar school students 'looked down on the Brooks schoolkids … they were the strugglers, the poor achievers'. However another Launceston resident, now a successful writer and academic, looks back with pride and affection on her schooldays at Brooks. She remembers the well-equipped science laboratories and the committed, energetic teachers and feels she had a first-class education there.[3]

By the 1970s, the school was just one among many 'comprehensive' schools in the city, now taking in a full range of children and known as Brooks High School. The original dream of a 'model village' had given way to the hard economic realities of a growing city where land was expensive and in high demand. Some of the school's land was taken over by the new College of Advanced Education and in the 1990s the school moved to a new site further north.

Margaret McIntyre did not live long enough to see the school expand and prosper, nor to see the changes that the 1960s brought in its wake.

The 1940s saw her engaged with other groups of a local and national character, including membership of the Queen Victoria Hospital in Launceston, representation on the council of the Australian Broadcasting Commission and presidency of the Tasmanian Women Graduates' Association. This last group was particularly interested in promoting further education and equal pay for women and in a better education for early school leavers. Her many community roles saw Margaret awarded the OBE in 1947 for services to the state.

She was president of the state council of the National Council of Women (NCW) from 1943 to 1947, when she was made a life member. At that stage, most of the council members were the wives of prominent citizens, comfortably off and well-educated. How could they address the needs of the marginalized: the migrant families on the hydro schemes, the unemployed? Their mission was a different one: it was to support women and children in their communities and promote their interests and welfare. Margaret McIntyre was a diligent and tireless advocate for the cause, judging by the Launceston NCW minutes. In June 1944, for example, a lengthy discussion took place on the need for public lavatories and rest rooms in the city for women and children – an issue that had been of equal concern to Cara David's feminist friends in Sydney in the 1900s. The issue had still not been resolved by April 1946, when Margaret led a deputation to Launceston City Council. (The Council, stirred into action, acquired land and submitted plans for the rest rooms to NCW in October.)

Margaret's interests extended beyond the domestic needs of women and their families. She had grown up in a family that supported women's full engagement in public and political life, so it comes as no surprise that she was also drawn into the post-war movement to field more women candidates for Federal and State parliaments and to have them represented on juries and city councils. In July 1943, the lobby group Women for Canberra invited her to consider contesting the seat of Bass, in northern Tasmania, for the House of Representatives. In an echo of Rose Scott's remarks about the corrupting nature of party politics, the Women for Canberra movement would not endorse any one party and chose women who were prepared to vote on matters according to their conscience. Margaret declined at this time, but by April 1948 had accepted an invitation from friends and supporters to stand as an independent candidate for the seat of Cornwall in the Tasmanian Legislative Council elections. Her platform was the creation of a democratic post-war society, with an emphasis on education, child welfare and housing, and support of the family as the basic unit of the community. After the upheavals and losses of the war, this conservative program of reconstruction and welfare must have struck a chord with many voters, and in the May poll for Cornwall Margaret received 35 percent of the votes cast, defeating the incumbent, the Labor Minister, William Robinson. This was a singular victory for a woman at a time when Legislative Council franchise was still restricted to property-owning men – and to nurses who had served in the armed forces. Anne Edgeworth recalls helping her mother door-knock in the electorate, and the sympathetic and interested response she received from many householders, disillusioned with the corruption that seemed to permeate affairs of state at that time.[4]

Margaret was the first woman to be elected to a Tasmanian legislature. She was voted in for a six-year period, so hopes were high among her supporters that she would be able to make her voice count. She was sworn in on 29 June 1948, a lone woman in a conservative bastion of pastoralists and merchants. In July, she refused to support Liberal Party councillors who were attempting to block supply and thus force a general election: she felt it was immoral to hold the state to ransom in this way. This move brought the wrath of Launceston's conservatives down on her head and she was even accused of being a Communist sympathizer.

In November 1947, Margaret had been appointed as convenor of the state NCW Council on Press, Arts and Letters. It was in this capacity that she attended a National NCW Congress in Brisbane in August 1948, travelling there by train after attending a drama festival in Sydney with her daughter, Anne.

A letter to her husband survives, written the day before her death. She was looking forward to returning to Sydney where Bill was staying, en route to Launceston for the next parliamentary sitting. Molly had theatre bookings for Bill and the two sisters to a Shakespeare performance. It was to be a brief and rare reunion of the three David women now that Mootie was housebound and Margaret so caught up in affairs in her own state.

After the four-day conference, Margaret boarded the Australian National Airlines (ANA) plane *Lutana* at Townsville on Thursday 2 September. It called at Mackay and left Brisbane en route for Sydney at 5.30 pm, carrying a crew of three and ten passengers, and was due at Mascot at 8.55 that night. It did not arrive. Through faults in the navigational aids, the pilot drifted off course and, believing he was near the coast, asked for permission to lose height as ice was forming on the aircraft. The radio controller in Sydney gave permission for a descent to 4000 feet, not knowing that the pilot's reading of his position was faulty. He was in fact well over a hundred miles west of the coast and approaching the New England mountain range. At about 8.15, according to watches found on victims on the plane, the *Lutana* clipped trees on top of the 4600 foot Square Peak and crashed. The wreckage was sighted two days later by a plane en route to Sydney. A subsequent search party arrived at the scene later that day, and found that all passengers and crew had been killed instantly.

Bill McIntyre drove in with Molly on Thursday evening to the ANA office in the city. There the nightmare unfolded: a four-hour wait in the office, confirmation after midnight that the plane was missing, a sleepless night at home waiting for further news. After a plane report of patches of oil on the sea, the family was haunted by the thoughts of the victims drowning, until Saturday brought news that the plane had been sighted, in rugged mountain country near Tamworth in the New England Range. A phone call from the company early on Sunday confirmed that the plane had exploded on impact and was burnt out.

Margaret's youngest boy, David McIntyre, flew up from Melbourne to support his father before returning to face a week of exams for his final year of medicine. Molly's brother, Bill David, travelled to Tamworth with his brother-in law and stayed on for the private burial he had arranged for his sister after identifying her body.

With Margaret's death, the very centre of the McIntyre family life crumbled. Bill McIntyre, five years her senior, had never visualized life without his partner, assuming that the hard pace at which he drove himself as a community doctor would shorten his own life and see him departing first. He knew he must carry on without Margaret as best as he could, but confessed to his elder son, Archie, that he didn't care how soon he followed her. For the next thirteen years, until his retirement at eighty, he kept up his strong work ethic and role as a respected and well-known family doctor, but in private life became depressed and withdrawn.

The two daughters, Peggy and Anne, lost the mother who had given them loving support through some difficult adolescent years and subsequent stormy marriages. Both women, by that stage, were bringing up children on their own, and it was their mother who provided a stable and loving base for them, often caring for their children when they were working or travelling. Peggy's elder daughter, Philippa, remembers her grandmother as the one constant, loving presence in her own childhood.

Molly lost the sister who was her dearest friend and companion. In her memoirs, *Passages of Time*, she wrote with great poignancy of the experience of loss:

> Everyone, of course, adjusts in time to the loss of someone who matters to them more than anyone else in the world, and it was not till about twelve years later when … there suddenly swept over me, for a brief flash, the memory of how I used to feel when my sister was alive, and I realized then that, since her death, I have never for one moment been really happy.[5]

She rarely visited Launceston after that. Bill McIntyre, troubled by increasing deafness as he grew older and withdrawn into his grief, was not able to relate with any great warmth to his children. Molly's brother

Billy paid for her to have a holiday there in 1952 but she confessed to her nephew Archie that 'being there without your mother was too hard … it was like losing her all over again'.

For Mootie, the death of her eldest child brought a grief too deep to find expression in tears or any outward way. Anne, Margaret's younger daughter, found in the coming years that through poetry she could give expression to the loss she had suffered, and the desolation Margaret's death had brought to her close-knit family:

> There was no hint of warning
> that she, strong ark
> of comfort and your store
> of grace, would disappear,
>
> The mountain's shrouded face
> reared up its silent wall …
> Nothing to be done at all
>
> as they searched for the plane's wreck,
> but stare at her empty place,
> watch the unopening door … [6]

There were many public ceremonies of remembrance and mourning for Margaret McIntyre. The Guides community, who had worked with Margaret since the 1920s, wanted to commemorate her great influence for good on the island. The year after her death, a fund was opened to establish a memorial in Launceston to her life's work, a building that would serve as a centre for training conferences and to accommodate visiting guides. In 1950, a large Victorian-era mansion in central Launceston was purchased with funds raised by guides throughout the country. Margaret McIntyre House served as northern headquarters for the Guides until financial pressures forced the association to sell the property in 2003.

A bronze plaque, made on behalf of the Tasmanian Guides, was placed on Margaret's grave in Tamworth, with the local Guides group taking on the care of the site.[7]

After Margaret's death, the Launceston Youth Players changed their name to the Edgeworth Players in memory of their beloved leader, and a plaque in her honour was erected at the Princess Theatre by the Launceston Repertory Players, who also created the Margaret McIntyre Memorial Library by donating their large collection of books and plays to the Launceston Public Library. The G.V. Brooks School, reorganized

The Guides farewell Margaret McIntyre (Girl Guides Tasmania)

Margaret McIntyre House, Launceston (Girl Guides Tasmania)

in the 1970s into a collection of 'sub schools', named one of these McIntyre School.

The Tasmanian legislature recorded their sorrow at Margaret's death. Some of her friends, remembering her idealism, reflected that if she had been longer in politics she might have found it a disillusioning experience, once she encountered 'the setbacks and frustrations that beset those who have visions of a better world'.[8]

Margaret McIntyre, 1947

Part Three: Molly

16   Younger Sister

After the publication of *My Brilliant Career* in 1901, Miles Franklin received letters from women all around Australia. To many of her readers, young women still in their teens as well as many older women, the book seemed to be the authentic voice of the new century, a woman's tale that expressed their own dreams and dilemmas.

Young Molly

Molly David, an artless, imaginative fourteen-year-old, wrote a long letter to Miss Franklin in August 1902, having met her once at Rose Scott's home in Sydney. Molly was at Woodford with her governess, envying Margaret the week away with her parents by the sea at Kiama where David was a running a geology camp for thirty

255

students. Molly expressed a wistful hope that the two of them might become correspondents. 'I love writing letters and I haven't anybody that I like writing to scarcely at all.'[1] She shared with the young author her own secret writing ambitions and expressed hopes that Miss Franklin would be able to visit them at Woodford.

Remnants of Molly's childhood stories survive: elaborate fairy tales and reference to a newspaper called *The Weekly Waratah* which Molly created and sent to a girlfriend in Sydney. There are also references to stories submitted to the children's columns of a Lithgow paper and the *Melbourne Sun*. Her mother encouraged these literary efforts in her child; but it is clear that both parents found the teenage Molly puzzling and rather unpredictable, posing dilemmas which they found hard to solve. In a letter to Touche in 1903, Cara talked about Molly 'taking up literature … at present she refuses a university career'. The words convey a sense of exasperation: why was this younger daughter so wilful in her choices? A later comment of Cara's about Molly is even more revealing, with a sting in it that expresses a mother's bewilderment: 'like everything else she takes up she has dropped it again'.

In 1903, Margaret was preparing to enrol in her studies at the University of Sydney. She and her sister had always been very close, having spent their girlhood years together in the mountains, their schooling undertaken side by side under the tutelage of their mother and governess, Miss Wilson. Fifteen-year-old Molly, distraught at the idea of their imminent separation, persuaded her parents to let her join her sister as a student in the Faculty of Arts, a strange decision that they were soon to regret. Cara arranged for the two girls to stay together in lodgings near the university: an unconventional move at a time when young women were still closely chaperoned. Their rooms at 3 The Avenue, Newtown, were owned by a widow, Mrs Keating, who lived there with two of her sons and a daughter. Two other university girls were also boarding there besides the David girls. Margaret and Molly ate one meal a day with the Keatings but for the rest of the time more or less fended for themselves, eating mostly out of tins, their contents washed down with cocoa heated on a spirit lamp. They were accountable only to themselves for much of the time. After a few months of heady independence, Molly was withdrawn from university, having come down with pneumonia after getting wet at a football match.

She was brought back to Woodford to convalesce once she was strong enough to travel. She was a trying convalescent, 'peevish, selfish and rude to those in authority', as she recalled. Her parents, no doubt after much soul-searching, decided she needed the discipline of boarding school and enrolled her for a year at Kambala, a girls' private school in Sydney's Eastern Suburbs.

Molly, so used to the glorious freedoms of Woodford, hated the place at first: the lack of liberty and solitude, the chatter and gossip of the girls, the regimented nature of the day where each activity was marked by a bell ringing. 'If any one dares to ring a bell when I am at home I'll fly at them and rend them,' she warned Margaret.

But the two women who ran the school soon won her over. Miss Louisa Gurney and Mlle Augustine Soubeiran were friends of Cara David, part of that energetic feminist network which made an impact in so many areas of Sydney's life in those years. They had established the school in 1887 and it had become one of the places favoured by wealthy colonial families to provide a 'cultured' education for their daughters before marriage and child-rearing. Music and French may have provided the polish that would have been missing in the emerging public schools, but according to Molly the girls also received a good grounding in English, history and mathematics. The Davids would hardly have been attracted to a school based on snobbery and social class and they chose to ignore the rumours about its reputation, including the story that girls were taught how to alight gracefully from a carriage kept in the school grounds – a rumour which Molly later dismissed as 'poppycock'. Cara had enough faith in the good sense and character of her two friends to entrust her daughter to their care for a year. Molly learnt to love the two women. Under Louisa Gurney's tuition she had 'a revelation of what music could mean' and Mlle Soubeiran's French lessons were equally absorbing. As Cara David had done, Mlle Soubeiran taught the girls not to despise menial work and to help in the kitchen and serve at table. In later years Molly recalled their poise and unaffected dignity and an unforced worldliness that must have fascinated the young country girl.

In 1906, Molly had another chance to enrol at Sydney University, with what her parents hoped would be a more mature and disciplined approach to her studies. By this stage Margaret was in the third year of her Arts degree. The two girls stayed with the Keatings and then at a small house their mother rented for them close by the university, with occasional hired help to cook for them. Molly later recollected her time at university as 'frivolous … I didn't go there to be educated – I went there to have a good time'.[2] One can read into those lines a sense of the fragile relations that must have existed at the time between the Davids and their teenage daughter. A 'good time' meant going to dances at the university men's colleges and to the Sports Union Ball at Paddington Town Hall, and Saturday morning coffees with friends at the Civil Services Store in the city; it also meant joining the newly formed Sydney University Dramatic Society (SUDS) which put on its plays at the now demolished Palace Theatre. Letters exchanged between Cara and the professor on his 1906 Mexican tour point to the family tensions that had arisen: by July, Cara had forbidden the two girls to take part in any further dramatic performances that year, as they had both had 'quite as much … as is good for them'. David warned his older daughter, 'Neither of you should think of taking up acting as a profession'.

He also worried about Molly's application to her studies. She was only studying Latin under sufferance and Physics was a struggle for her. A fatherly note of encouragement arrived from his ship off

Molly as Juliet (NLA MS 8890)

Newfoundland: 'I am sorry dear Molly you are finding Physics so difficult. It will be a great thing for you to get a University degree. They value it very highly in America.'

The female students, at that stage without a union of their own, used to gather in their small weatherboard common-room, a gas ring providing heat for their modest lunches. The Student Christian Union held meetings there which Molly attended once or twice out of curiosity. At one meeting the subject was 'The Character of the Virgin Mary', which Molly decided not to go to, as she did not feel qualified to comment.

Molly's final year studies, in 1908, must have been greatly affected by her father's absence in Antarctica and the shadow that it cast over their family life. In spite of her father's advice, she abandoned Physics and Mathematics and finally secured a modest degree with passes in English, History and Geology, after sitting for a few repeat exams.

Molly became friends with Jessie Lillingston, whose

Sophie Child, Lilian Butler, Molly and Margaret, Tyn-y-Coed (NLA MS 8890)

family had inherited a wealthy estate on the Clarence River in northern New South Wales. Jessie had behind her the confidence and vitality that came from robust physical health and her own strong feminist beliefs. She had travelled widely as a child and was assured of a substantial income once she turned twenty-one. She was very keen to attend university but her parents had been unwilling at first to let her go, worried that she would meet some fortune-hunting 'bounder' and be trapped into marriage with him. Their daughter was able to persuade them to let her sit for the matriculation exams and enter Sydney University; in exchange Jessie agreed to have a 'coming out' season, though she was supremely indifferent to the social expectations required of young women at the time.

Molly David was in her final year when she met Jessie. She remembered her as an attractive young woman seething with vitality. Jessie started a women's hockey club at the university and persuaded Molly to join the hockey team which Molly did reluctantly, hating the aggressive physical nature of the game. Jessie also helped form the University Women's Sporting Association and was soon involved with SUDS, serving with Molly on the committee in 1909. It was through this society that she met her future husband, the young law student Kenneth Street.

Cara and her husband must have had mixed feelings about Molly's friendship with Jessie Lillingston, worried perhaps by the strong-willed young woman's unsettling influence on their daughter. Jessie had energy, initiative and intelligence and was already making her mark at university, but she was also indifferent to conventional opinion and happy to pursue her own way. Left unengaged by the traditional subjects of Latin, physics and mathematics, Jessie dropped all three and in 1909 took up philosophy with Francis Anderson (by that stage married to Maybanke Wolstenholme) and history with George Arnold Wood. In her second and third years, swept up in the excitement of university life and sport, she just managed to scrape through the exams with a couple of posts and gained her degree in 1911. After her marriage to Kenneth Street in 1916, Jessie joined the Women's Club where she became a regular at lectures and discussions. Young enough to be Cara David's daughter, she joined her on equal terms in organizing the Women's National Movement that year. She was involved with Cara and Maybanke Anderson in the move to bring discussion of venereal disease and prostitution into the open.

The David family knew the Streets independently of knowing Jessie Lillingston. Justice Philip Street became a member of the University Senate in 1915 but before that the Davids often visited the Street family home in the Eastern Suburbs. Their younger son, Laurence Whistler Street, was to play a part in Molly's story during the coming war.

Dorothea Mackellar was another young woman whose family knew the Davids and who became friends with Molly. Her father, Sir Charles Mackellar, was a prominent medical man who had entered state politics and was involved in helping draft the child protection legislation of the early 1900s, laws of great interest to the early feminists including Cara. His daughter, Dorothea, who was four years older than Molly, had grown up in circumstances of extraordinary privilege. She travelled overseas with her parents as a child; she was educated by a governess and was fluent in four foreign languages; she learnt to swim and sail from their waterfront mansion at Point Piper. Her life moved easily between Sydney society, her family's country properties and holidays among family friends in London. At seventeen she enrolled in an Arts degree at Sydney University, not to obtain a degree but to further her own studies in literature. In 1907, she was taking art classes with Antony Dattilo Rubbo and singing lessons. Dorothea was to make her mark with the publication in 1908 of her poem, 'Core of My Heart', in the London *Spectator*, which appeared in later collections of verse as 'My Country'. It became one of Australia's best-known poems, frequently anthologized during World War I.

Dorothea published a number of novels and collections of verse but her biographer considers that she failed to achieve anything original in her later years, with an 'atrophy of talent and vitality ... typical of many Australian women of her generation.'[3] She did, however, become active in the Bush Book Club after the war and would have had much to do with Cara David in that capacity.

Molly was drawn into Dorothea's circle in her university days and became involved in designing dances – this was the time when Isadora Duncan was making her mark – and in amateur theatricals: a dilettante's life, her parents judged. Margaret David's comments to her fiancé in 1908 are a reflection of her parents' exasperation with their younger daughter: Molly was 'very exhausted after a typical day's work, two lectures in the morning and a matinee in the afternoon. She's a terror that girl!'

Nevertheless both Margaret and Molly were drawn to the excitement of the stage and were both involved in SUDS productions. (Molly continued to perform in productions in 1910 after her graduation.) In June 1908, they both had a role in Pinero's play *The School Mistress* with Margaret giving up the bigger role to her sister 'because I've had my share of fun out of that dramatic society over the last three years'. Margaret's trips down from Woodford for rehearsals were some of the only light-hearted times for her that year, much of which was spent up in the mountains with her mother.

Molly's graduation ceremony took place at the Town Hall in May 1909. Sydney was in a state of excitement at Ernest Shackleton's arrival in the city: here was another Antarctic adventurer to welcome, now that their beloved Professor David was safely home. It is recorded that 'Miss Mary Edgeworth David' was heartily cheered when she went up to collect her degree from the Chancellor. Shackleton was in the audience, but in spite of the crowd's loud acclamation of him and cries for a speech, he left without obliging the public. Molly remembered Shackleton as an 'attractive, magnetic personality with a hint of recklessness about him.'[4]

Cara and David must have wondered what the future held for Molly. She had not shown any strong interest in a career while at university. There was talk of her spending the year after graduation in Europe, learning modern languages and music. 'She would be snapped up at Kambala,' Margaret confided to Bill. A growing friendship with a young medical student, William Hamish Paton, made Molly reluctant to leave Australia at the time, but Paton was to marry one of the Maiden girls before war broke out.

In late 1910, Molly accompanied her father to England. He returned to Sydney at the end of the long vacation but Molly stayed on to help her sister and young family settle in to life in Edinburgh. 'Now our roles as leader and led were, for a time, reversed,' Molly reflected. Margaret was still run down after her illness and Molly was the one who arranged accommodation in London, then found them a flat in Edinburgh. After they were settled, Molly visited Aunt Ethel in Wales before returning to London. Ethel wrote to Ned Touche with an audible sniff of disapproval, 'She is *very* independent and I don't know much of her movements'. Molly had told her aunt that she intended to take up painting lessons in Dulwich Hill, where her Uncle Arthur lived at the time. Later that year she left for Canada to stay with her father's maternal relatives. That carefree winter in Canada was like a magical dream in her memory, a time of white silence broken only by the tinkle of sleigh bells. Her cousins took her skating on the ice at Ottawa and to dances where the northern lights shimmered above them as they rode home by sleigh. Back in England, Molly joined a Sydney friend who had been studying at a drama academy in London and was now taking whatever acting jobs she could get. Molly spent some days with Una, who was touring provincial towns in England with a third-rate theatrical company. The experience opened Molly's eyes to the hand-to-mouth existence entailed in this rather Bohemian lifestyle, for which she nevertheless felt a certain sympathy. She regarded her friend as both courageous and enterprising for setting out on such an unorthodox journey, so different from the safe conventions of life in suburban Sydney.

Molly was taken aback by the strict social conventions that governed the behaviour of young women of her class in England. 'Most girls of twenty-three in England are always under a chaperon's wings,' she wrote to her mother. She was also to come face to face with the snobbishness of the English upper middle classes when she travelled to Portsmouth for a special naval review. She went down on the train with an English friend and her friend's two nephews, a young naval engineer and his brother, an officer in the Territorials. A number of regular army officers and their wives, travelling in the same compartment, spent the time loudly chattering and laughing at the expense of the Territorial Army, which they obviously considered a rough outfit trying to ape its betters.

Molly found that the other blemish on English life was the patronizing and dismissive attitude of men towards women. Coming as she did from a home where she was always treated as an equal, and having moved in university circles where women were beginning to find their own voice, Molly was dismayed by this treatment of women as second-class citizens.

After returning to Sydney in late 1911, Molly was employed at home by her father as his secretary and was living with her parents when war broke out. In 1915, she accompanied the Davids when they moved to an inner-city apartment in Elizabeth Street, and like so many other young women of her generation, she threw herself with enthusiasm into fundraising for the men serving overseas (and was also involved in drama productions at the Women's Club). She had one special friend. Laurence Street was the second son of Mr Justice Street of the Supreme Court of New South Wales. He had graduated with a BA in 1914 and had joined his father as an associate in the court. Molly knew him well and often visited the Street family home. If she had dreams of marrying this young man, she kept her own counsel, only able to talk about it years later when she shared her memories of those days with a friend, Mary Walters.

Laurence enlisted once war broke out but he and Molly stayed in touch with regular letters in the early months. He was at the landing on Gallipoli on 25 April 1915 and was killed on the peninsula on 19 May, shot through the head by Turkish gunfire. Molly, calling at the Street home shortly afterwards, was confronted by a maidservant blocking the door with a brutal message. 'We have just heard that Laurence has been killed. You can't come in today.'

In later years Molly confessed that Justice Street and his wife 'didn't really approve of me'. She was four years older than Laurence and perhaps they saw the age difference as a barrier to their son's marriage.[5] Laurence's death must have left Molly desolate and aggravated the restlessness and moodiness that her parents had noticed in her teenage years. Margaret knew her sister was grieving: 'Poor old Molly, losing her greatest chum,' she wrote to Mootie. But Molly kept her feelings very much to herself. Her letters to 'dearest Margot' (Margaret) in Edinburgh in August 1915 are anything but melancholy and show a lively interest in people and a mischievous sense of humour. She talked of a 'spy play' she and Mootie went to see: 'feeble, but exciting in spots. The hero managed to wear three different uniforms in two acts.' She described the entertainments being put on in Sydney for the returned men from the Dardanelles, including harbour trips and dances: 'I am always there of course, being very attached to anything in khaki'.

When her mother offered their mountain home to the Red Cross as a convalescent home Molly threw herself into the project, travelling up to Woodford with Mootie and helping her prepare the place for its first visitors in September 1915. Cara wrote to Margaret in December that Molly was still very thin but 'is very interested in her work at the Home and works as hard as a general servant all day'. Molly had borrowed a trap and driven two of the soldiers back from an evening's outing through thick mountain mist, which reassured Cara that her daughter's

Molly David, 1918

'nerves' seemed to be improving.

The men shared their stories and what had brought them to Woodford. Horace Gage Wheeler was a Cockney from the London slums. He'd been a barman in London before emigrating to Australia and enlisting. Discharged from the AIF with a weak heart after illness on Gallipoli, he was convalescing at Woodford before being repatriated to England. His brother had been killed at Flanders and Wheeler was worried about his dependants in London, as his stepmother drank heavily and he knew the younger children were being neglected. Cara wrote to Margaret, enclosing a £10 note and asking her to try and get it to Wheeler once he was back. She told her daughter that Molly had taken a great interest in Horace Wheeler, 'chiefly because he was a bit cheeky I think'.

A photograph of those years shows Molly perched on the roof at

Molly on roof, Tyn-y-Coed (NLA MS 8890)

Tyn-y-Coed armed with a broom. She was cleaning the gutters and searching for leaks. 'She's a terror for doing all these unlikely things but gets very low-spirited at having the ordinary humdrum round of housework to do,' Cara wrote. There are references to days of poor health when Molly could barely drag herself from bed to complete the chores, and other occasions when, full of energy, she raced around organizing fancy-dress parties and games evenings for the men.

Molly's memoirs, *Passages of Time*, tells the story of how she mastered her natural timidity and became a proficient car mechanic and driver after her mother decided to purchase a car as transport for the men. Molly went to a Sydney driving school and 'teetered timidly about the metropolis in a ramshackle car accompanied by the instructor'. After gaining her driver's licence she had the charge of the family's new car, a four-cylinder Dodge tourer which was given the name Cuthbert. By a process of trial and error Molly gradually developed greater confidence and skill in driving it and was soon taking trusting convalescent patients on outings around Woodford.

In later years, Molly was to reflect on how much the decisive and energetic character of her mother had marked her childhood and young adult years. At times she felt like a minor character in the greater drama of her mother's life; merely an appendage being swept along in the wake of the latest bold and uncompromising project. She acknowledged, without bitterness, that at times Mootie 'hadn't the remotest idea' about her daughter's feelings.

Arriving with her mother in the United Kingdom in July 1917, Molly was determined to find work on her own account: she wanted to join the Women's Army Auxiliary Corps (WAAC) and serve as a driver, in France if possible or attached to the Flying Corps in Sussex. After enlisting in London, she was to be based, in the end, at Woolwich Arsenal near the docks. Mootie accompanied her daughter down to London in August to enlist. She watched Molly set off for the recruitment office with a mother's loving if irrational eyes. She wrote to Margaret that she 'felt very choky letting her go all by herself into the rough world. She looked such a mite.' (Molly was twenty-eight at the time.)

By late October, Molly had been promoted to acting sergeant in charge of a fleet of Ford vans and their women drivers. She battled the wintry weather and the London traffic on journeys that took her out through the East End and the city to Wimbledon, and through the Blackwell Tunnel under the river to an ammunition factory in the slums of Poplar. She wrote entertaining letters to 'dear Margot' in Edinburgh and to Mootie, who by late 1917 was serving as matron at the hostel in Kirkcudbright. There were observations about the women she worked with, the army hostel where she stayed and the politics and minor dramas of the workplace. In the garage and offices at Woolwich, men were coping with the very novel experience of working alongside women in an industrial setting and often having to take orders from them. Three men, 'a beastly sergeant called Crow', 'old Poyser' a former pawnbroker, and 'a horrible clerk called Collins', formed a jealous trio who resented Molly's success in the workplace and rejoiced when she was called into the company office to be charged for 'altering the detail' (the itinerary for the vehicles under her charge). Molly, more her mother's daughter than she realized, handled the accusations from the garage manager with aplomb and irony: 'I told him I hadn't realized before what an awful offence it was and that it would certainly never occur again, even if they detailed a car with only one wheel'.

From the beginning of 1918, all home-service motor drivers in the WAAC were to be transferred to the Women's Legion and would be able to choose where they wished to board. Molly hoped to get a transfer to Edinburgh to stay with Margaret and her family. Were there any Ford jobs going there, she wondered, because she was 'well up in the Ford genus now'. She confessed to being sorry to leave the garage at Woolwich and the men she worked with, especially a tough-voiced, much-travelled sergeant who'd lived in Canada and South America: 'We have yarns about San Salvador and wild Mexican miners that shoot their managers and it is nice to think of hot places and forget the muddy Thames and the muddier Arsenal and the biting wind that is generally blowing'.

During her time at Woolwich and as a result of her friendship with

Una from the drama school, Molly began reading some Labour Party literature and was very struck with it. Living in Woolwich had opened her eyes to English working-class life. She was surprised to find that the party was composed not just of working men but of professional people as well: she thought Margaret might be interested to read about Labour's aims and ideals.

In March, Molly received her transfer to Edinburgh but was to spend much of the remainder of the war in the countryside, based first at Kinross in the Highlands. Through the mild, rainy Scottish summer, she ferried patients from the railway station to Glenlomond War Hospital and delivered milk and bread to the hospital. This was one of the many institutions dotted round the United Kingdom that were to treat 'nerve' patients, those shell-shocked and traumatized survivors of the Western Front. For Molly the main challenge of the job was safely negotiating the narrow country lanes where erratic hens and herds of wandering heifers seemed always to have right of way.

In July she was transferred to another, much larger war hospital in the township of Dunblane. The place unnerved her: endless, echoing corridors and empty grounds patrolled by a fierce dog. The hospital was getting ready to receive its first patients, all other ranks as at Glenlomond. (Officers had their own hospitals.) A mob of curious villagers clustered round the station when Molly drove the ambulance down on the Monday morning to meet the train and the first patients.

Armistice Day saw her back with Margaret and her mother in Edinburgh. From the flat on Thirlstone Road they could hear the navy in the Forth Estuary tooting its sirens and see the flashing beams of searchlights swinging in mad triumph across the skies. In the privacy of her room, Molly knelt in the dark beside her bed and wept.

17   Writer

Molly travelled back to Australia on the *Eurypides* with her parents in March 1919. She was no longer a young woman: she turned thirty that year. All her family had felt the stresses and strains of war but Molly, in particular, carried a private grief about Laurence Street that remained largely hidden and unspoken. As well, in leaving England she was leaving behind the sister who was her soul mate. Margaret and Bill had expressed hopes of moving permanently to Tasmania but in the uncertain world they lived in after the war it was not easy to make definite long-term plans.

By 1920, Molly was preparing to move with her parents to Coringah, the newly purchased property at Hornsby. She remembered how her heart sank at the sight of the small and hideous cottage – as yet unrenovated – which Mootie had acquired, and wondered what kind of life awaited her in this bushland retreat with two elderly parents. As an experienced driver and mechanic, she was soon in demand as the family chauffeur. She drove her father to the station every day and took her mother, always so busy with Girl Guides work and other commitments, to her many appointments. There were also official visits for both parents to Government House. She would sit in the car, reading, knitting or doing crossword puzzles – or if it was night, just 'brooding' – while she waited for the function to end.

She also found herself helping to prepare tea for the many visitors who appeared at the Davids' residence, including scientists, Antarctic explorers, journalists and university academics. For an intelligent and active woman, it must have been a rather slow existence; in fact Molly herself confessed that her life at this time seemed rather empty of purpose.

In late 1920, Margaret and her young family returned to Australia. The highlight of every year after that for Molly was the three months of summer which she spent in Tasmania. She would drive the family car down the Princes Highway to Melbourne and then have it loaded onto the ferry – swung out on a sling over the wharf after the petrol was siphoned off – to be taken across Bass Strait. She recalled many adventures on the road while taking Margaret and her young children touring in Tasmania: a broken head-gasket temporarily patched up by a roadside mechanic; a steering bar broken in two and wired back in place with rod from an old iron bedstead; plenty of do-it-yourself mending of punctures in inner tubes while the car was pulled up on quiet country roads.

In the late 1920s, the two eldest McIntyre children, Peggy and Archie, came to stay at Hornsby while they completed their schooling and went to university. Peggy attended Abbots- leigh, a Church of England girls' school, from 1926 to 1928; Archie started at the boys' school, Barker College, in 1927. They both lived at Coringah with their grandparents

Molly's Standard, with Archie looking worried

but became boarders in 1927 when Molly and Cara went to England after David became ill.

In 1927/28, another house was built on the four acres of land at Hornsby, on the slope above Coringah. Having come into a family inheritance, David gave Molly £1000 towards the cost of a house of her own. It must have been clear to her parents that Molly would never marry, and that having her own home would give a stability and direction to her life. Molly designed the home with the help of an architect and moved into it in the winter of 1928. It was a Spanish style two-storey villa with a spacious sitting room on the top floor. Archie and Peggy moved up to the house with Molly on its completion.

Archie was Molly's favourite nephew: she loved him as a son. He was a studious, inventive boy: he liked to do his homework at the top of an old pine tree in the garden and to dabble in chemistry experiments in an old shed at the back of the house. In that Depression era in Sydney, Molly and her two housemates found an entertaining pastime that they all enjoyed and could pursue at home. This took the form of 'theatricals', with Archie being the mainstay of every performance as he was responsible for all the scenery, staging and light effects. With Peggy and other friends roped in as actors, the performances drew an audience of about twenty or thirty people, mostly families of the players. The theatre was set up in the large upstairs living room whose glass doors, opening on to both south and north verandahs, provided convenient access to the stage. Molly, the producer, prompter and occasional actor, was also cook and caterer and was proud of the hot suppers she was able to conjure up for her guests in her tiny kitchen. She found further outlet for her theatrical interests during a five-year stint as 'teacher of Diction' at Archie's old school, Barker College, from 1934 to 1939. The school principal had approached her with the offer of a position there as he was anxious to improve the boys' speech. Miss David seemed the ideal teacher, as she had an educated but neutral pronunciation 'offensive to neither Australian nor English ears'. During her time at the school, Molly produced a number of one-act plays, performed first at the local Killara Hall and then in the school's new Assembly Hall. One of her classroom exercises was an essay where the students could only use words with up to two syllables. She also wrote a number of plays for production at the school and – recalling her own childhood and the imaginative world she inhabited through story – she wrote and illustrated a charming story for her niece Anne's twelfth birthday.

The family drew together to cope with the pain of Edgeworth David's death in August 1934. Molly, her sister Margaret and son Archie, together with Mootie, attended the state funeral that the government had requested. The silent crowds who gathered, the address in the cathedral, the set sadness on the face of the pallbearers – all of them David's old Tunnelling Company officers – all reminded them of their own loss and showed them some of the many Australians who had loved this man.

As early as September that year, Mootie was talking about a plan to write a biography of her husband, whose adventurous life she had witnessed and largely shared. She discussed the plan with Margaret, who was staying on in Sydney after the funeral. Margaret took the step of approaching Angus & Robertson to see whether they would consider publication of such a book. There must have been a tentative expression of interest and the initial few chapters were dispatched not long after. Angus & Robertson returned a carefully worded but critical report. Their main criticism was with the rambling and unstructured form of the narrative, and they judged that the book's market would be limited to those who knew the subject. 'Though written from the rich store of a loving memory it cannot honestly be recommended.' The reader – editor of the *Sun* newspaper – would also have liked more anecdotes about David 'even if they weren't true'.[1]

Margaret, having read the draft after her return to Launceston, had more serious reservations. Her mother had more or less implied in the manuscript that Edgeworth David was at odds with Darwinian evolutionary theory (a theory which Cara herself never really came to terms with, according to Anne Edgeworth). Margaret realized what a serious error of judgment this was on her mother's part and that it would undermine the credibility of the book.

Anne Edgeworth recalls that there was general unhappiness within the family about the initial draft. Eventually Molly David was persuaded to take on the task of writing her father's biography, chiefly by Margaret and a long-term friend of the family, H.J. Carter.[2] Molly felt quite unequal to the task and embarrassed on behalf of her mother, but Cara, who had washed her hands of the whole affair, agreed that this would be the best outcome, though she must have struggled with resentments at first. So Molly tentatively set about what she called a 'difficult but fascinating task'. Over the period of a year in 1935/36, she combed through her father's papers at home and university and his great collection of memorabilia, photographs and letters. She received a great deal of support and encouragement in the project from the gifted and methodical Archie, who was boarding with her while pursuing postgraduate medical studies. She sent the first two chapters to her sister and was encouraged by Margaret's enthusiasm: 'my dearest old thing [it] moved me to tears and thrilled me – it is the real thing. Dad's character stands out clear and strong and if you can only go on as you began … You've got his clear mind for grasping things, and the imagination absolutely essential for appreciating him. It will be a great life work to have done – the finest memorial to Father that one could think of.'

In April 1937, Molly took the finished manuscript to England, feeling that a British publication would carry more weight, and also being unwilling to approach Angus & Robertson after their initial rejection of her mother's attempt. Her ship called at Adelaide, where she visited the university and lunched with Douglas Mawson and Cecil Madigan, a lecturer in the Geology Department and a man of whom her father had been very fond. Later Mawson drove them from Adelaide to visit the quarry where Professor David had done extensive investigation of Pre-Cambrian fossils. En route to the Cape the ship battled rough seas and driving rain and Molly found little on board to relieve the tedium of the days apart from her books. The shipboard company consisted mainly of smart, sophisticated people who dressed for dinner every night and consumed endless cocktails with the ship's captain. Molly played chess with the chief engineer, having discovered that they shared a fondness for 'coffee, Kipling and cats'. She also played rummy with the 'humble, ornery ones' on board most nights, then went to her cabin and read. 'I do so long for a bit of conversation with one of my own family sometimes,' she wrote to Mootie. The highlight of the voyage for her was getting cables from the McIntyres and from Mootie for her birthday.

As they neared London, news came through of the coronation proceedings of George VI. That night the company celebrated with a festive dinner which went on riotously until one in the morning. The lid of the piano and a window in the lounge were broken and the captain was very surly at breakfast the next morning.

Molly was a child of the Empire and loved returning to England. It was to be her last visit, the sixth she had made since childhood, all of them connected in some way with her father's work and career. The day after she arrived she had an appointment with Edward Arnold and Co., who were to publish the British edition of *The Geology of the Commonwealth of Australia*, at that stage being revised and completed by Dr W.R. Browne. She had the satisfaction of having her manuscript deposited with them that very day, and within a couple of weeks had a favourable response. Yes, they would publish it, though she was cautioned that 'there won't be much sale for that type of biography'. Thrilled with the outcome, she mailed the news to Mootie and Margaret. She would stay on in England to correct the proofs and booked her passage home in September, conscious of the expense of a prolonged stay overseas. She admitted to Margaret that things would be perfect if only her sister was there with her to enjoy the holiday: the London parks in all their summer glory, *King Lear* at Stratford, Canterbury Cathedral where she attended a performance of a Dorothy Sayers play, and a reunion in Edinburgh with Margaret's friends the Ritchies and Dorothy Crerer. In London Molly caught up with her brother Billy and his family but sensed the emptiness of the marriage: 'Poor dear Billy, I do feel sorry for him. What a pity he didn't marry someone nice. We don't really have anything in common now.'

Molly, 1938

The publishers were prompt and helpful and the book was ready for the autumn market in England. Molly was still in England when Cara received an advance copy. Writing tearfully and proudly to her daughter, she called it 'a perfect book – a perfect book … I've been immersed in it … my pride in your achievement overcoming the feeling of being second fiddle in your heart.'

Professor David was warmly reviewed in Britain and Australia, both on a scientific and a personal level. Cecil Madigan, who had been a close associate of David in his later years, wrote to Molly soon after the book's publication, 'You have struck the right note. It is not a paean of praise, but it rings true, right through, like him … It is a splendid life story you have put together. Thank you for writing it.' The book reminded Madigan of David's own life, 'his code, his industry, enthusiasm, loyalty and love. I can not tell you how I miss him in a selfish way.'

Edgeworth David's later biographer, David Branagan, considers the book 'an astounding achievement' despite the author's closeness to her subject.[3] Part of its success lies in the lucid and accessible language with which Molly summarized the scientific and technical achievements of her father. She wrote about his surveys for coal and tin for the Department of Mines, his discoveries on the coral reefs at Funafuti, his pioneering work on glaciation and his later, controversial studies of fossils in South Australia. She brought to life the enthusiasm of the young university lecturer with his quirky sense of humour and his ingenious 'practical experiments' that made his lectures so memorable to a generation of geology students; she described his popular 'field days' and camps where both men and women students tramped the hills and foreshores with their untiring teacher. Her book, Molly cautioned, 'tells of the man rather than the scientist', but in fact it does convey to the reader the romance of David's professional and scientific life: here was a man who, as his friends and colleagues acknowledged after his death, lived life to the full, a very powerhouse of ideas and inspiration for those around him.

The book was never to receive much publicity in Australia: the war years pushed aside any interest in the scientific endeavour and exploration of a past generation. By the 1970s, Molly had been given publishing rights to the book. Her niece, Anne, hoped that the book could be reissued as a paperback, but she was unable to find a publisher.

Molly was in Launceston with her sister, recovering from an appendix operation, when World War II broke out. She was to spend these war years living quietly in Hornsby, housekeeping for her elderly mother. She joined the Hornsby Women War Workers and started making camouflage nets for use over gun emplacements in the Pacific; she also joined the National Emergency Service as a volunteer car driver for ferrying possible air-raid casualties. None of her immediate family saw active service this time, as Margaret's children were still students, though Archie was to be employed on a number of air-combat research projects during the war.

In 1948, Molly lost the sister who had been her closest friend and confidante. Many years later, she shared with her friend and neighbour,

Mary Walters, the memory of that night when she and Bill McIntyre drove in to the city to await the arrival of the plane, only to learn that it was overdue. Dr McIntyre was called into the managing director's office while Molly was left alone in the outer office. As with the news of Laurence Street's death, Molly confronted this later tragedy on her own, as a door closed before her.

The terrible loss drew her closer to Archie, though at the time of his mother's death he and his young family were in England where he was studying for a post-doctorate degree at Oxford. When they returned to the Antipodes, it was for Archie to take up a professorial position at the University of Auckland. Archie became Molly's chief correspondent in the ensuing years as he and his wife, Anne, shared with his aunt the challenges of academic scientific work and pride in their three growing children.

In 1958, Molly wrote to him that she was 'battling along trying to write a bedside book for old ladies'. She worked at it from time to time over the next few years, but then abandoned it. Her niece, Anne, encouraged her to take up her writing again and suggested expanding the book into a memoir of her remarkable family. Anne had connections with the literary and publishing world and decided she would do her best to find a publisher for her aunt. In 1971, Anne sent Molly's completed manuscript to Angus & Robertson, who kept it for five months before sending a letter of rejection. Their reader, Douglas Stewart, had to report that the board felt such a book would not have a very wide sale. He added in a personal note that he had enjoyed the book very much and suggested Miss David write another book about the animals and wildlife at Hornsby. Privately he thought it the work of a 'first class mind'.[4]

The University of Queensland Press (UQP) accepted the book in July 1974 and it was in print by October. Molly's helpful editor suggested the title *Passages of Time* to replace Molly's rather enigmatic *Tryptich* and it was this title that appeared on the hardcover book, with the young Molly David's portrait on the front cover. Drawing on a currently fashionable theme, the publishers announced it as a 'women's lib' book, much to Molly's amusement. Many of the people who read the book, including a number of young women in their twenties, admired Miss David's many accomplishments as a single woman and wrote to her that they had found her life and example an inspiration.

The book's reception took UQP by surprise. There were numerous favourable reviews in Sydney and interstate newspapers and Molly found herself a subject of interest to journalists who requested radio and television interviews. She joined notable Australian 'battlers' Edna Ryan and Arthur Ellis as subjects of an ABC television program, 'On Their Own Terms', produced by Tim and Roz Bowden. Some of the other TV and radio interviews were either inaccurate or patronising – it was clear to Molly that TV presenter Mike Walsh had not read her book – but Molly accepted it all with a certain amused grace. She wrote to Anne, 'I feel I've done my duty to UQP. I hope the book is selling well to justify their rashness in publishing it.'

The two most informed and thoughtful reviews came, gratifyingly, from writers. Douglas Stewart chose it as one of his three favourite books for the year in the *Sydney Morning Herald* of 4 October 1975, liking especially its 'quiet humour and intelligence'. And the poet Rosemary Dobson reviewed it in *The Age* on 1 November that year. She noted the writer's 'delighted understanding of her [mother's] individuality'. She found the book illuminating, a wonderful reflection on 'human responsibility, religion and duty'. In October 1975, the National Book Council gave a special commendation in its yearly awards to *Passages of Time*, along with David Malouf's *Johnno*.

By May 1976, the first edition had nearly sold out and a reprint was on the way. The book 'is actually UQP's bestselling book ever', the promotions officer wrote to Molly. Its publication aroused a new interest in the life of her father: both the University of Sydney and the Mitchell State Library approached her with a request for more

Edgeworth David material for their archives. She was able to donate much valuable material, including David's letters from the Antarctic to his wife, and a copy of Douglas Mawson's *Home of the Blizzard* which included a poem Mawson had written for his old friend and teacher.

Molly received numerous letters about the book. A retired miner wrote to her from Newcastle, whose suburb near Wallsend had been renamed Edgeworth. 'My father, a coalminer in the pick and shovel days, was a great admirer of Professor David.' There were letters from former geology students, recalling the influence of their beloved professor on a new generation of university students in the 1920s, many of them returned soldiers resuming their studies. Former Woodford residents recalled their visits to Tyn-y-Coed where 'your mother told wonderful stories over the Sunday supper table' and young children set off on their own 'expeditions' into the bush, inspired by the tales they'd heard of the Antarctic.

In 1977, Ms N. Menetrey approached Molly with a request to paint her portrait. She was entering a local portrait competition and had been inspired by her reading of *Passages of Time* and by Douglas Stewart's comments on it.[5] There were other contacts concerning the book: it was recorded on tape (free of charge) for the use of blind or sight-impaired people; and excerpts were also included in an Australian school reader under the title 'Girl of the Bush'. (Molly would have been aware that her mother's book *Funafuti* had also been issued – in a severely edited form – as a school reader to an earlier generation of children.)

UQP continued to send Molly David a modest half-yearly royalty payment for the next ten years, by

Painting of Molly David (Author's photo)

which time the hard cover book was out of print. In April 1977, the firm of Rigby Ltd expressed an interest in reissuing the book as a paperback under the imprint of Seal Books. It was published in 1978 with a print run of 5000 copies. But the reading public wanted something more in tune with the boom times the country was experiencing. In July 1981, Rigby disposed of numerous titles that were not selling and they were offered at a remaindered price of 50 cents a copy to the author: Molly bought up the 2114 copies remaining.

At Anne's insistence, Molly kept on with her writing. Perhaps her niece understood the energizing role it played in the life of her aunt who, confronting the usual physical assaults of old age, was still marvellously alert and engaged with life. Molly began to write a series of letters from 'Sarah' to her sister 'Meg' who lived 'in a far country'. They were, of course, a tribute to her lost sister Margaret. In a collection of no more than a score of letters, she recalled their young lives together in a now vanished Australia. In May 1979, UQP returned the manuscript which Anne had submitted on her aunt's behalf: it was too slight for publishing as a book. They suggested that it might be suitable for a magazine series. Anne, a valiant supporter of her aunt, approached a number of other publishers, with no success. Molly, feeling already 'the frustrations and humiliations of old age', promised her niece to battle along with her on this last project, even though she admitted to feeling rather used up and drained of ideas. The book needed illustrations, Anne decided; and so Molly, now in her nineties, set to this final task, a series of lightly sketched and whimsical drawings that captured the worlds she was describing: an Edwardian childhood and the bush creatures who were her constant friends in Hornsby.

Redress Press was a cooperative feminist press with about a hundred members in 1983. Its energetic director, Pat Woolley, ran the enterprise from a Sydney office, seeking partnerships with commercial publishers who would distribute works that Redress Press had chosen, edited, designed and printed. *Letters to Meg* was chosen as one of the first eight books to bear the Redress logo, and in December that year Molly was sent a contract for the book, with its details appearing in a 'Forthcoming Titles' handout. Sadly, the promised book did not make it to publication at the time, as no commercial publisher could be found to distribute it. Molly confessed that she was now resigned to not having the book published before her death.

Letters to Meg was eventually published in 2002 by an independent Canberra publisher, Ginninderra Press, at Anne Edgeworth's instigation. Anne remained a lifelong supporter of her aunt's work and achievements and was to become custodian of the Edgeworth David Papers after Molly's death in 1987.

Letters to Meg has a nostalgic look about it but it is not sentimental. Molly David's own self-deprecating humour sets its tone. As the book opens – 6 am on her eighty-ninth birthday – she reaches for her dentures, 'the top plate grinning at me with an "Alas poor Yorick" suggestion that I usually find amusing'.

Certainly there is nostalgia for the passing of pleasant and valuable social customs: the writer sees a decline in neighbourliness, in family gatherings, in the backyard vegetable plot and poultry run, in the skills of home baking. But the book has a critical edge to it that is unexpected. In a chapter entitled 'The Itchy Rib', the elderly Miss David denounced the historic attitudes of the church to women, recalling how much she was discomforted by the practice of confirmation: 'I resented the patronizing laying of hands on my head by a strange man'. Having grown up in a family with a grandfather, an uncle and great-uncle in holy orders, she admitted that the two David daughters should have been zealous churchgoers, 'but we were both inclined to do our own thinking about religion'. She confessed that she now felt quite alienated from the established churches and their rituals, and her own moral and spiritual code was expressed in some of the closing lines of the book: 'I believe that we should worship with our lives, by being kind to our co-inhabitants of the earth, and honest in thought, word and deed'.

Her mother's friend, Maybanke Wolstenholme, whose passionate humanism led her to a life in the service of others, had affirmed at the age of eighty, 'Religion is doing what you can for the welfare of humanity and developing your own spiritual life'.[6] As far as we can gather, Cara David's own conclusions were similar. Molly David was an inheritor of the values of that generation of strong-minded women.

18   Homecoming

In 1951, shortly before her mother's death, Molly wrote to Archie's wife, Anne, who wanted very much to study architecture:

> Farming … is the greatest comfort to me. If I had only housework to do, and the (mostly) very sad task of tending Granny's declining years, I would probably go all nervy as so many women in my situation seem to. But with my two acres of rock and sand there is a continual battle to step up fertility and always a new season to give one hope and plenty to occupy both mind and body.

She encouraged Anne to go ahead with her studies – an unorthodox step to take in 1950s Australia – reminding her that all women, once their children were no longer little, needed challenges in their lives beyond household chores.

Molly's two acres of land were the remnants of bushland that formed part of the Coringah property. The four-acre block had been subdivided in 1928 when Molly's house was being built on the upper half. Mootie herself had done a lot to develop the land, establishing fruit trees (some grown from seeds she'd collected), a vegetable garden and chicken run. By the 1940s her painful arthritis and a prolapsed womb kept her largely confined indoors upstairs in Molly's house, though she was still mentally alert and still receiving many visitors.

In 1947, Molly began keeping sheep and goats. The goats were to keep down the honeysuckle and blackberry that were invading the property and would supply fresh milk to the two women who were finding the locally delivered milk was thin and unsatisfactory. A sheep, Mow, was added to the household and the animals grazed the overgrown paddocks, tethered on a long chain to a peg during the day. As Molly's livestock expanded in numbers – she began breeding goats herself – she built up connections with the local vet and with friendly tradesmen. The local blacksmith showed her how to scythe and mow her long grass and the ironmonger sold her tools and machinery for the farm. There were regular visits in her little Austin A4 utility to collect supplies for her livestock and garden from the seed merchant, whose

Molly and goats

store was home to a number of blue-tongue lizards. In time, Molly's neighbourhood network grew wider. Schoolgirls came to agist their ponies in the spare paddock and stayed to help her feed the livestock. Young mothers with delicate babies came to her to buy goat's milk and she regularly donated fresh eggs to local nursing homes and to her kindly neighbours. Living in an area still remote from big-city development, Molly came to know and care for the bush inhabitants of her block. She was an early member of the NSW National Parks and Wildlife Foundation and held views well in advance of her time about the importance of preserving native forests and pasture topsoil. (She subscribed to a New Zealand society dedicated to 'safeguarding what is left of the world's soil'.) Her rambling garden was home to numerous native bird species as well as possums which she warily befriended, conscious of the damage they could inflict on fruit and vegetable crops. One became a regular visitor to her upstairs verandah for a nightly feed of bread and jam and, learning to trust her, soon brought her young babies in tow. The world of invertebrates fascinated Molly and she conducted a correspondence about her garden inhabitants with helpful scientists at the Australian Museum and with local writer/ naturalist Densey Clyne.

Her parents had both left their mark on Australian life and after their deaths Molly was often approached in connection with their work. The Edgeworth David name was still well known in the Hunter Valley region. In April 1958, Molly attended a lecture by W.R. Browne in Newcastle to mark the centenary of her father's birth and later that year she was guest at the opening of the Edgeworth David library in Cessnock, a town born of the pioneering years of coal exploration in the region. The Department of Geology at the University of Sydney, conscious of the debt they owed to one of their founders, stayed in touch with his daughter and invited her to special occasions. In May 1979, Molly learnt that over a hundred graduates and friends of the department had met to form the Edgeworth David Society which would hold annual lectures in his honour. Her ninetieth birthday was celebrated with a fine luncheon and a tour of the new Geology and Geophysics building, to be named the Edgeworth David Building, its gleaming modernity so different to the old brick building she remembered.

During those years the Antarctic was attracting renewed interest as Australians, enjoying unprecedented prosperity and leisure, sought out faraway places to visit. Molly was bemused to learn that tourists could now take a luxury flight over the polar regions; she wondered if from their comfortable seats they would look down on the ghosts of three weary, frostbitten men dragging their sledge along the coastline.

The larger world remained a source of interest and inspiration to her. Watching the Russian spacecraft, Sputnik, circle the skies above the goat paddock one summer night in 1957, Molly felt like standing up and cheering, it seemed such a promise of an exciting age to come. As her mother had done, Molly became more open to change and new ideas as she grew older. In 1968, she was donating money to a program to advance the cause of Aboriginal education. That year, she also began supporting the Reverend Ted Noffs and his Wayside Chapel (a drug rehabilitation program run from Kings Cross). She approved of his practical approach to Christianity: 'helping people *is* religion – so that's where my church money is going in future.' She continued to be a faithful supporter of the Ashfield Infants' Home, but her pension was often dispatched to one needy cause or another – in the new year of 1975 it was paid into the Darwin Cyclone Relief Fund. While her mother was still alive, family records in the form of receipts show that both Lady David and Miss David were supporting the Australian Labor Party campaigns in New South Wales in 1943 – a far cry from the imperial loyalties of a past generation of Davids. In January and May 1944, there were donations from Lady David and Miss David to the campaign funds of the Friendship with Russia League, whose president was Bishop Burgmann.[1]

The Guides Association stayed in touch with Molly, wanting to keep Lady David's memory alive. In October 1983, Molly received an invitation to the fiftieth anniversary of the dedication service which her mother had organized on that bright spring day in 1933. After *Passages of Time* was published, Molly received letters from women who had been guides in the 1920s, remembering the spirited influence Lady David had on their young lives, with campfires and overnight stays in a bushland setting at Tyn-y-Coed. In a reminder of her mother's book on Funafuti, in September 1982 Molly received a request from the Department of Foreign Affairs for a copy of the book: they planned to present it to Queen Elizabeth on her visit to the Gilbert and Ellice Islands for their independence celebrations.

Other stories from the past became significant. The Samurai sword, gift to Professor David from the Shirase expedition in 1912, had been put away in a cupboard and largely forgotten by the family. In 1978, Anne Edgeworth, reading about the new interest in Samurai swords among collectors, decided to have it assessed and possibly restored for display. Major Ian Brookes, an Australian expert, was able to establish the ancient pedigree of the sword and its great cultural significance in Japan. In fact one of that country's leading sword polishers offered to restore the sword without charge and later came to Australia to return it personally to Molly David.

The strenuous but always interesting demands of her farming life kept Molly engaged every day. She learnt how to operate on crop-bound chickens, how to slaughter and prepare roosters for the table, how to milk goats and trim their hoofs. She stayed with her animals through difficult births, buried those who succumbed to illness or misadventure, and rejoiced in the growth of healthy and lively offspring. She especially loved the goats and hotly decried their reputation as evil-smelling, randy and bad-tempered creatures. The playful and affectionate young kids were a special source of joy.

As well as the livestock there were the garden and fruit trees to look after. (She wore her old World War I tin hat while picking plums in the rain.) Like her mother, Molly was skilled in all the traditional domestic arts and always made her own bread, kept the pantry stocked with jams and preserves and made her own soap. She had learnt the art of spinning wool during Woodford days and now that skill came in handy, allowing her to spin and knit her own clothes from wool produced in her very backyard; she engaged a reliable man to shear the sheep with his petrol-driven machine.

Molly at her spinning wheel

Other skills were mastered in time: mixing cement, basic carpentry, splitting wood, working a petrol-driven cultivator. This latter machine was always approached with some trepidation but Molly was gratified to learn that she could still haul the tarpaulin cover off and get it to work in her ninetieth year, 1978. Until 1980, she ran half a mile around the house each day: she would have run around the property but found the goats always wanted to race with her and got in her way.

Her life began to close in as the infirmities of old age made themselves felt. In 1980, she had a hip operation, and limping everywhere with the aid of a stick in its aftermath, she realized that her livestock would have to go. Kate Moss, a farmer in southern New South Wales who had started a correspondence with Molly about farming life, offered a kind and loving home to the remaining sheep and goats and kept Molly informed of their welfare, but the rambling Hornsby garden seemed strangely empty once they were gone. A further blow to her independence came with a minor stroke in 1983, and the need for a daily visit from a nurse. Correspondence with her nephew Archie, and regular visits from her niece, Anne, were now her lifeline to the wider world. 'It is now a bit after 4.30 – a lonely time of day,' she wrote to Anne, 'especially when there's what Jane Austen would call a small thin rain falling.' Anne drove up every second weekend from Canberra to visit her aunt and was later to record in poetry the image of a woman whose bright and eager intellect was increasingly trapped inside a frail body. Anne urged her aunt not to abandon *Letters to Meg*, and the book that finally saw publication in 2002 was the work of these last years of physical struggle and loneliness, when her thoughts turned increasingly to the sister she had lost. Writing the letters, Molly found, seemed to bring back a faint echo of the time the two had lived together, but also recalled the agony of bereavement: 'When you died, all those thirty years ago … I remember standing at night on the balcony … looking out into the immensity of space – a great depth of darkness lit only by stars, and crying in my head "Meg! Meg! Where are you?"'

The darkness gave back no answer, but as her own life drew to a close, Molly told Anne, 'I have lately felt your mother's presence very strongly from time to time.'

Molly died on 9 April 1987, in her ninety-ninth year. She died peacefully in her sleep in her own home, where she had found 'anchorage', as her memoirs tell us. The funeral notice contained a simple epitaph: 'That which drew from out the boundless deep, turns home again.'

Bibliography

Abbreviations
A&R: Angus & Robertson
AWM: Australian War Memorial
ML: Mitchell Library, Sydney
MUP: Melbourne University Press
NLA: National Library of Australia
OUP: Oxford University Press
SU: Sydney University

Manuscripts and Albums
Amy Lewis Papers NLA MS 6147
David Family Papers ML MS 3022
David Family Papers NLA MS 8890
Edgeworth David Papers SU P011
Franklin Papers ML MS 364
Henry Parkes Papers ML A 871-1052 (CYA 907)
Journals of W.K. McIntyre AWM, PRO 1127
Letters and Diaries of W.K. McIntyre AWM PRO 84/109
Maybanke Anderson Papers ML MS 4539
Mort Family Papers ML MS 2859
Scott Family Papers ML MS 38 (CY 4302 -38/9)
Women's Club Archives ML 367

Official Records/Archives
Annual reports Australasian Home Reading Union
Annual reports Bush Book Club
Annual reports Girl Guides Association Tasmania 1924–1949
Minute books Abbotsleigh Archives, Abbotsleigh School, Sydney
National Archives Australia, AIF Base Records, B2455 1st AIF, Laurence Whistler Street
National Archives UK, WO 95/4867 and WO95/4868 War Diaries 80 Field Ambulance 1916–1919;
 WO95/1945 War Diary 45 Infantry Brigade: 6 Battalion Cameron Highlanders
National Council of Women Minute Books 1895–1904 ML MS 3739 (MLK 03009)
NSW Electoral Rolls 1909, 1913

NSW Legislative Assembly, Votes and Proceedings, Department of Public Instruction, Annual reports, 1881-1886

State Records NSW: Department of Public Instruction, subject files 'Cookery' and 'Teacher Training Colleges' 1882–1895

Suffolk County Council, Girls' Log Books, Southwold National School, 1863–88

Sydney University Dramatic Society records, SU Archives

University Oral History project, Interview with Miss Mary Edgeworth David, 23 March 1981, SU Archives

Whitelands College Archives, UK

Newspapers and Journals

The Age
The Armidale Express and New England General Advertiser
Ashfield Advertiser
Australasian Home Reader
Australian Christian World
Australian Teacher
Bathurst Times
The Blue Mountains Echo
Casino and Kyogle Courier and North Coast Advertiser
The Daily Telegraph
Glen Innes Examiner
The Grafton Argus and Clarence River General Advertiser
The Inverell Times
Launceston Examiner
The Lawson Souvenir
Leader and Orange Stock and Station News
Moree Gwydir Examiner and General Advertiser
Raymond Terrace Examiner and Lower Hunter and Port Stephens Advertiser
Sydney Mail
Sydney Morning Herald
The North Western Courier
The Tamworth Daily Observer
The Tenterfield Star
The White Ribbon Signal
The Woman's Voice
Waratah
Western Suburbs Courier

Books, journal articles, theses, websites

Ackerman, Jessie, *Australia From a Woman's Point of View*, Cassell, London, 1913

Allen, Judith, *Rose Scott: Vision and Revision in Feminism*, Oxford University Press, Melbourne, 1994

Anderson, Maybanke, *Maybanke, a Woman's Voice: The Collected Works of Maybanke Selfe –Wolstenholme – Anderson, 1845–1927*, ed. Jan Roberts and Beverley Kingston, Ruskin Rowe Press, Avalon, 2001

Baachi, C., 'Evolution, Eugenics and Women', in *Women, Class and History: Feminist Perspectives on Australia, 1788–1978*, ed. E. Windschuttle, Fontana, Melbourne, 1980

Babkenian, Vicken, 'Edith May Glanville: Champion of the Armenian Relief Fund', *Journal of the Ashfield & District Historical Society*, Ashfield, 2008

Baldock, C.V., and Cass, B., *Women, Social Welfare and the State in Australia*, Allen & Unwin, Sydney, 1988

Bayley, William, *Miss Dorothea Mackellar O.B.E.*, Sydney, 1968

Bean, C.E.W., *Anzac to Amiens*, A&R, Sydney, 1946

Beaumont, Jeanette, and Hole, W.V., *Letters From Louisa: A Woman's View of the 1890s, Based on the Letters of Louisa Macdonald, First Principal of the Women's College, University of Sydney*, Allen & Unwin, Sydney, 1996

Blue Mountains Official Guide and Souvenir: Lawson, Hazelbrook, Woodford, W. Lowden, Sydney, 1905

Branagan, David (ed.), *Rocks, Fossils, Profs: Geological Sciences in the University of Sydney, 1866–1973*,

Science Press, University of Sydney, 1973

Branagan, David, *T.W. Edgeworth David: A Life*, National Library of Australia, Canberra, 2005

Brooks High School 1948–1988 Anniversary Magazine, http://freepages.genealogy.rootsweb.com/~ricksmith61/brooks/brooks.html

Bygott, Ursula, and Cable, K.J., *Pioneer Women Graduates of the University of Sydney, 1881–1921*, University of Sydney, 1985

Cable, K., Turney, C., and Bygott, U., *Australia's First: A Pictorial History of the University of Sydney, 1850–1990*, University of Sydney, 1994

Campbell, M.A., *Hazelwood Heritage: A Social History of Hazelbrook and Woodford*, Hazelbrook Public School P&C, 1989

Carter, H.J., *Gulliver in the Bush: Wanderings of an Australian Entomologist*, A&R, Sydney, 1933

Carter, Jennifer, 'Portrait of a Lady: Caroline Martha David', *NLA News*, September 2002

Clarke, Patricia, *The Governesses: Letters From the Colonies, 1862–1882*, Hutchinson, Melbourne, 1985

Cole, Malcolm, *Whitelands College: The History*, Whitelands College, London, 1982

Coleman, Margaret, *From a Flicker to a Flame: The Story of the Girl Guides in Australia*, Girl Guides of Australia Inc., Sydney, 1989

Coltheart, Lenore, *Jessie Street: A Revised Autobiography*, Federation Press, Annandale, 2004

Commonwealth Office of the Status of Women, *Our Centenary of Women's Suffrage*, Canberra, 2004

Coupe, Sheena, *Speed the Plough: Ashfield, 1788–1988*, Ashfield Council, 1988

David, Cara, 'Housewifery Schools', *Australasian Nurses' Journal*, 1906

David, Cara, 'Mission Work in Funafuti', *Australian Christian World*, Sydney, 1897

David, Cara, *Funafuti, or, Three Months on a Coral Island: An Unscientific Account of a Scientific Expedition*, John Murray, London, 1899

David, M.E., *Professor David: The Life of Sir Edgeworth David*, Edward Arnold, London, 1937

David, M.E., *Mary Edgeworth David's Passages of Time*, Rigby, Adelaide, 1978

David, M.E., *Letters to Meg*, Ginninderra Press, Canberra, 2002

Dunstan, Keith, *Wowsers*, Cassell Australia, Melbourne, 1968

Dutt, William, *Suffolk*, Methuen & Co., London, 1917

Edgeworth, Anne, *Poems for Off-Duty Hours*, Ginninderra Press, Canberra, 2007

Eldershaw, Flora (ed.), *The Peaceful Army: A Memorial to the Pioneer Women of Australia, 1788–1938*, Women's Executive Committee, Australia's 150th Anniversary Celebrations, Sydney, 1938

Feminist Club of NSW, *Silver Jubilee Souvenir, 1914–1939*, B.H. MacDougal, Sydney, 1939

Feminist Club of NSW, 1914–1920, programs and related material collected by the National Library of Australia

Fitzgerald, Ross, and Jordan, T.L., *Under the Influence: A History of Alcohol in Australia*, ABC Books/HarperCollins, Sydney, 2009

Fox, Brian, *Blue Mountains Geographical Dictionary*, B. Fox, Bathurst, 2006

Fussell, Paul, *The Great War and Modern Memory*, OUP, New York, 1975

Gilbert, Lionel, *The Little Giant: The Life and Work of Joseph Henry Maiden, 1859–1925*, Kardoorair Press, Armidale, 2001

Goodlet, Ken, *Hazelbrook and Woodford: A Story of Two Blue Mountains Towns*, Ken Goodlet, Hazelbrook, 2006

Griffiths, G., *The Feminist Club of NSW, 1914-1920*

Griffiths, Tom, *Slicing the Silence: Voyaging to Antarctica*, Harvard University Press, Cambridge, Mass., 2007

Guides Victoria, *Guides Can Do Anything: The Guide International Service, 1942–1954*, Guides Victoria, Melbourne, 1996

Hawthorne, Fifi, *Kambala: A History*, Wentworth Press, Sydney, 1972

Haygarth, Nic, *Joe Fagan's Waratah: Celebrating the Life of a Great West Coaster*, Tasmania, c. 2009

Hill, Brian, 'Training State School Teachers in NSW, 1880–1904', in *Australian Teachers*, ed. A.D. Spaull, Macmillan, South Melbourne, 1977

Hole, W.V., and Treweek, A., *The History of the Women's College Within the University of Sydney*, A&R, Sydney, 1953

Hooper, Florence Earle, *The Story of the Women's Club: The First Fifty Years*, Women's Club, Sydney, 1964

Horn, Pamela, *The Victorian and Edwardian Schoolchild*, Alan Sutton, Gloucester, UK, 1989

Howley, Adrienne, *My Heart, My Country: The Story of Dorothea Mackellar*, University of Queensland Press, St Lucia, 1989

Huntford, Roland, *Shackleton*, Atheneum, New York, 1986

Inglis, Ken, *Sacred Places: War Memorials in the Australian Landscape*, MUP, Carlton, Victoria, 2005

Johnson, Hewlett, *The Socialist Sixth of the World*, Victor Gollancz, London, 1939

Kingston, Beverley, *My Wife, my Daughter, and Poor Mary Ann: Women and Work in Australia*, Thomas Nelson, Melbourne, 1975

Kyle, Noeline, *Her Natural Destiny: The Education of Women in New South Wales*, NSW University Press, Kensington, 1986

Kyle, Noeline, 'Caroline Edgeworth David: A Short Biography', *Unicorn, Bulletin of the Australian College of Education*, Vol. 15, No. 1, February 1989, pp. 4–5

Kyle, Noeline, 'Can You Do as You're Told? The Nineteenth Century Preparation of a Female Teacher in England and Australia', *Comparative Education Review*, Vol. 36, 1992, pp. 467–486

Kyle, Noeline, 'Cara David and the "Truth" of her "Unscientific" Travellers' Tales in Australia and the South Pacific', *Women's Studies International Forum*, USA, Vol. 16, 1993, pp. 105–118

Kyle, Noeline, 'Cara David: A Leading Woman in Australian Education', *Women in Management Review*, Vol. 9, No. 3, 1994, pp. 23–36

Kyle, Noeline, 'Women Teachers and Travel: The Case of Eliza Darling, Cara David and Euphemia Bowes', *Mary Wollstonecraft Conference, Sweden*, 1996

Lake, Marilyn, *Getting Equal: The History of Australian Feminism*, Allen & Unwin, Sydney, 1999

Lambert, L.T., *A Short History of Woodford Academy*, Woodford, 1975

Larry, Tracey, *An Account of the Lives and Careers of Miss Caroline Mallett and Miss Margaret Pollard*, School of Education, Roehampton Institute, 1986

Lawson, Olive (ed.), *The First Voice of Australian Feminism: Excerpts From Louisa Lawson's The Dawn, 1888–1895*, Simon & Schuster in association with New Endeavour Press, Sydney, 1990

Liddell Hart, B., *A History of the World War, 1914-1918*, Faber & Faber, London, 1934

Limerick, Brigid, and Heywood, Eileen, *Purists, Wowsers, Do-Gooders and Altruists: The Construction of Female Stereotypes in Australian Volunteer History*, Program on Non-Profit Corporations, Queensland University of Technology, Brisbane, 1992

Lorne-Johnson, Susan, *Betrayed and Forsaken: The Official History of the Infants' Home, Ashfield*, The Infants' Home, Ashfield, 2001

Luffman, Laura B., *In Memoriam: Hilma Molyneux Parkes*, Women's Liberal League Monthly Record, Sydney, 1909

Macdougal, B.H., *The Feminist Club of NSW: Silver Jubilee Souvenir, 1914–1939*, Sydney, 1939

Mackinolty, J., and Radi, H (eds), *In Pursuit of Justice: Australian Women and the Law, 1788-1979*, Hale & Iremonger, Sydney, 1979

Magarey, Susan, *Passions of the First Wave Feminists*, UNSW Press, Sydney, 2001

Maggs, James, *The Southwold Diary of James Maggs*, ed. A.F. Bottomley, Boydell Press, Suffolk, 1983

McKernan, Michael, *The Australian People and the Great War*, Collins, Sydney, 1984

McNicoll, Ronald, *The Royal Australian Engineers: The Colonial Engineers*, Vol. 2, Corps Committee of the Royal Australian Engineers, Canberra, 1977

Mitchell, Bruce, *Teachers Education and Politics: A History of Organizations of Public School Teachers in New South Wales*, University of Queensland Press, St Lucia, 1975

Neill, Norm, *Technically and Further: Sydney Technical College, 1891–1991*, Hale & Iremonger, Sydney, 1991

Paine, Harry R., *Taking you Back Down the Track, is About Waratah in the Early Days*, Tasmania, 1994

Parkes, Sir Henry, *Fifty Years in the Making of Australian History*, Longmans, London, 1892

Pink, Kerry, *100 Years of Western Tasmanian Mining*, West Coast Pioneers' Memorial Museum, Zeehan, Tasmania, 1975

Pratten, Chris (ed.), *Ashfield at Federation*, Ashfield & District Historical Society, Ashfield, 2001

Priestley, Raymond, 'Sir Edgeworth David: An Appreciation by an Old Student and Comrade', reprinted from the *Australian Quarterly*, June 1938

Radi, Heather (ed.), *200 Australian Women: A Redress Anthology*, Women's Redress Press, Sydney, 1988

Rich, R.W., *The Training of Teachers in England and Wales During the Nineteenth Century*, Cambridge University Press, London, 1933

Rich, Ruby, 'Ruby Rich on Feminist Club', Tape 10, sound recording by Hazel Berg, National Library of Australia

Richards, P., Valentine, B., and Dunning, T., *Effecting a Cure: Aspects of Health and Medicine in Launceston*, Myola House of Publishing, Launceston, c. 2006

Roberts, Jan, *Maybanke Anderson: Sex, Suffrage and Social Reform*, Hale & Iremonger, Sydney, c. 1993

Roe, Jill, *Stella Miles Franklin*, Fourth Estate, Sydney, 2008

Ruhen, Carl (ed.), *Ashfield, 1871–1971*, Horwitz, Cammeray, 1972

Shackleton, Sir Ernest, *The Heart of the Antarctic: Being the Story of the British Antarctic Expedition, 1907–1909*, Heinemann, London, 1910

Smith, S.H., and Spaull, G.T., *History of Education in New South Wales (1788–1925)*, G.B. Philip & Son, Sydney, 1925

Somerville, Hedley, *A Taste of Ginger*, Hedley and Del Somerville, Hornsby, 2002

Spaull, A.D. (ed.), *Australian Teachers: From Colonial Schoolmasters to Militant Professionals*, Macmillan, Melbourne, 1977

Spaull, G.T., *The Educational Aims and Work of Sir Henry Parkes*, Sydney Teachers College, 1920

Strange, Carolyn, *Griffith Taylor: Visionary, Environmentalist, Explorer*, University of Toronto Press, 2008

Street, Jessie, *Truth or Repose*, Australasian Book Society, Sydney, 1966

Summers, Anne, *Damned Whores and God's Police*, Penguin, Camberwell, Victoria, 2002

Sydney Water, *Blackheath, Katoomba and Woodford Special Areas: Draft Plan of Management, January 1997*, Sydney Water in association with National Parks and Wildlife NSW, Sydney, 1997

Teniswood, Barbara, *Guiding in Tasmania, 1911–1973*, Girl Guides Association of Tasmania, Hobart, 1974

Thomas, Martin, *The Artificial Horizon: Imagining the Blue Mountains*, MUP, Carlton, Victoria, 2003

Travers, Robert, *The Grand Old Man of Australian Politics: The Life and Times of Sir Henry Parkes*, Kangaroo Press, Sydney, 2000

Veale, Veda, *Women to Remember*, V. Veale, St Helens, Tasmania, 1981

Walker, M.L., *Development of Kindergartens*, Unpublished MEd thesis, University of Sydney, 1964

Warner, Philip, *The Battle of Loos*, Kimber, London, 1976

Whitford, R.L., 'The Community School', *Tasmanian Education*, February 1949

Williams, Roma, *The Settlement: A History of the University of Sydney Settlement and the Settlement Neighbourhood Centre*, University of Sydney, 1988

Woodward, Oliver, *The War Story of Oliver Holmes Woodward, Captain 1st Australian Tunnelling Company, Australian Imperial Force*, O.H. Woodward, Adelaide, 1932

Websites

Australian Dictionary of Biography: http://adbonline.anu.edu.au/biogs

Times Digital Archive: http://nla.gov.au/app/eresources/item/1088

Trove: http://nla.gov.au/trove

UK Census records 1841–1901: http://Ancestry.com

University of Sydney registers of graduates: http://heifer.ucc.usyd.edu.au/as/

Notes

Part One: Cara
Prologue
1 NSW Legislative Assembly, *Votes and Proceedings*, 1882, Vol. 2, 'Training School Hurlstone', p. 854.

1 Early Years
1 The Whitelands College records list Cara Mallett as an orphan.
2 The two Skinner children were brought up by their mother, Pamela Mallett, until her death in 1877. They then went to live with their father, Richard Skinner. The 1881 UK census shows Skinner, by then aged fifty, living in Southwold with his pensioner father and mother, with his unmarried brother Robert, a 'mariner', and with his children, Richard and Elizabeth, and a third child, Emma. The records state that he was married, but no wife is entered in the census. Perhaps she left him, tiring of the indignity of bringing up her husband's two illegitimate children.
3 Whitelands College Archives, *Regulations for the Admission of Students*, 1875.
4 Molly David records this anecdote in her memoir, *Passages of Time*. She also recalled: 'Mother disapproved of the English habit of addressing [working men] by their surname. She always addressed the old miner who worked for us sometimes as "Mr…" This would have scandalized our English relations.' (*Letters to Meg*, p. 74)
5 In 1996, a Mallett descendant now living in Canada wrote to Anne Edgeworth: see endnote chapter 3.

2 Lady Principal
1 *Votes and Proceedings*, p. 855.
2 Noeline Kyle, *Comparative Education Review*, November 1992, p. 476.
3 Parkes Correspondence, 6 October 1882.
4 Times Digital Archive 1786–1986,
5 State Records NSW: Department of Public Instruction, 20/1335, Training Schools and Colleges 'Hurlstone College', April 1883.
6 *Votes and Proceedings*, 1884, Principal's Annual Report, p. 903.
7 SRNSW, op. cit., 12 June, 1883.
8 SRNSW, op. cit., 12 June 1883.
9 *Sydney Mail*, 12 May 1883.
10 SRNSW, op. cit., 5 September 1884.
11 SRNSW, op. cit., 5 September 1884.
12 SRNSW, op. cit., 9 September 1884.
13 SRNSW, op. cit., 19 September 1884.
14 SRNSW, op. cit., 15 November 1884.

15 Votes and Proceedings, 1884, p. 419.

3 Courtship and Marriage
1 M.E. David, *Professor David: The Life of Sir Edgeworth David*, p. 23.
2 Parkes Correspondence, 6 October 1882.
3 Cecil Sharp was an accomplished musician who was later to become well-known as a collector and arranger of folk music.
4 Perhaps the debonair young Sharp was also courting Cara. He gave her a necklace, purchased in Colombo on the journey out to Sydney. It is now in the possession of Cara's great-granddaughter, Louise McIntyre.
5 *Professor David*, pp. 26–7.
6 M.E. David, *Passages of Time*, p. 38.
7 Pers. comm. from Anne Edgeworth.
8 University Senate minutes, 18 May, 1891. (Quoted in David Branagan, *T.W. Edgeworth David: A Life*, p. 61.)
9 Elsie Carter, the baby whom Cara David offered to adopt after the death of Elsie's mother Sarah, survived to marry and raise a large family. Elsie was widowed twice, took in boarders and later ran a pub and then a farm. Her father, the widower Elgin Carter, never remarried. Elsie's granddaughter, Pat Chamberlain, seeking information about her family's connection with Professor Edgeworth David, wrote to Anne Edgeworth from Canada in 1996 and sent Anne copies of Cara David's letters, which are quoted in this chapter. Pat mused on how different Elsie's life might have been if she had come out to live with the Davids in the colony

4 The Professor's Wife
1 *Australasian Home Reader*, Vol. 1, May 1892.
2 *AHR*, August 1892.
3 *AHR*, September 1894.
4 *AHR*, September 1893, pp. 196-97.
5 Cara may well have purchased some of these leaflets when she returned from England. Her granddaughter, Anne Edgeworth, recalled, 'My mother did tell me that Cara endeavoured conscientiously at one time to impart the facts of life to herself and Molly, but as it was all about bees and flowers the girls failed to understand what their mother was on about!'
6 *A Woman's Voice*, 21 December 1895.

5 Funafuti
1 It was actually seven miles long.
2 The drilling program continued under Sweet's leadership and with another expedition under A.E. Finckh in 1898. A final depth of over 1114 feet was reached, still in coral, though much valuable core material was brought up which broadly substantiated Darwin's theory about atoll formation.
3 *Passages*, p.17.
4 *The Age*, 11 August 1900.
5 Ibid., 22 September 1900.

6 The Blue Mountains
1 Three local features are named after David: Edgeworth David Head and David Crevasse on the northern side of the Grose River, and Sir Edgeworth David Lookout at the northern end of Woodbury Street, Woodford.
2 *Passages*, pp. 25–26.
3 In 1894, *A Woman's Voice* ran a 'rational dress for women' campaign.
4 *Passages*, p. 31.
5 Another fault she learned of was his tendency to leave rock specimens lying about. Staying in Hobart one year for a geology conference, David left his rock specimens on his hostess's grand piano, much to Cara's horror. This incident prompted David to tell his hostess a story (surely exaggerated in the telling?) about their wedding night when Cara, finding the bed covered in rocks, had retreated up onto the canopy. (Amy Lewis Papers)
6 *Passages*, p. 32.

7 Ibid.

8 Cara worked long hours indoors and outdoors at Tyn-y-Coed. Nevertheless she could afford to employ men as builders and handymen and there was always casual help available in the village. Her domestic projects were generally embarked on as interesting challenges, not submitted to as inevitable and enslaving chores.

9 *The Souvenir*, Friday, 18 December 1903.

10 Clement Wragge, Queensland meteorological observer, established a weather station on Mount Kosciuszko in 1898, but after his ongoing disputes with the NSW government the bureau was closed in 1903.

7 New Directions

1 *Australian Teacher*, May 1894.

2 These diploma courses ceased in 1909 after the opening of Sydney Teachers College in 1907.

3 *Australian Teacher*, September 1899.

4 SRNSW: Department of Public Instruction, 20/12605, Subject Files, 'Cookery', file 46680.

5 *Daily Telegraph*, 28 July 1915.

6 Cara did not want to restrict the life chances of young women and lobbied, unsuccessfully, for the establishment of an agricultural college to train women.

7 Franklin Papers, MLMS 364/8 22 June 1902.

8 Ibid., December 1903.

9 Franklin Papers, MLMS 364/9A, 7 November 1903.

10 Jill Roe, *Stella Miles Franklin*, p. 85.

11 Franklin Papers, ML MS 364/9A, April 1904.

12 Scott Papers, ML MS38 (CY 2640), P.255.

13 C. Bacchi, 'Evolution, Eugenics and Women', in *Women, Class and History*.

14 The Davids met Mrs Marie Stopes when they were in England in 1927. Dr Stopes was an early champion of contraception; she also had a doctorate of science in fossil botany. According to Branagan (p. 397) they all 'got on famously'.

15 *A Woman's Voice*, 8 September 1894.

16 *White Ribbon Signal*, 9 August 1907.

17 Ibid., 10 September 1907.

8 Antarctic Mission

1 Papers of Lady David, ML MS 3022/9, 23 September 1908.

2 Raymond Priestley, 'Sir Edgeworth David: An Appreciation', p. 7.

3 They left the second sledge with a cache of supplies before climbing on to the ice plateau.

4 The David Papers in the National Library, Mitchell Library and Sydney University archives contain many of David's fine photographs of landscapes and geographical features but very few of his own family.

5 Priestley, p. 6.

9 The War Years, Australia

1 Cara was indifferent to the latest fashions and was known to often wear the same dress to official university dinners. At one such dinner a Sydney matron approached her to ask if the dress was a uniform. Not one to retreat in the face of such a comment, Cara retorted that at least the dress was paid for. The woman hurriedly left the scene and Cara later discovered that the woman was being sued by her dressmaker for unpaid bills. (Anecdote from Anne Edgeworth.)

2 Faunthorpe must have kept all her letters. When he came to write his memoirs he wrote to Cara asking for permission to quote from them. She replied that 'she did not wish her letters to be quoted and that her name was not to be mentioned in the book'. 'Illicit', unpublished MS of Faunthorpe's memoirs, courtesy of Noeline Kyle.

3 Pencke was not interred as an enemy alien in Australia as he was over military age. However, it was later discovered that he had been covertly spying on the harbour defences at Newcastle during his stay in Australia.

4 In August 1915, Dorette MacCallum offered to resign from the National Council of Women because of her German nationality. President Rose Scott received unanimous support from the council in asking Mrs

MacCallum to stay on.

5 Throughout the early stages of the war, Cara kept a detailed diary which would serve as a source of letters to family overseas. This is the source of much of the material in this chapter.

6 The Voluntary Aid Detachment was an arm of the Red Cross. It consisted of women, mainly from leisured and middle-class homes, who received training to work as volunteers in hospitals and rest homes, thus freeing trained nurses to join the war effort overseas.

7 *Daily Telegraph*, 18 January 1916.

8 Bentley eventually withdrew from the campaign, advising his supporters to vote for the Liberal candidate.

9 *Daily Telegraph*, 18 December 1915.

10 *Grafton Argus*, 26 March 1916.

11 *Daily Examiner*, 24 March 1916.

12 *Casino and Kyogle Courier*, 22 March 1916.

13 While Cara had little time for Councillor Waterhouse, the Davids were to become good friends with one of his sons, also named Gustavus Waterhouse. Gustavus studied geology under David and became a distinguished entomologist. He accompanied David on his 1907 trip to the Snowy Mountains.

14 Michael McKernan's survey in his book, *The Australian People and the Great War*, found only one anti-conscription newspaper in rural Australia, the *Maryborough 'Alert'*.

15 *North Western Courier*, 25 October 1916. Billy Hughes, confident that the referendum would be a success, had already established 'exemption courts' in September in rural areas. Thus far relatively few men, however deserving their case, had been granted exemptions from call-up.

10 The War Years, Abroad

1 David informed his family that the Australian battalion of which he was so proud, in fact only contributed 2 percent of the total number of Allied troops engaged in mining the Western Front.

2 Harvey, Chief Inspector of Mines for the British Armies on the Western Front, was later to say of David, 'I had the privilege of calling him "friend"; his great knowledge and experience was of untold value to the Tunnelling Service'. (Letter in the possession of Ian Morse)

3 The Australian film, *Beneath Hill 60*, released in 2010 and based on Oliver Woodward's memoirs, dramatically portrays this incident.

4 David Papers, ML MS 3022/9, 10 May 1916.

5 David Branagan (p. 301) refers to the belief that the Messines multiple mine system may have been David's concept. Of the twenty-two mines, nineteen were successfully exploded.

6 Captain David was awarded the Military Cross for his war service, gazetted in the New Year Honours of January 1917.

7 David Papers, University of Sydney Archives, PO 11 Series 25, June 1916.

8 Ibid., March 1918.

9 David Papers, ML MS 3022/9, 9 March 1918.

11 A Public life

1 David Papers, ML MS 3022/9, 21 November 1918.

2 Branagan, p. 458.

3 Ibid., p. 364.

4 One of the few published articles about Cara David, Jennifer Carter's 'Portrait of a Lady', is a serious misreading of Cara's attitudes and motives, portraying her as a 'social climber'. Carter claims that the orphaned Cara was determined to find status and prestige in married life, and 'pushed and promoted David socially', putting much of her energy 'into bringing and keeping her husband before the public eye'. *NLA News*, September 2002.

5 The house was destroyed in a bushfire in January 1945.

6 *Sydney Morning Herald*, 17 September 1913.

7 Throughout the 1920s and 1930s, referenda were held in each Australian state. A substantial minority supported statewide prohibition during this era. Victoria had the largest vote (42%) in March 1930. In other states, about one-third of the electorate voted 'Yes' but this was not enough to allow the legislation to be passed. But the 1930s saw alcohol consumption drop dramatically throughout Australia, due mainly to the Depression.

8 A.W. Jose, correspondent in Australia for some years for the London *Times*, had a distinguished career as a journalist and historian. He worked with C.E.W. Bean on compiling the official history of the war.

9 *Bush Book Club Report*, 3 May 1923.
10 Ibid., 1936.
11 Ibid., 1937–38.
12 The Davids had a personal interest in this memorial because of its connection with the Governor General's wife, Lady Helen Munro Ferguson, who had established the Red Cross in Australia in 1914. The memorial, built on the initiative of Helen and her husband, was modelled on her ancestral home in Ulster.
13 C.E.W. Bean, *Anzac to Amiens*, p. 264.
14 Branagan, p. 407.
15 *The Waratah*, November 1933.
16 Ibid., August 1934.
17 Ibid., April 1934.
18 Ibid., November 1934.

12 Loss. Cara's Later Years
1 Priestley, p. 7.
2 It is now Mosman Uniting Church.
3 *Poems for Off-Duty Hours*, p. 17.
4 Mort family papers, Box 4, letter to Grace Eunice Graham, 8 January 1950.
5 Recollections of Diana Jones, Blue Mountains Historical Society, 2 May 2009.
6 Mort Family Papers, 30 December 1950.

Part Two: Margaret
13 Youth
1 David Papers, University of Sydney Archives, PO 11 Series 25/1, 1882 (undated).
2 David posted them a yearly cheque of £200 for five years.

14 Scotland
1 There were anxious times if the Davids' cheque was late. According to Anne Edgeworth, her mother would pawn her engagement ring and Bill's medical books until the cheque arrived, so that food could be bought.
2 During her father's visit to the UK in 1913, Margaret had a ticket for a lecture he was giving in Edinburgh, but as she wrote to Mootie, 'I am not sure yet whether they consider womenfolk intellectual enough to be allowed to attend the Royal Society meetings here.'
3 Journals of W.K. McIntyre, PRO 84/109, 23 October 1915.

15 Launceston
1 Dean Hewlett Johnson's book created great controversy after its publication. Dubbed the 'Red Dean' by his critics, he was accused of advancing the communist cause in the West by acting as a propagandist tool for the Russian state. His visit to Australia in April 1950 was organized by the Peace Council. Margaret McIntyre was one of many idealists who were attracted to the program he was proposing, with no understanding of the conditions in Russia at the time.
2 G.V. Brooks was the Minister for Education when the school was being planned.
3 Interviews with Cynthia Breheny and Jillian Koshin.
4 In December 1947, a Royal Commission was held in Tasmania into bribery allegations and the Labor Premier, Robert Cosgrove, stood aside for six weeks while facing criminal charges.
5 *Passages of Time*, p. 141.
6 *Poems for Off-Duty Hours*, p. 16.
7 A memorial plaque for the victims of the plane crash was erected at the small settlement of Nundle, near the site of the crash, in May 1983.
8 Veda Veale, *Women to Remember*, p. 35.

Part Three: Molly
16 Younger Sister
1 Franklin Papers, ML MS 364/8, 24 August 1902.
2 SU Oral History Project, Interview with M.E. David, March 1981.
3 Beverley Kingston, *Dorothea Mackellar*, DAB, online edition.
4 Oral History Project, op. cit.
5 Judge Philip Street was particular about his family's public profile. The AWM records of Laurence Street include a ten-year correspondence between the judge and the Department of Defence. He tried, unsuccessfully, to have the words 'Chief Justice of NSW' added to the family details on his son's Roll of Honour inscription.

17 Writer
1 Notes in the David Family Papers, MS 8890, Box 10, folder 45.
2 Carter and his wife lived near the Davids at Hornsby. They acquired the private school Ascham, in 1902, and ran it on enlightened educational principles.
3 Branagan, notes on the text, p. v.
4 Stewart's notes to the committee of Angus & Robertson, David Papers, MS 8890, Box 11, folder 18.
5 The portrait now hangs in the meeting rooms of the Hornsby and District Historical Association.
6 Jan Roberts, *Maybanke Anderson: Sex, Suffrage and Social Reform*, p. 202.

18 Homecoming
1 Cara and Molly resigned from the Australian-Russian Society in August 1948. Molly was reported in the Broken Hill *Barrier Miner* on 31 August as saying they had joined 'to try and get wider cultural relations and understanding between nations. When we found the society had a political flavour we resigned.'

Index